GUARDSMARK®

HOW TO BE
SAFE

PROTECT YOURSELF, YOUR HOME, YOUR FAMILY, AND YOUR BUSINESS FROM CRIME

IRA A. LIPMAN

FOUNDER AND CHAIRMAN, GUARDSMARK, LLC

THE READER'S DIGEST ASSOCIATION, INC.

NEW YORK, NY / MONTREAL

About the Author

Protection of people and their property has been a lifelong career for Ira A. Lipman. As founder and chairman of Guardsmark, LLC, one of the world's largest security companies, he directs an international network of protection professionals. Guardsmark team members are responsible for the security of thousands of people and billions of dollars in assets. Following many of the procedures personally developed by Mr. Lipman, the firm serves many leading multinational corporations and institutions, protecting people, assets, and classified, intellectual, and proprietary information in such diverse sectors as aerospace, defense, transportation, energy, manufacturing, financial, health, mining, and other areas and enterprises.

Known throughout the industry for his innovative approach to security problem solving, Mr. Lipman is frequently sought as a source for information on crime prevention techniques, addressing audiences at conferences and universities across America and writing for the public on a wide range of security topics. He has been editorially praised by the *New York Times* for his leadership in the security industry, and his individual, corporate, and industry achievements have received acclaim in a wide range of global publications, such as the *Washington Post, Reader's Digest,* and *People.* Mr. Lipman is also publisher of The Lipman Report, a monthly newsletter that is visionary on the challenges facing the world, including terrorism, sabotage, cybercrime, drug abuse, employee theft, workplace violence, and espionage.

Guardsmark's reputation for excellence has led author Tom Peters to describe Guardsmark as the "Tiffany's of the security business" in his book *Liberation Management.* In addition, *Time* magazine has referred to Guardsmark as the company "which many security experts consider to be the best national firm in the business."

Mr. Lipman has chaired or led well-known national organizations, including the National Council on Crime and Delinquency, for which he now serves as Chairman Emeritus, and he is also a member of the Council on Foreign Relations. He and his wife, Barbara, live in New York. They have three married sons—Gustave, Joshua, and Benjamin—and four grandchildren.

Praise for How to Be Safe

"A valuable guide to what each of us can do to protect our loved ones and our property." —Carl Levin, U.S. Senator from Michigan

"*[How to Be Safe]* should be required reading for every family member."
—Dr. Lee P. Brown, formerly: Director, White House Office of National Drug Control Policy; Police Commissioner of New York City, Public Safety Commissioner of Atlanta; Police Chief and three-term Mayor of Houston

"An important addition to anyone's library."
—Christie Whitman, former Governor of New Jersey

"Ira Lipman has combined rigorous research with common sense to create a comprehensive guide to the range of issues around personal safety."
—Dr. Joseph E. Aoun, President, Northeastern University

"...an excellent guidebook and tool to make us safer in our homes, neighborhoods, and businesses."
—Bill Gibbons, Commissioner, Tennessee Department of Safety and Homeland Security

"Ira Lipman's 2011 updated version of his book is entirely relevant and important."
—Howard H. Baker, Jr., former U.S. Senator from Tennessee

"...an invaluable guide to protecting individuals, families, communities, and businesses from crime."
—Charles F. Wellford, Professor of Criminology and Criminal Justice, University of Maryland

"...*How to Be Safe* is required reading for all to feel secure in the 21st century."
—Andrew H. Marks, Senior Insurance Industry Executive

"This tour-de-force could have only been authored by the nation's single most knowledgeable authority on security and safety—Ira Lipman. A must read."
—Dr. Bernard Cohen, Professor of Sociology and Criminal Justice, Queens College and The Graduate Center, City University of New York

"The best guide yet to help families keep themselves safe."
—Lamar Alexander, U.S. Senator from Tennessee

"This comprehensive, clear, and coherent book deals with virtually every situation in which personal safety and security might become an issue."
—Dr. Rock Jones, President, Ohio Wesleyan University

"Without hysteria, but with great insight, *How to Be Safe* is a security blanket for your family, your home, and your business...."
—Michael Douglas, Actor

"For three decades *How to Be Safe* has been the bible for anyone looking to prevent themselves, their families, and their businesses from being victimized by crime. This new edition continues that tradition...."
—Dr. Edmund F. McGarrell, Director, School of Criminal Justice, Michigan State University

A READER'S DIGEST BOOK

Copyright © 2012 Ira A. Lipman

All rights reserved. Unauthorized reproduction, in any manner, is prohibited.

Reader's Digest is a registered trademark of The Reader's Digest Association, Inc.

READER'S DIGEST PROJECT STAFF

U.S. Editors: Susan Randol, Barbara Booth
Indexer: Andrea Chesman
Cover Designer: Jennifer Tokarski
Designer: Nick Anderson
Senior Art Director: George McKeon
Executive Editor, Trade Publishing: Dolores York
Associate Publisher, Trade Publishing: Rosanne McManus
President and Publisher, Trade Publishing: Harold Clarke

Library of Congress Cataloging-in-Publication Data
Lipman, Ira A.

    How to be safe : protect yourself, your home, your family, and your business from crime / Ira A. Lipman.
      p. cm.

    Includes index.

    ISBN 978-1-60652-169-4

1. Safety education. 2. Dwellings–Security measures. 3. Crime prevention. 4. Preparedness.
    5. Self-protective behavior. I. Title.
    HV675.L49 2011

613.6–dc22

               2010028280

The previous edition of this work was published as *How to Protect Yourself from Crime*
(4th edition), ISBN 0–89577–931–5.

We are committed to both the quality of our products and the service we provide to our customers.
We value your comments, so please feel free to contact us.

    The Reader's Digest Association, Inc.
    Adult Trade Publishing
    44 South Broadway
    White Plains, NY 10601

For more Reader's Digest products and information, visit our website:

    www.rd.com (in the United States)
    www.readersdigest.ca (in Canada)

Printed in the United States of America

1 3 5 7 9 10 8 6 4 2

Acknowledgments

Indicative of my position as founder and chairman of Guardsmark, LLC, my name on the title page of this book simply reflects the names of the many Guardsmark people responsible for this collective effort. The fine work of those who assisted with the previous editions of How to Protect Yourself from Crime has been greatly enhanced in How to Be Safe by the efforts of world-renowned criminologist Dr. James Alan Fox. I am grateful to all those who made this book project possible.

—Ira A. Lipman

For Barbara, Gus, Josh, Benjamin and our entire family,
and for my beloved late parents, with love

CONTENTS

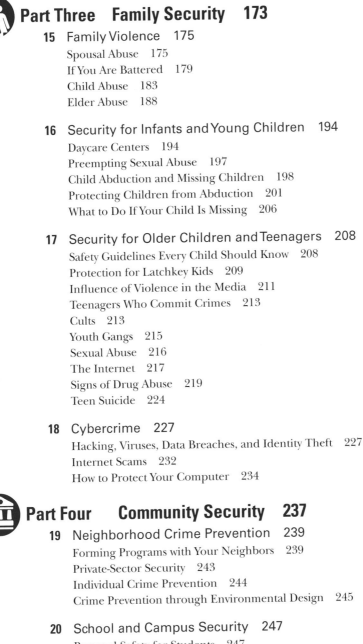

 **Part Six Protection from Violent Crimes 313**

FOREWORD

Crime statistics rise and fall, but safety and effective law enforcement remain among our primary concerns—a truism whether we're parents or grandparents, homeowners or renters, friends or neighbors, teachers or students, businesspeople or clients. And for all of us, Ira A. Lipman's book *How to Be Safe* is an exceedingly thoughtful, comprehensive, and practical guide for ensuring personal safety.

Ira and I have been friends for more than two decades. We served together for many years on the board of governors of the United Way of America, where he passionately supported community health, personal and organizational service to others, and not-for-profit organizations benefiting the community.

In Memphis, Tennessee, and other locales where his family and business colleagues have lived and worked, Ira proved to be a leader with impeccable values, character, and integrity. The solid ethical standards he demonstrated as a member of the board of governors of the United Way of America nationally earned him a reputation as the "conscience of the board." For almost half a century he has brought the same qualities to Guardsmark, the private security enterprise he founded and developed into one of the world's leading companies.

As for myself, I was born and raised in Jersey City, New Jersey, then lived and raised my own family in the nation's capital. I also called New York City home for a number of years. Fortunately, my 1989–2006 term as commissioner of the National Football League (NFL) gave me the opportunity to visit communities throughout America—urban, suburban, and rural. In all of them I observed firsthand the importance of personal safety and security for citizens of every age and in all walks of life.

GUARDSMARK AND THE NFL

As NFL Commissioner, I frequently consulted with Ira and his Guardsmark colleagues about safety and security issues pertinent to the league, stadiums, and other facilities—especially after tensions rose in the wake of the September 2001 attacks on the World Trade Center.

Among other things, Guardsmark conducted thorough audits of the quality, safety, and security of stadiums throughout the league; evaluated the people and plans responsible for the safety and security of fans and others present in the stadiums; and reviewed the relationship between team and stadium organizations and local, state, and federal law enforcement agencies. These invaluable assessments provided benchmarks of excellence that both the league head office and individual NFL teams strive to achieve to this day.

ABOUT HOW TO BE SAFE

The same commitment to quality that has made Guardsmark a paragon of the security business has gone into *How to Be Safe*. Two of the things I find most impressive about the guide are its no-nonsense directness and its comprehensiveness, as in the following examples:

- In chapter 2, a discussion of the pros and cons of keeping a gun as protection doesn't shy away from the hard truth that a family member or friend is statistically more likely to be shot than an intruder in homes where a gun is kept. At the same time, the text lays out the information in such a way that it's clear that the decision "to arm or not" is yours and yours alone.

- Two whole chapters devoted to security for the young—from infants to teenagers—cover everything from the preemption of sexual abuse to the actions to take if a child goes missing to recognizing the telltale signs of teen drug abuse.

The book also stresses how staying informed is of utmost importance: The more educated you are about the ways of criminals, the better your chances of staying out of harm's way. These are wise words indeed, and advice we would all do well to follow.

—Paul Tagliabue

INTRODUCTION

People from all walks of life occasionally come face-to-face with criminal activity, and almost always when they least expect it. A theft or assault (or worse) can happen at any moment, anytime, anywhere—unless, that is, we stay one step ahead of the criminal.

Crime has been with us from time immemorial, but we could hardly have imagined the many new forms it has taken over the past 20 years: Electronic communications have brought identity theft; workplace and school shootings have generated far too much "Breaking News"; and overseas political upheavals and instability have made "terrorism" a household word.

Recognizing how much the world has changed over the more than 35 years since the first edition of this book (then entitled *How to Protect Yourself from Crime*) was published, and even since the last edition of the book some 14 years ago, we have thoroughly revamped this all-new fifth edition to reflect these new threats. Each page conveys the same central message: The way to reduce crime is for each of us to become more educated about multifarious criminal activities and to arm ourselves with tactics that help us outwit the bad guy.

AWARENESS AND PREVENTION

If there is a recurring theme running through all editions, it is that people make crime too easy for the criminal. Unless we educate ourselves on how to avoid scams and schemes, guard our personal information as if it were gold, and learn to recognize a physical threat when we see one, we are, in effect, accomplices.

Simply put, the first step toward staying safe is to be aware. Take crime close to home, for instance. You're probably already aware of

Neighborhood Watch programs, alarm systems, personal safety devices, and other preventive measures. But do you know that burglars often drop in at open houses when homes go on the market or that tall hedges are an intruder's dream come true?

In businesses, prevention measures aren't always as obvious. Simple orderliness and cleanliness are more helpful than you might think:

- A shopkeeper whose store is messy or cluttered leaves the impression of carelessness, giving potential robbers the idea the store is an easy target.
- In offices large or small, desks piled with papers can invite unwanted attention, especially after hours. Keep important documents (including personal ones) either out of view or locked up so that confidential information won't fall into the wrong hands.

ELECTRONIC THREATS

As technology grows apace, the world grows smaller and more unpredictable. Although we can connect with people globally as never before, the new interconnectedness is a boon for the cybercriminal.

Numbers tell the story: It is estimated that computer crime costs organizations in excess of $64 billion a year. The traditional embezzler gleans $19,000 from company books on average, while his modern counterpart nets nearly $500,000 for each computer offense.

Likewise, as we conduct more of our personal and professional lives online, we become more vulnerable not only to identity theft but to other electronic crimes as well. People with malicious intent can lurk anywhere from online dating services to the most innocent chat room.

NEW DIRECTIONS

Now the good news: As criminal activity evolves, so does our ability to protect ourselves. Technological advancements have led to vast improvements in alarm systems and personal defense weapons. GPS, Firefly phones, and other new devices can also help keep us free from danger. Then there are the new communications systems such as Amber Alert, which enable whole communities to come together to combat crime.

Through continued education and awareness, we can stay at least one step ahead of crafty predators and crooked profiteers, allowing us to live more confidently in a secure, protected environment.

Be smart. Protect yourself. And stay safe!

PART ONE

SECURITY IN YOUR HOME

CHAPTER 1

DOORS AND WINDOWS

Did you know that a burglary happens somewhere in the United States every 14 seconds? This amounts to more than 2 million burglaries each year. Although properly secured doors and windows should not be the primary piece in your overall security plan, it is key to your first line of defense in the fight against crime—and essential in keeping your family and possessions safe.

BEST DOOR-SAFETY STRATEGIES

The easiest and most common way for someone to enter your home is simply to open an unlocked door. In fact, one-third of all burglars enter homes through an unlocked door or window. But believe it or not, very few families take the number one precaution of locking exterior doors. Children who are in and out of the house all day leave doors unlocked, as do people who go next door for a visit or go out to walk the dog. Moreover, it is not only important to keep doors locked when the house is vacant but when someone is home as well. The safest bet is to get into the habit of keeping the doors locked at all times.

The Weak Truth behind Doors

Locking your doors actually provides little defense against the determined criminal. Intruders are adept at forcing open doors, which need to be reinforced and strengthened to be truly effective. Here's why:

- Doors often have small glass or light plywood panels, which can easily be broken or cut with a rasp or keyhole saw. An intruder can open the lock very easily simply by reaching through the hole.

- A door that doesn't fit its frame properly can be forced open by wedging a prying device between it and the frame and then "spreading" the frame away until the bolt moves free from the strike (the hole in the door frame into which the bolt slides when the door is locked).

- Some older homes and apartments have doors that open outward. These can often be opened by removing the hinge pins and lifting the entire door from the frame. Multipoint locking systems, such as Mul-T-Lock (page 12), which bolt into all four edges of the door frame when engaged, are useful in protecting doors of this type.

- Certain locks can easily be picked, removed, or destroyed.

- Determined intruders who have the skill, are provided enough time, and are concealed from view will more than likely accomplish the task.

- Sliding and French doors are constructed for elegance, not safety. They need to be reinforced with deadbolts and multipoint locking systems in order to be fully secure. Even when locked, many can be pried open with a good shove.

Mapping out the Crimes in Your Area

Crime mapping is used in many municipalities to provide a detailed picture of where crimes have occurred. This information is commonly made available as a public service that allows individuals to access information—often through the Internet—regarding reported crimes in their immediate neighborhoods. Check to see if this information is available in your community—it's an excellent resource for staying informed about potential dangers.

WHAT YOU CAN DO

If you can't entirely eliminate the possibility of criminals breaking into your home, then what's the next best thing to do? Make breaking in as difficult, time consuming, and noisy as possible. Install and use deadbolt locks with a minimum 1-inch (2.5-cm) bolt throw on all perimeter doors, and ensure that your windows and doors are locked when you are away. In addition, install low illumination lighting on the exterior and inform a nearby relative or trusted neighbor of any extended absence.

What Is the Criminal Thinking?

Social psychologists suggest that burglars weigh five sets of questions before committing a crime:

- Am I detectable? For example, where are the doors and windows positioned, and what is the distance from the street to the house?
- Are any meaningful barriers present? Does the structure have a gate, strong locks, or an intrusion alarm?
- Are there any signs or symbolic barriers, like Neighborhood Watch or private patrols, that define territoriality and vigilance?
- Are residents active in the streets and yards? Are lights on in the homes? Are newspapers still lying in the driveway?
- Is there a positive social climate in the area? Are people suspicious of me, or can I go about my business without interference?

Consider these questions when thinking about which precautions will offer you maximum security.

If the burglars still succeed, at least you will have forced them to destroy the lock or part of the window or door, leaving clear evidence of illegal entry. This is vital when filing an insurance claim to recover your loss.

Guidelines for Strong Doors

Strengthening outside doors is not difficult. Most important, the door should be as sturdy as possible. A hollow-core metal or solid wooden door is best. Follow these excellent tips to keep doors strong and criminals out.

Install double-cylinder locks. Although many people prefer the look of doors with heavy glass or wooden panels, these offer considerably less protection than solid doors, but you can make them more secure by installing double-cylinder locks. This kind of lock requires a key to open it from the inside as well as from the outside, which prevents an intruder from unlatching the lock by reaching through broken glass or a hole in a wooden panel. That much delay—unless the burglar is especially determined—will very often send them off to easier targets.

Caution: In the event of fire or other emergency, double-cylinder locks can delay occupants from getting out. Consequently, a key to the inside lock should always be kept conveniently at hand (for example, on a chain or string attached to the wall near the door). In some jurisdictions, double-cylinder locks are illegal in multiple dwellings. If double cylinders are installed, make sure the family has a well-defined plan of escape in case of fire (see "Practice a Home Fire Escape Plan," page 39). Check the local laws in your community before installing these locks. In locations where double-cylinder locks are prohibited, doors with glass panels should use non-breakable glass at least 3 ½ feet (1.07 m) from the lock.

Reposition mail slots. An aggressive kick may be all it takes to break in doors that have a mail slot. This is because mail slots tend to weaken the horizontal integrity of the door. But if you insist on having one, position it on the bottom of the door, no higher than a quarter of the way up.

Replace flimsy strike plates. In many cases with forced entry, the deadbolt holds but the door frame around the strike plate splinters. Unfortunately, most doors come with a light-duty strike plate. These should be replaced with heavy-duty strike plates and 3-inch (8-cm) screws, or the builder should install steel door frames so that the deadbolt protrudes into metal and not wood.

If you rent your home or an apartment, this may not be practical. Your landlord might not permit you to replace an existing door, or you might not want to go to the expense of installing a high-quality door on someone else's property. In this case, consider reinforcing your door with a sheet of steel or heavy plywood. It may not be a thing of beauty, but it might save your TV and DVD player.

Light up hidden doors. Be especially meticulous with exterior doors that provide cover to an intruder—such as doors inside vestibules or enclosed porches. Here a criminal can work at leisure, safe from observation by neighbors or passersby. Install lights near these doors for added security and keep them on at night and when you're away.

Place hinges on the inside. Door hinges should always be placed on the inside. If the hinge pins are on the outside, a burglar can easily remove the pins and, with them, the door. This can be prevented by removing one pair of parallel screws on each of the leaves that connect the door to the door frame. Then insert a single screw or concrete nail that protrudes about a half inch (1.27 cm) from the leaf on the door. When the door is closed, the protruding screw or nail will connect into the screw opening on the hinge leaf connected to the door frame. Even if the hinge pin is removed, the door will be held in place by the protruding screw or nail.

Reinforce the frames. No lock can prevent a door from being opened by brute force, but this is especially true with a weak door frame. Every exterior door should fit its frame snugly. Most don't. Builders sometimes take shortcuts by making the openings oversized, and even a well-fitted door can develop problems as a house settles on its foundation. The best way to remedy a poor fit is to reinforce the door frame or replace the door with one that fits. If this is too costly, at least use locks with bolts that slide a minimum of 1 inch (2.5 cm) into the frame, or attach a common thumb lock with a long bolt to the inside face of the door. Better yet, ask a locksmith about an L-shaped metal strip that can be attached to a door frame to protect an inward-swinging door from being jimmied with a crowbar.

A flat plate attached to an outward-swinging door can be used to cover such an opening, but it should be attached with flat bolts or non-retractable screws so that it cannot be removed from the outside.

Add storm doors. Storm doors are good energy savers, and when equipped with adequate locking devices, they add an element of security by introducing a delay factor. The glass and/or wrought-iron features serve as another deterrent.

Keys and Entry Codes

As mentioned earlier, the easiest and most common way for a burglar to enter your home is through an unlocked door or window. One of the simplest and most obvious ways to protect yourself and your home is to place locks and/or alarm devices on your doors and windows—and remember to use them. Although a determined offender may still find various means to enter your home, these devices ensure that only those individuals who possess keys and/or entry codes can enter your home with ease. If a key or entry code gets into the wrong hands, they can and will be used against you.

Many people hide a spare key somewhere outside their home, just in case they get locked out. If you do this, be sure not to place the key in an obvious location, such as under a potted plant or doormat. Instead, give a spare key to a trusted neighbor or nearby friend whom you can call or go to for assistance. Similarly, do not pick entry codes that are incredibly obvious, such as 1-2-3-4. Be sure to have DO NOT DUPLICATE stamped on all copies of your keys, and make sure there is no personal information—such as your name, address, or phone number—attached to them.

Provide keys and entry codes only to those people whom you know well and trust. This list should not include carpenters, electricians, and painters. But if you must give a key to someone doing extensive work on your home, be sure to repin the locks after the renovation.

If your family has an "attached garage" and multiple vehicles, make sure all vehicles are locked, even when parked in your own driveway. Criminals will not hesitate to use a garage door opener in an unlocked vehicle. Always use a layered approach for security, keeping the garage door closed and the interior garage door to the residence locked.

If you have houseguests coming to stay with you, change the entry codes for the duration of the visit and then change the codes again once these houseguests are gone.

You obviously wouldn't give your keys and entry codes to strangers; however, how many times have you given your entire key chain to a valet parking attendant or auto mechanic? Instead, keep a car key separate from other keys solely for this purpose.

When it comes to children, it is vitally important to teach them the importance of security and that a key or entry code is something that can

Choosing a Locksmith

be misused and must not be shared with others. If you have houseguests coming to stay with you, change the entry codes for the duration of the visit and then change the codes again once these houseguests are gone.

Key control is an especially important issue for apartment dwellers. There are several steps you should take in order to ensure that you have maximum control over entry to your apartment. First and foremost, make sure that the locks have been changed or the lock cores repinned since the last tenant moved out—otherwise, any number of people associated with the previous tenant may have keys to your apartment. And while the landlord usually has a master key to your apartment, try to limit how often and under what circumstances he or she may give it out to various workers (plumbers, electricians, pest control, and so on). Finally, make sure that any master keys are kept in a safe, locked location. (See chapter 9 for more information on apartments and condos.)

New types of keys, which resemble credit cards (like those often used in hotels), are now being offered to the homeowner. These keys can be password-protected at many levels and cannot be easily reproduced. These systems are primarily used in very high-end homes. Locking system brands, specifications, and costs may be obtained from a professional bonded locksmith.

Another advance in lock design uses personalized fingerprint recognition as a means for keyless entry. But until this technology reaches a reasonable price point, more conventional designs and security measures must suffice.

Chain Locks

Chain locks are generally not effective in preventing someone from entering your home. A good kick could easily pull the lock away from

Key advice for maximum protection

☐ Do not place hidden keys in an obvious location, such as under a potted plant or doormat.

☐ Stamp DO NOT DUPLICATE on all copies of your keys.

☐ Be sure there is no personal information—such as your name, address, or phone number—attached to them.

☐ Always keep a separate key on hand for valets.

☐ Tell children keys and entry codes should not be shared with others.

☐ If at all possible, do not give in to convenience and provide carpenters and housecleaners with a key.

☐ Before moving in, renters should make sure locks have been changed or repinned.

☐ Make sure spare keys are kept in a safe, convenient location.

the wall, and the chain itself can be cut with a hacksaw or bolt cutter. To maximize the effectiveness of such locks, anchor them with long screws or, better yet, bolts. A wedge-shaped rubber doorstop inserted beneath a door can provide substantial protection against unwanted entry.

One advantage of a chain lock is that when engaged, a burglar knows someone is home, generally causing him or her to move on. One distinct *disadvantage* of a chain lock is that burglars, once inside your house, can engage the lock themselves to avoid being surprised on the job. The value of a chain lock is thus debatable, but on balance a good one is worthwhile, if for no other reason than its effect of delaying entry. Also, if you have solid doors without peepholes, a chain lock enables you to speak to visitors without fully opening the door.

Peepholes

A solid exterior door should be equipped with a peephole to help you ascertain who is outside before you open it. Ideally, the peephole should have a wide-angle lens. If at all practical, a convex mirror should be installed opposite the door. With this device, you should be able to see anyone attempting to hide beyond the vision range of the peephole.

Night Latches and Doorknob Locks

The night latch or rim spring latch commonly found in most older homes, and the cylindrical lock or doorknob lock found in many apartments and newer houses, do not offer a great deal of security. The doorknob device is easily defeated by prying the entire assemblage loose with a crowbar. Night latches are very common because they are inexpensive and convenient and can be engaged simply by shutting the door. But often they can be opened by sliding a credit card or similar piece of plastic into the gap between the door and the frame.

Newer night latches have protection to prevent the "credit card entry." However, this represents little if any protection, because doors of this type can often be compromised by forcing them open with a screwdriver. You can prevent this by equipping the lock with an effective dead-latch plunger, which prevents pushing back the latch's beveled edge. Unfortunately, the faceplate can be pried loose and the cylinder removed quite easily.

Deadbolt Locks

A key-operated deadbolt is, dollar for dollar, the best means of defense that you can enlist in securing your home. You should install one on each outside door, either in place of or supplementary to whatever locking devices you are now using.

A deadbolt usually features a square-faced (rather than beveled) bolt, which is engaged from the inside by a key (double cylinder) or is operated by a thumb turn (single cylinder). If the bolt is long enough [a 1-inch (2.5-cm) throw is recommended], the door becomes very difficult to jimmy open.

> A key-operated deadbolt is, dollar for dollar, the best means of defense that you can enlist in securing your home.

A variation on this theme—the rim, or surface-mounted vertical deadbolt lock (the ring-and-bar lock)—is an even more effective protection measure. For high-risk situations, the Mul-T-Lock is a deadbolt lock that, when engaged, bolts into all four edges of the door frame.

Other Locking Devices

There are a number of virtually pickproof locks available, but they are expensive and, except in the most extraordinary of circumstances, unnecessary for the average homeowner. Few burglars are skilled at picking locks, so unless there are items of unusual value in your home, installing pickproof locks generally would constitute overprotection. Nevertheless, here are a few to keep in mind.

Push-button combination. Although these are secure from lock pickers, the combination can be read even from great distances. These locks are therefore much more effective for interior security than for exterior use. A five-pin tumbler lock is considered adequate for home use.

Police brace. This serves as an anti-intrusion device the way wedging a piece of furniture under a doorknob does. It consists of a long steel bar that reaches from the floor to the door at an angle. The top edge of the bar fits into a lock mechanism on the door, and the bottom fits into a metal socket in the floor. Another version of the police brace is a horizontal steel bar mounted across the center of the door that fits into jamb braces attached to both sides of the door frame. It can be removed or put back in place in a few seconds. While these devices are useful only for security from the inside, they have the very real advantage of being completely pickproof.

Tubular keyway lock. This type of device is similar to the round locks found on many vending machines and has the advantage of being extremely difficult to pick and, for all intents and purposes, is impossible to force open with a screwdriver or wrench.

Sliding and French Doors

Of all the types of exterior doors, the most hazardous are sliding glass doors. In general, these doors have ineffective locks. Even if the lock works, an intruder can cut or break a piece of the glass and disengage the lock.

You can strengthen your doors by attaching locks with vertical bolts that fit into holes in the floor and upper frame and hold the door in place when it is engaged. You can also substitute the panes of plate or tempered glass with polycarbonate or other shatterproof glass, or some impact-resistant glazing material. In addition, you can cut a broom handle to fit the track in which the doors slide. Even if the lock were forced, the door would not slide open.

You can further protect sliding glass doors by inserting screws into the upper track of the door assemblies. Properly placed, these screws can prevent an intruder from lifting and removing an entire door—glass, frame, and all—from the lower guide track.

French doors should be made of solid wood that is at least 1 ¾ inches (44 mm) thick. Locks should always be installed at a right angle to the grain of the wood in order to lessen the chances of the wood splitting if the lock is under pressure.

For added security, install slide-rod locks to the top and bottom of one or both of the doors. If you've got an outward-opening French door, add hinge bolts as well. These bolts should be fit 4 to 6 inches (100 to 150 mm) below the top hinge and above the bottom hinge.

Garages

Garage doors that lead directly into the house are considered entry doors, like your front door. However, they represent a more serious threat to your security because an intruder, hidden from sight in the garage, can take his or her time breaking into your home. At the very least, this door should be solid core and contain a deadbolt lock, secure hinges, and if warranted, an intrusion alarm sensor (a magnetic contact switch set).

Obviously, you should keep your garage locked shut whenever practical. All garages should be protected with good padlocks when away for an extended period of time. A good padlock has a hardened (or, better yet, a stainless) steel shackle (the loop). This should be no less than ¾ inch (1.9 cm) in diameter. It should have a double-locking mechanism (heel and toe), a five-pin tumbler, and a key-retaining feature. This last feature, sometimes difficult to find, prevents you from removing the key unless the shackle is secured in the lock body. To test the garage-door locking mechanism, aggressively strike the lock with the palm of your hand to see if the jolt causes the lock to open.

Roll-up garage doors should have two good padlocks for acceptable security, one on either side of the door. (Upward pressure on one side of the door may cause the other side to raise enough for someone to crawl under.) Many garage-door assemblies, electric or mechanical, have predrilled holes on the tracks for a padlock. Also, if you have an electric garage-door opener, change the factory designated code to a personal code immediately. This can be done right on your keypad. Refer to your owner's manual for instruction.

To test the garage-door locking mechanism, aggressively strike the lock with the palm of your hand to see if the jolt causes the lock to open.

WISE WAYS TO REINFORCE WINDOWS

Any windows large enough for an intruder to crawl through should be secured regardless of what level it's on. Burglars usually don't opt for

Window-Unit Air Conditioners

An especially vulnerable access point is the window-unit air conditioner. Thwart potential intruders by ensuring that the unit is secured by long screws to both the window and the window frame. When this is not possible, place a horizontal metal strap across the exterior face of the unit, again ensuring that it is firmly secured to the window frame and/or exterior walls.

breaking glass, because it makes too much noise and can cause injury. So securing your windows with good locks is your best bet against entry.

Windows that are used for ventilation or as an emergency exit, especially those on the ground floor, should be secured by key-operated locks, which are readily available from hardware stores and locksmiths.

Although intruders are less likely to break the glass, they could still easily remove a small piece of glass with a glasscutter and reach through to unlock the window. As with sliding glass doors, you may want to replace the glass with laminated glass, special impact-resistant plastics, or assault-resistant film, as developed for schools and store windows.

In many homes glass is held in windows by putty. This material deteriorates with age, making panes easy to remove with no more than a pocketknife. Usually a contractor will replace all putty when painting your house. Make sure to include this in your contract and double check afterward to make sure that this was done.

TYPES OF WINDOWS

Homes have many types of windows. Unfortunately, however, burglars are wise to how they operate and can still easily break in even if they are locked. Below are a few ways to boost the security on typical windows.

Double-Hung Windows

The windows in many older homes are double hung, made of two frames, one or both of which slide up and down. A two-piece device, resembling a butterfly, locks it shut. An intruder can easily open this lock by sliding a thin piece of metal, such as a knife blade, vertically through the crack separating the two sashes.

Safeguarding Windows from the Ground Up

Regardless of the type of window, some general commonsense measures should be taken to thwart intruders.

Ground-floor windows should be covered with blinds, shades, or curtains to obstruct a potential thief's view of your home's contents. If not, a burglar may look in your windows and see valuables that may encourage a break-in. Mini blinds should be closed tightly, with slats up, so that at most, the only view available from outside is of your ceiling. If a service employee has been in your home, check the windows—burglars have been known to enter through windows that service people left unlocked for them. (See chapter 5— Service Employees and Invited Strangers.)

Plant thorny shrubs under windows. Rose bushes are not only beautiful but are a great deterrent.

Second-story windows pose less of a problem than ground-level, but they still require attention because they may be accessible from outside staircases, fire escapes, roofs of porches, or even trees. Don't store ladders outside unless they are secured by a padlock and chain.

In some cities, windows may be close enough to neighboring buildings to allow a plank to bridge the gap between the structures. In some high-rise apartment buildings, intruders might gain access by lowering themselves from a rooftop or higher floor to an unprotected or open window. Protect these windows as you would ground-level windows.

In evaluating your window security, pay special attention to basement and storeroom windows, attached garages, ventilation exhausts, access to crawlspaces opening into partial basements, coal chutes, storm cellars, attics, and all other spaces that provide access to little-used areas inside the home.

Some dwellings have ash cleanout doors on the exterior of the chimney at ground level, used to remove ashes from the fireplace. These rectangular doors should never be larger than 16 inches wide by 8 inches high (41 cm by 20 cm) to minimize the possibility of entry into the dwelling.

Windows become considerably more secure when a hole is drilled completely through the lower window sash and halfway through the upper while the window is in the closed position. A bolt or nail inserted into the drilled hole will effectively lock the windows in the closed position. Similarly, you can drive nails or bolts into the window tracks to prevent the window from being raised high enough to admit an intruder. For maximum security, employ these steps on both sides of the tracks.

When a window has been "frozen" shut by paint and is not needed for ventilation, leave it that way as a simple anti-burglar precaution.

Caution: If windows are secured by bolts or nails or immobilized because of layers of paint, ensure that these observations are included in the fire escape plan (see "Practice a Home Fire Escape Plan," page 39), especially if children are living in the dwelling.

Storm Windows and Guards

Storm windows provide an impediment to the would-be intruder. Although they can usually be removed with little more than a screwdriver, this takes time and can create noise, which will generally send the intruder on to easier targets.

Window guards—lockable folding metal screens—provide excellent security yet still provide for emergency evacuation of the home, as long as the key to unlock the screens is readily at hand. It should not be placed within reach of the would-be intruder on the outside.

Casement Windows

Casement windows are more secure than most double-hung windows because they are opened with a geared-crank arrangement and often are too small to allow human entry even when successfully opened. Intrusion is usually possible only after smashing or cutting the glass. A number of key-operated locks are available for casement windows.

CHAPTER 2

MAINTAINING SECURITY INSIDE

Keeping your home secure with proper locks and lighting is paramount to keeping your family and valuables safe. Sixty percent of burglaries occur when the house is occupied. So should an emergency situation arise, it is important to know how to respond and to be savvy enough to always stay one step ahead of an intruder. Here are a number of simple rules you can follow to keep burglars at bay and significantly enhance your safety and well-being.

KEEPING STRANGERS OUT

Most of us know that if you don't know who is standing on your doorstep, you should *never* let them in. But many of us are too trusting, especially in broad daylight or if they are wearing an official uniform. The fact is, if a burglar or other type of criminal intends to invoke harm, they are not going to be obvious about it. Here are a few tips to stay safe.

Always be cautious when answering your door.   If your door has glass panels, a peephole, or a window nearby, you can easily see who is on the doorstep. If you have a solid door, fit it with a good chain lock and *always* use it. As an added precaution, place a wedge-shaped rubber doorstop, available at variety or discount stores, underneath the door. This will add support to your chain lock if a caller tries to forcefully break in. He or she will probably recoil from the initial thrust, leaving you time to slam the door and seek help. If you live alone, consider installing an intercom so you can communicate with visitors without opening the door.

Install high-tech security devices. All-in-one units consisting of a camera, monitor, intercom terminal, and phone allow you to view and communicate with visitors. Weather-resistant cameras provide a number of views, such as your driveway, home entrances, backyard, patio, guest-house, garage, or pool area. This system can be connected to your television monitor so you can view these areas on a designated TV channel. This interior security system can even be connected to a digital recorder and programmed so that selected areas and activities are captured on disc when you're not home. Some cameras even have built-in infrared LEDs to light up the area for the camera without requiring a high level of visible lighting.

You can even buy an inexpensive device that works on a timer and simulates the flickering glow of a television (go to www.faketv.com).

Don't always believe that a visitor is who they say they are. It is best to assume that the caller is lying and ask for at least two or three items of identification, such as a driver's license or company photo ID. This applies even to a person in police uniform.

Tune in to Intruders

You can easily trick a thief into believing that someone is home simply by turn-ing a radio on to a talk show (as opposed to music) and positioning it so that it can be heard from outside the front door. Another radio, near the rear, will en-force that belief. Tuning the radios to different stations could easily convince the thief that two people, at least, are home. You can even buy an inexpensive device that works on a timer and simulates the flickering glow of a television (go to www.faketv.com).

Don't Be Lured away from Home

Burglars are skilled at luring people out of their homes. In one such instance, a woman's purse was stolen at a restaurant. The following day, she received a call from a woman who said she had taken the purse by mistake. The caller asked if the victim would meet her at a convenient location so she could return the purse. Upon returning home, the victim, thrilled to recover her property, found her home burglarized. It had been entered by an accomplice, who had duplicated a house key found in her purse.

What could the victim have done differently? She could have avoided the burglary by keeping her house keys separate from any form of identification. Failing that, she should have changed her locks immediately after realizing her purse was gone.

If an unfamiliar person in another kind of uniform appears—to read your gas or water meter, for example—shout through the door or intercom to wait while you call the utility company to determine if readings are being taken in your neighborhood that day. Also be wary of the door-to-door salesperson. Call your neighbors to see if they have been visited. If they haven't, the caller will probably be gone by the time you hang up the phone. If not and you are still suspicious, suggest that he or she call for an appointment at a later date. Legitimate salespeople may call you in an attempt to set up an appointment to see you at home. If you do agree to an appointment, confirm the salesperson's identity with the caller's office, using the phone directory number rather than the number given to you by your visitor.

TAKING INVENTORY

Identifying items of value that are likely to be stolen—TV sets, stereo equipment, radios, computers, cameras, binoculars, and firearms—makes life a lot tougher for burglars. Set aside a Saturday or Sunday to go through your home room by room, and list every item therein, noting also the approximate value of each and, where possible, serial numbers. Always save your receipts when you purchase an item of value. They come in handy when evaluating your valuables for the insurance company.

Operation Identification

Operation Identification is a nationwide project that encourages people to mark their property to combat burglary and theft. In some cities burglary rates for Operation Identification households were significantly lower than those of non-participants. Why? People who join a community-wide crime-prevention activity, like Neighborhood Watch and Operation Identification, are the same ones who install adequate lighting and deadbolt locks and who use and practice overall self-protection.

Use a form like the inventory sheet provided on page 22. Photograph items of extraordinary value, such as jewelry, silverware, and art. Then take the inventory to your insurance agent and discuss your existing coverage. You may also want to videotape each room in your home to have a visual record of contents. To prove the date of the video, record the front page of a newspaper or a television channel that shows the date and time.

Keep this inventory list up to date and put it in your safety deposit box or non-bank depository (see page 24) or give it to a trusted friend or relative. Do not keep a copy at your office or anywhere else that might serve as a shopping list for a burglar.

Another way to protect your belongings is to etch your name and the last four digits of your Social Security number or driver's license number onto your belongings with an electric pen that has a hard tip capable of scratching most metals. These pens are readily available; many crime-prevention bureaus will let you borrow one, or they can be purchased at any hardware store. (*See also* "Individual Crime Prevention," page 244.)

Devious Decals

Many people attach decals to their front doors to indicate that the home is protected by a patrol or alarm service or other type of security device. In many cases the homeowner purchased only the decals and no actual service or device. An accomplished thief is not fooled, but a less-experienced thief might be, so the decal itself may or may not be an effective deterrent.

Inventory Sheet

Use this chart to list all your valuable possessions room by room, or download one from the Internet. Keeping a running list on your computer is beneficial when it comes to adding and subtracting items. Be sure to save your data on a disk or USB drive and store it in a safe place, such as a safety deposit box or nonbank depository.

Room: _____

Date: _____

Item/ Serial Number	Date Purchased/ Cost	Current Value/ Insurance Coverage	Comments

Etching makes your household goods harder to fence. Also, etched goods must be defaced to remove any evidence of etching. People are less likely to buy defaced property, and fences will either not handle damaged goods at all or only at ridiculously low prices. Finally, thieves caught with etched merchandise are easily convicted. That said, some thieves will avoid etched property entirely.

Burglars almost never venture into kids' rooms. Your child's sock drawer is a safer bet to hide valuables than the medicine cabinet and master-bedroom night tables and dresser drawers.

Some assets defy etching, though, so other protective measures can be used, such as placing copies of expensive gems in your jewelry box and keeping the real ones hidden in a safe, marking the skin side of furs (after loosening the lining, of course), or requesting auto manufacturers to attach unique identifiers to automobile components. You can protect your vehicle's highly desirable, easily removed accessories, such as the CD player, by etching them with identifying information.

SAFEGUARDING VALUABLES

Burglars almost never venture into kids' rooms. Your child's sock drawer is a safer bet to hide valuables than the medicine cabinet and master-bedroom night tables and dresser drawers. However, it's best to take extra precautions when it comes to preserving important documents and jewelry. These small items can easily get lost or stolen and are sometimes impossible to replace.

Home Safes and Security Closets

Some people rely on a small safe to store valuable items. These are relatively inexpensive and protect your valuables against fire, but most can be removed by a skilled and determined burglar. Therefore, they provide no guarantee against theft. Also, most safes cannot protect larger items, like furs.

Storing Your Will

One document that should *not* be placed in a safety deposit box is your Last Will and Testament. The law in many states requires that a safety deposit box be sealed after the owner dies. It may take several days to obtain the necessary court authorization to open the box, so your family would not have immediate access to your will.

Instead, entrust your will to your lawyer. Attorneys have safes for these documents, and they can make your will available when necessary. Keep a copy of your will at home in a strongbox or in a nonbank depository.

However, there are ways to overcome some of these limitations. A small safe can be hidden, bolted to the walls or floor, or otherwise made a permanent addition to a structure. Setting the safe in concrete in the basement is one approach. You can also install an alarm.

One effective alternative to a safe is the home security closet. This requires lining the floor, walls, ceilings, and door of a suitable space with fire-retardant or fire-resistant material and then providing adequate locks for the entry door. Fire-resistant building material and adequate locking devices are generally available, so an accomplished handyman could create a security closet. An ordinary closet door should be rehung because the hinges of most are on the outside, where the hinge pins can be taken out, enabling the door to be removed. Bracing or otherwise strengthening the door frame is usually necessary so it cannot be removed along with the door.

It would be difficult, if not impossible, to construct a safety closet with walls as impenetrable as those of a safe. Thus, an alarm system is highly recommended. Or, for a more sophisticated installation, consult a general contractor or bank vault/safe installer.

Bank Services and Nonbank Depositories

One particularly valuable service offered by banks is a safety deposit box. There are also specially secured commercial 24-hour-a-day nonbank depositories. These locations are generally as secure as bank boxes—many have

Securities and Valuable Documents

Do not assume that stock certificates are not negotiable simply because they are issued in your name. Stolen stock certificates are frequently used as collateral for loans, which are then defaulted. Obtaining reissuance of a stock certificate to replace one that has been lost or stolen is a laborious and time-consuming process. There is also the distinct possibility that you might suffer a loss from being unable to sell a security while it is tied up for months in a reissuing process.

The best way to protect certificates is to leave them in your safety deposit box, in a non-bank depository, or in the custody of your broker. A federally sponsored insurance program protects investors from loss, within specified limits, of securities held by brokers for their clients.

It is also a good idea to keep important papers together in a fireproof box should you ever need to evacuate.

around-the-clock armed guards—and are accessible at any time, day or night. Virtually all these services are insured for the protection of clients; be sure to ask about the extent of any insurance coverage. Both kinds of depositories are recommended for storing valuable jewelry, stock or bond certificates, and all other valuable or important documents.

POSSESSING HANDGUNS AND FIREARMS

However comforting a gun might seem as a protective measure, it also increases the chances of an accident or homicide. Unless you and every member of your household know exactly how to keep and use a firearm safely, it is probably more hazardous to you than to any intruder.

The National Rifle Association (NRA) offers a number of common-sense suggestions for safeguarding a weapon in the home.

- Keep firearms out of the reach of children, the immature, and the irresponsible.
- Lock up unloaded firearms in the home.
- Keep weapons out of sight so that a thief is not tempted to use it.
- Lock up ammunition in a hidden place.

Gunning for Protection

As many as 220 million firearms can be found in U.S. homes, many of them handguns. But guns are deadly. About 30,000 Americans die each year from gunshots due to suicide, homicide, or accidents. More than 80 percent of these deaths are due to handguns. Guns kill more people between the ages of 15 to 24 than all natural causes combined.

To Arm or Not to Arm?

About 30,000 Americans die each year from gunshots due to suicide, homicide, or accidents. Over 80 percent of these deaths are due to handguns. Guns kill more people between the ages of 15 and 24 than all natural causes.

At present, the majority of states have passed legislation that requires a permit to carry a concealed firearm or other weapon for protection. Citizens who have passed a background check and completed a course in the safe use of firearms can get a permit. Many believe it is important to preserve the Constitutional right of citizens to keep and bear arms and that the ultimate protection of the people should rest in the protection available within the family unit.

Others, however, insist that the loss of lives from handgun use and abuse is too dear a price to pay, especially when it involves the lives of your own family members. One study found that keeping a gun in the home increases the residents' risk of murder by about three times and that these murders are more likely to be committed by family members or intimate acquaintances rather than strangers. Tragically, the lives lost are often children, many of whom locate their parents' handgun and are killed either by their own hand or by a family member. So ask yourself this question: What do I fear more than the possibility of my child's having access to a loaded firearm? Your answer to this question will dictate your course of action.

Handguns are extremely dangerous, not only to intended victims but also to owners and their families.

Guns kept in the home can fall into the hands of people who consciously intend to use them against others or sell them. This could include a family member, such as an angry spouse who uses the gun in the heat of a passionate argument. However, it can also include strangers. Research has found that about 500,000 guns are stolen from private citizens each year.

Guns in the home also bring an increased risk of suicide. In fact, the most common form of gun-related death in the home is suicide.

The overwhelming reason for having a handgun in the home is for protection of lives and assets. However, while many people keep guns in the home for protection, very rarely are they used for this purpose. Guns pose far more of a threat to your safety than any sort of protection. If assets are what you are trying to protect, then consider securing them in a bank or, more conveniently, in a non-bank depository. And also keep in mind that a home without a gun is not necessarily an *unarmed* home. Weapons such as knives and baseball bats are, in fact, used to thwart crimes in the home more than guns.

Handgun Safety

If you decide to keep a gun in your home, you must keep it safely away from unauthorized users, particularly children. Toward this end, you should take these precautions.

- If you decide to keep a loaded handgun in your dwelling for protection, be absolutely certain it is stored where children can't get to it.
- Keep all ammunition in boxes that are clearly and accurately marked.
- Purchase and use a trigger lock for the gun.
- Keep your finger out of the trigger guard unless you are ready to fire.
- Check your weapon to see if it is loaded before you use or store it.
- Remove the firing pins of guns that are part of a collection or are used for decorative purposes.
- Open the action immediately upon removing the gun from its case or rack.
- Ensure that your weapon is free of rust.
- Treat all weapons as if they are loaded.

- Carry your weapon with the muzzle under control at all times.
- Ensure that the bore is unobstructed.
- Make certain that all metal parts are free from accumulations of heavy grease.
- Be certain the action works freely.
- Be certain the trigger works freely.
- Be certain the safety works properly.
- Store only the type of ammunition prescribed for your weapon.
- Ensure that your weapon is cased, or its action opened, whenever you enter or leave an automobile.
- Follow local laws when transporting firearms, making certain they are not loaded.
- Enroll in a weapons safety course.
- Study your instruction manual thoroughly before using your firearm.
- Never handle firearms while under the influence of alcohol or drugs.
- Never give your child a toy that looks like a real gun.
- Store ammunition separately from the gun.

Licensing and Registration

Depending on the state in which you reside, if you do decide to keep a gun in your home, you may need to become a licensed gun owner. All federally licensed dealers require buyers to fill out a federal form. Gun control and regulation is an area subject to frequent changes in the law, so check the most recent laws in your state to make sure that you have met all its legal requirements before purchasing a gun and bringing it into your home. State requirements may also include a waiting period between the purchase of the firearm and the time the gun is physically given to you.

Legal Requirements for Safekeeping

A majority of states have enacted safe-storage gun laws, also known as child-access prevention (CAP) laws, imposing criminal liability on adults who negligently allow children to gain access to their firearms. The content of these laws varies from state to state. In some states the gun owner is liable if a child gains access to a firearm—loaded or unloaded—while in others the law applies only if the child actually uses the firearm. CAP laws also vary with respect to the age of the children who are covered. In most states the laws apply to children under the age of 16 and only to loaded guns; however, in Massachusetts, California, and Hawaii the laws also apply to unloaded guns.

While all CAP laws are concerned about safe gun storage, most do not provide exact requirements for storage. The law simply states that extreme caution must be exercised so that a child is prohibited from gaining access to a gun.

Practice safe gun storage (see "Handgun Safety," page 27) whether or not you have children. An improperly stored gun can still become accessible to other children, such as family members or neighbors who come to visit.

Firearm Locking Devices

All firearms in the home should be equipped with lockable trigger guards or a cable lock through the weapon's action. Trigger locks most commonly consist of two metal or plastic pieces that clamp down around the trigger mechanism on either side, completely covering the trigger and rendering it immobile. The locks are secured either by a key or by a combination-activated locking mechanism. Cable locks are inserted through the weapon's action and handle, then padlocked, thereby preventing the action from being closed and functioning. The lock also prevents the insertion of the magazine into the handle of a semiautomatic handgun.

Trigger locks should never be used on loaded firearms, since they have been known to cause a gun to fire. In addition, you run the risk of accidentally firing the weapon when installing or removing the trigger lock from a loaded gun. And even when using trigger locks on unloaded weapons, be aware that the lock does not prevent the weapon from being loaded—so along with using trigger locks, keep the ammunition in a separate, secure location. Some trigger locks can be easily broken by children, so store the gun in a locked cabinet. Also, keep in mind that not all trigger locks are created equal: Avoid cheap, plastic locks.

Although federal law does not require the use of firearm locking devices, several states are now legally requiring them.

Guns at Friends' Homes

Your children may have access to guns in their friends' and neighbors' homes. Nearly 40 percent of shootings of children under the age of 16 occur in the homes of friends and relatives. Talk to the parents of your children's friends to find out if they keep any firearms in their home, and if they do, make sure they are taking adequate steps to safely store them. Moreover, talk to your children about the dangers of guns so that should they somehow gain access to them, they will be less likely to touch them.

RELYING ON DOGS FOR PROTECTION

Dogs are an excellent source of protection and can serve as both a warning device and a deterrent. The question is, What type of dogs offers the best protection? And should a dog be stationed in the yard or in the house? A yard dog is likely to be a better deterrent, but a house dog is likely to be a better defense if an intruder gains entry inside your home. Consider also that yard dogs are more susceptible to being harmed or set loose by would-be intruders.

Whatever you decide, make sure that your dog is fully vaccinated and that the vaccinations are up to date. Proper identification and microchip ID implants are also essential in case of injury or disappearance.

Perhaps even more important than size and strength, however, is the dog's "voice"—the louder and more persistent its bark, the better.

Specially Trained Security Dogs

Specially trained security or attack dogs generally are not suitable for the average household. They are expensive, require periodic retraining, and must have constant practice and handling in order to retain their specialized skills. Also, these dogs must be kept away from welcome visitors.

A security-trained dog that gets loose and roams the neighborhood can become a menace and a liability, especially if it becomes confused in unfamiliar territory. Lack of regular training and handling can cause a dog to lose some of its "fail-safe" restraints. Thus, only people who are

Pet Doors

While pet doors may be a convenient way to allow your pets to freely enter and exit your home, keep in mind that they may also provide a very convenient point of entrance for intruders. Any opening that is larger than 9 inches by 10 inches (23 cm by 25 cm) can be used to gain entrance inside.

What's the solution? Don't have a pet door. However, if it's a must-have, outfit the door with a frame so that you can slide a security plate into the opening to prevent entrance when you are out. There are also one-way pet doors that enable cats and dogs to exit through the door but nothing (including the pets) to enter. Electronic pet doors can be opened only by a signal sent out from a transmitter placed in the cat's or dog's collar. When the animal gets within a few inches of the door, the signal is transmitted and the door opens. However, you still run the risk of a burglar catching your pet and wrestling the collar away from it. Finally, consider placing your pet door in a wall rather than in a door—this way, intruders may not even realize that you have one.

subject to extortion, kidnapping, or other very serious crimes, or those who keep extremely valuable items around the house, should consider housing these animals. Even then, owners should be aware of the risks involved, including the very heavy liability they face if the dog attacks an innocent person. These dogs can be hazards, both to their owners and to other people, especially young children. Never treat a trained guard dog as the family pet. Dogs raised as attack dogs can "snap" at any time, even against their owners.

The recent increase in crime—especially aggravated assaults, rapes, and robberies—has given rise to charlatans who pass off ill-trained or untrained animals as trained security dogs. Conversely, unscrupulous kennels may sell you an overtrained dog, aware that you lack the ability to handle the animal.

The personality of most dogs reflects their upbringing, so enlist the aid of a veterinarian, the head of the police dog squad, and other qualified individuals before deciding where to buy an attack dog.

The legal requirements for owning an attack animal can vary by city or state, so research regulations in your local area before getting one.

In most cases the animal must be registered and wear a tag that identifies it as an attack animal. In addition, the premises on which the attack animal is kept must have a sign or notice that clearly warns the public of the animal's presence. To reduce potential liability, it is prudent that you go through handler training in order to learn commands for protection and how to control the animal. Be aware that some specific breeds and types of attack dogs—including pit bulls, rottweilers, German shepherds, and Dobermans—may be outlawed in certain areas.

Common Breeds

Most people don't require specially trained guard dogs for proper security; many common breeds can be just as effective. Which one you select is largely a matter of personal preference. For security purposes a large dog is generally more intimidating than a small one. Rottweilers, Doberman pinschers, and German shepherds are most frequently preferred. Pit bulls have also become popular due to their immense strength, despite some widely reported incidents involving them in unprovoked attacks. Several states, in fact, have restrictions on keeping pit bulls and other potentially dangerous animals.

Perhaps even more important than size and strength, however, is the dog's "voice"—the louder and more persistent its bark, the better. A small dog that barks a lot, especially when people approach your residence, can be a great deterrent. Female dogs are reputed to be more territorially protective. Like the wolves and foxes from which they descend, dogs are nocturnal animals by nature, but they often adapt to the rest patterns of their masters. Nevertheless, their innate sense of nighttime hunting makes them particularly valuable protectors when the rest of the household is asleep.

ENCOUNTERING AN INTRUDER

Even if you have done an excellent job securing your home, a skilled and determined intruder may still find a way to break in. Whether you come home to find an intruder inside your home or you are at home when you realize someone is breaking in, you need to know the safest way to respond to the situation at hand.

What to Do during a Home Invasion

- [ ] If there are other family members in the house, make sure that everyone stays together.
- [ ] Go to as secure an area as possible that has a landline you can use to call for help, or be sure to take your cell phone with you. If using a cell phone, be prepared to give the dispatcher your address.
- [ ] Dial 911 immediately. If you have a silent panic alarm, activate it.
- [ ] Escape the dwelling if at all possible.
- [ ] If required, barricade yourself and your family inside a room so the intruders cannot reach you.
- [ ] Home invasions generally last only for a short time—minutes, in fact. Continue to buy time in any way that is practical.

Would You Recognize a Burglar?

If you were asked to describe a burglar, you'd probably portray a hardened criminal, not the fuzzy-cheeked teenager who comes around weekly to ask if you want your lawn mowed. Or the neighbor who carries around the Swiss Army knife, perfect for removing a small pane of glass from a front door, providing access to the night latch (as opposed to the deadbolt lock, which would provide more reliable protection). Even worse, the nice boy who once dated your daughter and gave her an expensive stereo for her birthday.

The point? Appearances can be deceiving, even when it comes to burglars.

To Flee or Not to Flee?

If you arrive home to find an intruder, your first reaction will almost certainly be fright, plus an impulse to protect your possessions, leading to the temptation to yell. Confrontation is not a good idea, if only because you might block the intruder's only avenue of escape. You are an obstacle to the intruder's survival—a very dangerous situation if the intruder is armed, desperate, or violent.

A much better way of handling the situation is to go as quickly and as quietly as possible to a neighbor's house and call the police. Then call a neighbor within view of your home and ask them to watch your house while you await the police. If you come home to find your house has been broken into but you do not see a burglar, do not enter the house—the intruder may be hiding somewhere inside.

If an intruder breaks in while you are home, again, it is far safer for you and your family to escape and get to the safety of a neighbor's house as quickly as possible rather than stay behind to confront the intruder. Escape is always the best option.

If you are forced to confront the intruder, stay calm and wait for the right moment to take action. Attack fast and with force. As soon as the intruder is immobilized or momentarily stunned, make your escape. If you want to heighten your defense skills, consider enrolling in a self-defense or martial-arts course.

Entering an Empty House

When entering an empty dwelling, whether it's your residence or a friend's house that you were asked to look after in their absence, be aware of the interior environment. Look for any item that is out of place and could suggest an intruder—a rug that is askew, a light on that shouldn't be, or some dirt or grass at an odd location. Also be aware of unfamiliar smells in your environment. If suspicious factors are present, leave immediately, go to a neighbor's house or public place, and call the authorities.

Create a family security plan detailing what to do and where to go should a home invasion occur (see "What to Do during a Home Invasion," page 33). Create a plan with your neighbors, too, so that you can help each other in an emergency.

If you want to heighten your defense skills, consider enrolling in a self-defense or martial-arts course.

LIVING ALONE

People living alone, especially women, must take special precautions because criminals will likely perceive him or her to be vulnerable. The home will often be empty, so extra measures must be taken to make it appear occupied. Here are just a few ideas to fool intruders:

- Use timers to turn on lights, radios, and televisions at preset times, and use an answering machine so callers won't know if you're home or not.
- Get a dog—it serves as an excellent deterrent—or simply pretend you have one: Purchase a barking tape from an alarm company, place a BEWARE OF DOG sign on your door or window, and leave a water and food bowl outside.

Filing a Police Report

There may come a time when you have to report a criminal or crime to the police. Below is some essential information you should include to help police apprehend a suspect.

☐ Where—the address or the street intersection.

☐ When—time of day.

☐ What—the type of crime, injury, shots, fight, and so on.

☐ Who—the persons involved, including how many and their descriptions.

☐ Escape details—if the person fled the scene in a car, give the license number, make, and model, as well as where the suspect headed, toward what nearby intersection, and so on.

- Keep a telephone in the bedroom—a cell phone is your best bet, because it allows emergency calls even if the telephone lines are cut, and it's portable. A disadvantage to using a cell phone is that the 911 dispatcher will not have automatic access to your address when you call. Be prepared to report your address when calling for help.
- Install a strong deadbolt lock on the bedroom door. The lock should be key-operated, and a duplicate key should be left with a friend or a trusted neighbor in case of sudden illness or other event necessitating quick assistance.
- Keep doors locked at all times, even if you're home, and be especially cautious about strangers at your door. Install a peephole in your door if you don't have one and use it to verify the identity of visitors before allowing them in.
- If your building has a locked entrance, don't let strangers in behind you, and avoid getting into the elevator with a strange person. If you are embarrassed and need an excuse, say something like, "I forgot my mail" or "I forgot to buy something at the store."
- Reside in a building or complex that provides adequate security and be sure that the locks on the doors are changed with every new tenant. If your building is lacking in security measures, complain to the building manager and persuade your neighbors to do the same. (See chapter 9 for more information on apartments and condos.)
- In both the telephone listing and on your mailbox or intercom, list your last name and only a first initial to avoid disclosing your gender.
- If possible, make your schedule unpredictable, and don't reveal it to anyone.
- Avoid telling people you don't know very well that you live alone. Tell them you have a roommate or that you live with a relative.

Keep Your Keys Next to Your Bed at Night

If you hear a suspicious noise outside or you think someone is trying to break into your home, grab the keys off your nightstand and press the Panic button. The alarm will immediately sound off and the horn will continue to sound until your car battery dies. Odds are the burglar won't stick around with all that racket.

CHAPTER 3

ALARM SYSTEMS

More than ever before, homeowners and renters are investing in home security, and a residential alarm system is one of their top priorities.

SECURITY FUNCTIONS

An alarm system does two things: It detects and it communicates. Some alarm systems function both as fire alarms and as intrusion alarms. Panic or silent duress buttons add a third function—manually communicating the need for assistance. High-tech systems may also control the temperature of a wine cellar; monitor a vital piece of equipment, such as a home furnace; or warn of a flooded basement.

Fire Detection

You're more likely to have a fire than an intruder, so it is important to understand this function of the alarm system first.

Fires develop in four stages: the incipient stage, the smoldering stage, the flame stage, and the heat stage. Naturally, the earlier in its development that a fire can be detected, the better the chances to limit the damage it will cause. Different sensors on the market are designed to

Practice a Home Fire Escape Plan

More than 6,500 people die each year from fires, most of them children and senior citizens. So when a fire breaks out, every second counts. That's why it's so important to plan ahead. Unfortunately, though, a recent study found that more than 80 percent of families don't discuss fire safety with their children at home. Here's how you can be prepared:

- Install smoke detectors and make sure they are in good working order.
- Attach rope ladders to upstairs bedroom windows and practice using them.
- Create a floor diagram of your house, mark all possible exits, and talk about possible escape routes.
- Open all the windows in the house to see if they function properly. Any jammed windows should be repaired.
- Explain the importance of closing bedroom doors when family members are sleeping; it takes a fire about 15 minutes to burn through a wooden door.
- Discuss the dangers of smoke, and practice crawling on your hands and knees to the nearest exit.
- Warn never to open any doors that are hot.
- Role-play what you would do if you were trapped—close all doors between you and the smoke; cover vents and openings under doors with towels; if a telephone is nearby, call the fire department with your exact location.
- Establish a safe meeting place, like a neighbor's yard, a mailbox, or a specific tree.

detect a fire in these different stages. Unfortunately, however, there is no one detector that can detect all of these stages. The following systems provide a relatively inexpensive and effective means of fire protection, and many insurance companies discount premiums for customers who install them.

Ceiling-mounted ionization detectors. In its incipient stage, a fire doesn't produce any smoke or flame. It does, however, generate products of combustion—microscopic particles that rise on air currents. Ceiling-mounted ionization detectors can identify these particles and set

Choosing a Carbon Monoxide Detector

Here are some things to keep in mind when purchasing a carbon monoxide detector.

☐ Always have a battery backup for any plug-in detector so that the unit will continue to function even in the event of a power failure.

☐ Look for a detector that sounds a warning when just a low level of carbon monoxide is detected, since even low-level exposure to carbon monoxide over a long period of time can be hazardous.

☐ Make sure the alarm you purchase is UL-approved. (Underwriters Laboratories is an independent, nonprofit testing organization.)

off an alarm. This is the most expensive kind of sensor available. Due to its method of detection, though, it may sound a false alarm in a dusty atmosphere.

Photoelectric detector. The photoelectric detector will sound an alarm during the fire's smoldering stage. This type of detector is not good for areas that normally have smoke, such as a kitchen or areas near a fireplace, since the detector will cause a false alarm if excessive but non-threatening smoke is produced. These units are relatively inexpensive.

Rate-of-rise or temperature-change detector. This type senses the rapid temperature increase that occurs as the fire progresses from the smoldering stage to the flame stage and then to the heat stage. A heat or fixed-temperature detector, which activates when the air around it reaches a designated temperature, may be incorporated into a single unit with the rate-of-rise detector.

Carbon Monoxide Detectors

Just as you need to protect your family from intruders trying to invade your home, you also need to protect your family from dangers that can emanate from within your home, including carbon monoxide. Carbon monoxide is an extremely hazardous gas with no smell, color, or taste. Because it is so difficult to detect, it is the most common cause of fatal poisonings, with about 50 percent of all carbon monoxide poisonings occurring in the home. The only way to truly protect yourself and your family is to install a carbon monoxide detector.

What to Do If Your Carbon Monoxide Detector Goes Off

Simply having the carbon monoxide detector is not enough—you must also know how to respond if the alarm sounds. Your first response should be to open all windows and doors in order to ventilate your home. If anyone inside your house is experiencing headaches, dizziness, or any other flulike symptoms, immediately evacuate everyone from the house and call the fire department. Do not reenter the house until a firefighter tells you that it is safe to do so.

The best place to install one is where people will be able to hear it, even when they are sleeping, but do not install in kitchens or bathrooms, where smoke from cooking or steam from bathing may cause the alarm to malfunction. Nor should it be placed in very cold or hot rooms, because these extreme temperatures may also cause the detector to malfunction.

Because it is so difficult to detect, carbon monoxide is the most common cause of fatal poisonings, with about 50 percent of all carbon monoxide poisonings occurring in the home.

Intruder Detection: Alarming Doors and Windows

There are two broad categories of devices used to detect intruders: point protection and space or volumetric protection. Point-protection devices detect an intrusion through a specific location, such as a door or window and even through a wall. Space-protection devices detect movement within a particular area (see "Intruder Detection: Alarming Rooms,"page 43).

Point-protection devices include:

Magnetic contact switches, which can either be surface-mounted or concealed. When the magnet is attached to a door or window, and the switch is attached to the door jamb or window frame, the magnet keeps the contact points apart. When the door or window is opened, the magnet can no longer hold the spring-loaded contact to prevent the switch from engaging, and the alarm sounds. The surface-mounted version of the switch can be defeated by using another magnet to hold the switch contact, even when the door is opened. Using another magnet configuration can negate this possibility.

Shock or seismic detectors, which provide protection for the specific object upon which they are mounted, such as walls, safes, file cabinets and closets. They also guard window frames, glass panes, and patio or French doors. Any vibrations resulting from pushing, knocking, banging, touching, or kicking will upset the equilibrium of the device and sound the alarm.

Pressure detectors, which use something like a doormat that is installed under the carpet inside the doorway, in a hallway, or on stairs. An individual's weight on the mat brings electrical contacts together and activates the alarm. Some self-opening doors at supermarkets and discount stores employ the same principle.

A beam of light shining across the inside of a door or window to a photoelectric sensor, like those that prevent elevator doors from closing on passengers. The alarm is activated by the interruption of the beam. However, an intruder could circumvent a photoelectric sensor merely by stepping over or sliding under the beam or by shining a light beam at the sensor. To overcome this vulnerability, many photoelectric sensors use infrared light, which is invisible to the human eye. (This technology can also be used for space protection by placing the transmitter at one end of a room and the receiver at the other.)

A fiber-optic wire mesh built directly into the walls of especially sensitive areas, such as a silver closet or safe room. The breaking of the wire triggers the alarm.

Glass-breakage detectors, which can either be ceiling-mounted or attached to windows. These sound when an intruder tries to enter the home by breaking a glass window or door. This type of detector is highly effective. There are many types on the market today. Some respond to sound, others to vibration, and still others to both. Some glass-breakage detectors need to be placed on every window, while others use just one to cover multiple windows. These detectors have replaced the silver-colored foil tape in the past on glass doors and windows. Some are designed to work with certain kinds of glass. With almost all glass-breakage detectors, however, you run the risk of false alarms, because these detectors may go off in response to other sounds, such as bells or tinkling tableware.

Intruder Detection: Alarming Rooms

Space-protection devices detect movement within a specific area, alerting you to an intruder in a particular room of your house. Here are some types to consider.

Ultrasonic sensors generate high-frequency sound waves. These waves are too high in pitch to be heard by the human ear, so intruders are not aware of their existence. When the waves bounce off an intruder, the pattern of the waves is altered, activating the alarm. Unfortunately, some individuals—and many pets—are irritated by these ultrasonic "noises." In addition, these sensors are subject to false alarms caused by the flapping of a curtain, a ringing telephone, or even a rush of air from a heater or air conditioner starting up. Loud noises in adjacent spaces might also activate this system. Two sensors, tuned to different frequencies, may cause false alarms if installed too near one another.

Electromagnetic microwaves, rather than sound waves, are used in a similar system. While this eliminates the irritation to sensitive ears, these waves can penetrate walls rather than bounce off them like the ultrasonic waves. This means that movement in the next room or outside the building can activate this detector.

Passive infrared (PIR) sensors detect an intruder's presence by sensing the contrast between an intruder's body heat and the temperature of the surfaces within the space. There are drawbacks to this type of system. Obviously, a PIR detector would be impractical for protecting an area often frequented by people. Animals, heating ducts, electric motors, and even television receivers are capable of emitting sufficient heat to affect its operation. Also, these devices become less reliable at room or ambient temperatures approaching normal body temperature, because at such levels the body's temperature would be masked by that of the surrounding air.

Audio detectors are used to protect entire rooms. These detectors consist of wall- or ceiling-mounted microphones. The detectors are set at a certain noise level, and if that level is exceeded, a signal is sent to a central station. Keep in mind that the central-station operator can open a circuit and listen to activity in the monitored space, even if nothing warrants attention.

No single-sensor technology can be considered effective on its own. A free-standing residence may have magnetic contact switches on all exterior doors and windows, space protection in hallways, and a magnetic contact on the door to a silver cupboard. A good system uses a number of technologies, so that an intruder who defeats one layer of protection will be caught by the next one. A qualified professional can help determine which mixture of alarm system devices is best for you.

SIGNALING THE MONITORING STATION

Once a detector has sensed a fire or intruder, the system must be able to communicate an alert. The detectors can be set to activate a bell or siren on the premises or to activate a device that transmits an emergency message to a monitoring station. Alarm systems typically use a telephone line to transmit a signal to a central station where personnel on duty alert the police or fire department. Cell phones are also used as transmitters for alarm systems and as backup for landline alarm notification.

False alarms—as high as 98 percent of all alarm signals transmitted—are a major problem. The alarm industry has made a determined effort to reduce this rate by improving the products and by educating dealers and installers in proper installation techniques and use of effective alarm components and location, as well as in user understanding of system activation and deactivation.

In most communities, due to high rates of false alarms and limited response resources, police and fire departments no longer accept alarm signals directly from residential or most commercial alarm control units. Instead, the signal must travel from the protected premises to a central station, where personnel then telephone the appropriate public agency. In some jurisdictions the alarm company must confirm that the intrusion alarm is not false before the police will respond.

ARMING AND DISARMING THE SYSTEM

Regardless of how sophisticated your alarm system may be, there is always one potential problem—you. You must remember to turn the alarm system on and off. This is called arming and disarming the system. The greatest false-alarm hazard lies in your failure, upon reentering your protected premises, to identify yourself properly to the alarm control unit, either with a key or your code number, within the allotted time.

All intrusion-alarm arming-and-disarming processes include a time-delay feature. Time delay lets you activate the system from inside the residence and then have a set amount of time to exit before the system is armed. On reentering, the time delay provides a certain amount of time to shut off the system before an alarm is activated. The system will sound a pre-alarm tone to remind you to disarm the system and to let an intruder know that an alarm has been activated.

Common Types of Arming Mechanisms

You must be able to turn the alarm on and off and enter your home without triggering the alarm or compromising its effectiveness at detecting an intruder. Here are the three arming (or disarming) mechanisms generally used with an alarm system.

- Permanently installed push-button keypad arm/disarm systems, which are more convenient and secure than key-operated systems. But if the code numbers are discovered, then the security of your system is compromised. The key-operated system is used less frequently, since possible theft of the arm-disarm key creates a system vulnerability. If a key-operated system is utilized, the key should be of cylindrical design to minimize success in picking the lock.
- Portable handheld keypads that resemble a calculator, television remote control, or key fob to arm/disarm, bypass selected parts of the system, transmit a silent duress (panic) alarm, and query the system from distances up to 100 feet (31 m) from the system control unit. You must enter your personal code before the system will acknowledge commands.
- Alarm systems that let you telephone in from anywhere in the world to arm/disarm, bypass, and query the system. Again, your personal code must be entered for the system to acknowledge commands.

PURCHASING AN ALARM

When you set out to buy an alarm system, begin by seeking objective advice. Many police crime-prevention units and fire departments have alarm system specialists. Your insurance carrier probably has a specialist who will not only be able to recommend special equipment but also be able to tell you how to lower your insurance premiums by installing it. If you aren't satisfied, contact the Better Business Bureau, who may be able to steer you away from some of the fly-by-night firms. Of course, alarm manufacturers and installers will be more than happy to offer advice. It may not be totally objective, but if it is the only advice available, it is better than nothing.

Some alarm systems are worse than none at all. You can't afford to have a system that delivers only false security. In selecting a source for your alarm system, remember that the equipment is complex and that you must have good service available. Generally, this rules out buying a system by mail from a distant supplier or from any firm other than one that specializes in the sale, installation, and service of such systems. As a rule, the longer the warranty, the better the system. But if the system is issued by a "here today, gone tomorrow" firm, the warranty, regardless of terms, is suspect.

Check parts inventories. If a critical part is available only from a single manufacturer located in a remote or far away location, you may be asking for trouble. If your dealer doesn't have the parts on hand, your system may be useless.

Features to Look For

Certain features should be a part of your alarm installation. Keep these things in mind when purchasing your system:

Look for the system's self-check capability. This enables you to check the "health" of your alarm system and be certain it is in proper operating condition. Of course, you must remember to make these capability checks. Even if you forget, an alarm with a system-in-trouble warning signal will probably jog your memory.

Require that the system have a line-interruption monitor. This will activate the alarm in the event the telephone line is cut or damaged.

Insist on a provision for emergency power when normal power supplies are interrupted. In the event of a fire, which may interrupt your power, your auxiliary power could save your life. If an intruder deliberately interrupts your power, auxiliary power could prevent loss of property, injury, or death at the hands of the thief.

Install the control panel within a locked cabinet or an area not accessible to an unauthorized person. Installing the control panel in the garage, for example, will make you an easy target for anyone who comes to work on your home. And since many homeowners don't alarm the garage doors, it is easy for an intruder to break in and disarm the alarm without your knowledge.

Make sure that entrances such as crawlspace doors into basement areas are alarmed. These entrances are often overlooked by residents but are hot spots for intruders.

Follow the manufacturer's recommendations for battery replacement to ensure its viability. Some auxiliary power systems employ non-rechargeable batteries; others use rechargeable batteries, which can malfunction, too. If your system has this type of backup, you should determine proper testing procedures. You may need to contact the manufacturer of the batteries to obtain the information, since the equipment installer may not have it or may claim that the batteries never need replacement. If you contract for quarterly or semi-annual system inspection, battery inspection will be part of the process.

Make certain that your alarm's signal horn is loud enough to be effective. Ideally, the horn should be mounted in the attic and sound through a vent to the outside. Before you sign any security system contract, arrange to see an installation that has been performed by your chosen contractor. Check for its appearance, workmanship, and customer satisfaction.

Consider the tax consequences of your system. Certain types of installations may affect the tax treatment you receive when you sell your home. For example, a permanent, hard-wired, through-the-wall installation may be more expensive initially, but it may pay off handsomely in the long run.

Wired or Wireless?

Alarm systems can be wired, wireless, or a combination of the two. A "wired" alarm system is one in which all the individual sensors are connected to the system control cabinet, while the components of "wireless" systems communicate via transmitted radio signals.

Wired alarm systems have proved to be very reliable. Wireless systems are increasing in popularity but have disadvantages. For example, the transmitters are battery-operated, and the batteries need to be changed every four to five years. Although some systems are self-checking, others have no way of letting you know if one of the transmitters is not working, giving you a false sense of security. In addition, you must be certain that the wireless signal is unimpeded by structural barriers or extended distance from sensors to the base transmitter. On the other hand, wireless systems have many advantages. Wireless equipment can be placed exactly where you want it, without having to worry about drilling into walls or ceilings in order to run wires. Wireless systems are also easier to install and are portable, so they can be brought along if you move. Wireless systems are often less expensive and less costly to install than wired systems.

If you want to purchase a wireless alarm system, here are some things you should look for:

- The system should be supervised, meaning that the control panel and sensors are in constant communication with each other via transmitted signals.
- The transmitters should also be tamper-proof.
- The sensors should send two signals in order to activate the control panel. These signals communicate to the control panel the alarm status and provide an ongoing diagnosis of the system condition.

CHOOSING A PROVIDER

Now that you've decided to purchase a particular alarm system, you need to select the alarm provider. But there are a few things you should know about before signing up.

Buyer Beware

You may find unscrupulous opportunists during your search for an alarm company. Beware of companies that use scare tactics to sell alarm systems, particularly through unsolicited direct-mail advertising or door-to-door salespeople. Don't allow yourself to be stampeded into immediate action. The best response to a now-or-never sales approach is "Never!" Instead, take the time to do the following:

Find out if your state requires an alarm company or dealer to be licensed. If so, make certain that the company or dealer has a license. Ask if the establishment has its own central station, who manages it, and its location. Find out who is expected to respond to an alarm signal. Does the alarm company have its own security force, or are the local police expected to respond? And, of course, ask for the average response time to an alarm signal.

Beware of companies that use scare tactics to sell alarm systems, particularly through unsolicited direct-mail advertising or door-to-door salespeople.

Beware of installation charges. Many unscrupulous operators quote absurdly low prices (for absurdly inferior equipment) plus a "nominal installation fee." Your definition of *nominal* may be a lot different from theirs. If possible, contract a set price for all services, including installation.

Research the dealer if you are financing your alarm system. The dealer may offer to finance the installation and cost of the system. In most instances the dealer will then sell the contract to a bank or finance company, which becomes its holder. The dealer is then responsible for carrying out the contract. If the dealer defaults on the contract, you will probably be liable for the payment. You could very well get fleeced under such an agreement, especially if there is collusion between an unethical contractor and equally unethical holder. You must be sure you are dealing with a completely reliable, ethical contractor.

Carefully select the communication phase of an alarm's operation. Find out how the alarm signal will be carried from the protected premises to a monitoring/response point. If you buy a system that the installer programs to dial the police or fire department with an emergency message, make sure your town's departments will respond. Also, confirm that radio-transmitted messages don't violate FCC regulations.

Beware of extended service contracts. While good service from a reliable contractor is the main consideration when you purchase an alarm system, contractual prepayment for this service may be unnecessary and expensive. Be certain to investigate total costs before making your commitment. Insist on a clear explanation of the warranty and ask whether or not alarm components are manufactured in the United States or out of the country. If out of country, inquire about the extent of the contractor's equipment inventory.

Narrowing It Down

Once you've honed in on a few possible providers, you must meet with them, obtain references, and agree on the installation costs. Here are some guidelines to follow before you sign the contract.

- Make sure the alarm company will meet with you in person at your home. Be sure to ask the company representative for proper identification before allowing him or her into your home.
- Ask for an inspection, recommendation, and a quote in writing. Get quotes from at least three or four different installers, including the prices of setup, equipment, monthly monitoring fees, and warranties.
- Get a list of references from each provider so that you can contact current clients and find out if they are satisfied with their service. If possible, view the installer's workmanship on other systems he or she has installed.
- Find out how long the company has been in business; select a home-security provider that has been in business for at least five years.
- Make sure the company carries general liability, worker's compensation, and errors/omissions insurance, and ask to see the company's business license.
- Contact the Better Business Bureau to see if any complaints have been filed against the company.
- Find out where the alarm system's monitoring center is located and if they have redundant monitoring locations in the event of monitoring disruptions, such as severe weather.
- Make sure that all alarm system equipment to be installed is your own property rather than leased property. All installed equipment should be certified as industry-standard compliant, such as UL-approved. This certification may qualify you for a homeowner's insurance discount.
- Select a company that provides 24-hour customer support and services.

CHOOSING A MONITORING SERVICE

An alarm system isn't worth anything without a reliable monitoring service. Once the alarm sounds, it is up to the monitoring service to communicate with the authorities. You must be able to depend on them 24/7. Below are several specific features to look for when making your selection.

- Look for cell phone backup. Most home alarm companies offer 24-hour monitoring, which is usually conducted via phone lines. However, in the case that your phone line becomes disconnected, it is important that the alarm system has cellular backup.
- Make sure the alarm company is UL-approved and conducts system testing on an interval basis (usually once per day) in order to ensure that your alarm system is working and the phone lines are operable.
- Find a company that offers annual maintenance so that your alarm system gets tested and cleaned at least once per year.

If your front entrance consists of decorative glass, never install the key pad where it can be seen from the doorstep. Then burglars can easily determine if it's set.

KEEPING YOUR SECURITY SECRET

Do not advertise everything you do to make your home secure, because every defensive action you take can be countered, subverted, or bypassed when a would-be intruder knows exactly what to expect. So should you display an alarm decal that highlights the type of alarm system you installed? It may deter an amateur burglar, but a professional burglar can possibly circumvent it, given enough time. If the residence is isolated or in a rural area, the intruder will likely not care if there is an alarm system— betting that the intrusion can be completed before the arrival of law enforcement. If the residence is located in a neighborhood around other dwellings, a decal may be more effective in intimidating a burglar.

In addition, if your front entrance consists of decorative glass, never install the key pad where it can be seen from the doorstep. Then burglars can easily determine if it's set.

Relying on Webcams for Home Monitoring

More and more people are able to watch over their young children, elderly parents, vacation homes, dogs, and even fish using their laptop's webcam. By purchasing software such as HomeCamera, which has motion detection and automatic recording times, users can monitor what's going on and receive e-mail alerts about possible intrusions. Homeowners can also purchase individual cameras with built-in webcams to be placed in several different rooms.

You need to strike a balance between deterrence and total disclosure, revealing enough to discourage the random burglar but not so much that you make it easy for the skilled and determined pro who singles you out. And obviously, do not let others know you own items of value.

Wireless and GPS technology now offer an array of personal asset-protection systems, both portable and stationary, that can be applied to various situations requiring enhanced security. For example, personal duress alarms, which can be carried, will immediately alert a monitoring station of an adverse personal situation such as a medical emergency or physical assault. Such system capabilities now can signal not only duress but also specific locations under certain conditions. Surveillance monitoring of the location of your personal vehicle is also available.

Valuable assets at your residence, such as artwork, may now incorporate additional security protection utilizing radio-frequency devices that signal to alarm base monitoring or to a local alarm that the asset has been tampered with. Technology now can assist in recovery of a missing asset by transmitting tracking information to a monitoring operation or directly to law enforcement. Property tracking can now be accomplished on outdoor assets such as farm equipment or household emergency generators, which can be fitted with asset protection devices that signal if the equipment is moved.

Site security, including the perimeter of your house or yard, can be monitored, alerting if anyone entered during your absence. Actually, only the imagination now limits the use of wireless/GPS technology for personal and domestic security applications.

CHAPTER 4

THE TELEPHONE

The telephone is essential for communicating in today's world. But it is also an instrument of crime—in fact, possibly the most widely used criminal instrument.

ESSENTIAL RULES

Telephones are in everyone's home, but unfortunately criminals rely on them all too often for stealing identities, gathering information for a break-in, or simply to harass unsuspecting individuals. The cardinal rule with regard to the telephone is that you should always use it on your terms, not those of the caller. In other words, never talk on the phone unless you do so willingly.

Guard What You Say

Never say anything over the telephone that you don't want a stranger to know. For example, a caller who asks for the man of the house should never be told that one doesn't exist or that he is out of town. Tell the caller that your father or husband is asleep and will return the call when he wakes up. It is vitally important that this lesson be taught to children, as well as ingrained as a habit in adults.

Keep an Emergency Phone List

It is always a good idea to keep a list of emergency numbers right next to all your phones or taped to the back of the handset. If you have children, you should teach them how to dial 911 in case of an emergency and define what a "real" emergency is. Below is a list of the most notable ones to include:

- police department
- fire department
- poison control
- parents' cell numbers
- parents' work numbers
- pediatrician

answering the phone at all. All children should be taught never to talk to strangers on the phone, and if they do, never to tell them they are home alone or provide their address.

Children should also be told who to call for help if they receive unusual or threatening phone calls, and this number should be kept on speed dial. You must also teach your child how to dial 911. Never instruct a child to "Call nine-eleven." Always use the numerals nine-one-one. Children may become confused since there is no eleven on a phone.

Keep a list of all emergency numbers (police, fire department, poison control, etc.), both parents' cell and work numbers, and your home address on the back of the phone.

Unlisted vs. Unpublished Numbers

Many people protect their privacy by having their phone numbers either unlisted or unpublished. These aren't the same thing. Having an

Keep the Phone On

Never disconnect the telephone while you are away from home. A temporary disconnection message is a clear indication of one of two things: You haven't paid your bill or you are out of town, neither of which is information you want to share.

Answering Machine Dos and Don'ts

Telephone answering machines indicate that you cannot take calls at the present time, and many people use them to screen their calls. But they're not so safe if you inadvertently provide too much information in your message. Always be as brief and generic as possible so that the caller cannot determine anything about your personal status. For example,

- Do not indicate that you are away from home.
- Use your first name only, to avoid revealing your surname to a caller who doesn't already know it.
- Don't repeat your phone number in the message.
- Never leave seductive messages, and always use "we" instead of "I."
- If you are a woman living alone, have a male relative or friend record your message or use the preprogrammed automated message that comes as an option with most answering machines.
- If you travel extensively, purchase an answering device that enables you to receive messages from another telephone. This way, you can return your calls from far away and avoid revealing that you are out of town.
- Never disclose the date you will be arriving back home in your message.

unlisted number means that your name, address, and telephone number are excluded from the phone book but can still be found through Directory Assistance. An unpublished number, on the other hand, means that this information is excluded from both the phone book *and* Directory Assistance. Both of these services add an extra cost to your telephone bill, but many people believe that this is a small price to pay for dodging unwanted telephone calls.

CELL PHONES

Although cell phones are designed with security in mind, don't forget that someone will undoubtedly devise a method or piece of equipment to defeat your safeguards. You must continually upgrade the safety and security of your phone in case it is stolen.

Built into the system are theft-prevention protocols, including a user-entered password to operate. If, however, an owner chooses not to use password security or carelessly leaves the code on a nearby scrap of paper, a thief can make all the free calls he wishes. But when you notify the cellular service provider of the theft, the service will be deactivated.

Controlled-Use Phones for Children

Cell phones aren't just for adults anymore. More and more parents are giving cell phones to their children as a safety precaution. Controlled-use phones, such as Firefly, are cell phones that are specifically designed for young children. They have only five keys rather than a regular number pad, and they are designed for a child's small hands.

Parents can program up to 20 phone numbers into the phone, plus two speed-dial keys for both parents, giving them control over whom their children are able to call, as well as whom they can receive calls from; the phone rejects any call that doesn't come from a preprogrammed number. In addition, a button enables children to easily access a 911 operator in case of an emergency.

HANDLING UNWANTED CALLS

It is almost impossible to live without a telephone, but it can quickly become an annoyance when you get bombarded with unsolicited calls.

Nuisance and Obscene Calls

Under federal and most state laws, it is a crime to make harassing or obscene telephone calls.

If you do receive an obscene call, hang up immediately and forget it! Most obscene calls are isolated one-time occurrences, possibly placed by someone dialing numbers at random. Often the callers are adolescents, although annoyance callers can also include neighbors, acquaintances, or fellow employees. Should the calls continue, do not broadcast your displeasure. If you are not expecting important calls, remove the receiver from the hook for a short time. The caller will likely be frustrated and turn his or her attention elsewhere. Maintain a log of the calls, and notify your telephone company immediately. Usually a pattern of calls must be documented before action can be taken. Report calls to your local telephone company's Annoyance Call Bureau.

Under no circumstances should you attempt to debate or get into a shouting or cursing match with your caller—unless, of course, law-enforcement or telephone security personnel ask you to do so to assist in their investigation. (Confirm the identity of the person requesting your assistance, since some obscene callers get someone to call first and pretend to be from the phone company.) To excite or inflame anyone is a certain invitation for a repeat performance. Do not talk to the caller at all. Anything other than hanging up or leaving the receiver off the hook encourages the caller to continue.

The best way to avoid obscene or nuisance calls is to get an unlisted number. However, changing your telephone number won't be effective if the caller is an acquaintance who will learn your new number. One expert suggests having two numbers—a new number and an answering machine to pick up your former number—so that your harasser will not be able to contact you anymore. After a while he or she may give up.

A common tactic to discourage such calls is blowing a loud whistle into the receiver. However, some experts caution that this will agitate the caller and make the problem worse.

If you are a woman living alone, have your telephone number listed with only your first initial. If you answer the phone and nobody responds, hang up. Repeated hang-ups or wrong numbers may come from someone checking if you are home, including a criminal. A common tactic to discourage such calls is blowing a loud whistle into the receiver. However, some experts caution that this will agitate the caller and make the problem worse. If someone calls and asks for your name or what number they have reached, do not tell them. Tell them they have a wrong number. Some women have brought their obscene calls to an end by having a male friend answer their telephone.

Fortunately, the telephone companies are offering more and more services to thwart nuisance or obscene callers, although some may not work for cell phones or be available in certain areas. Here are a few to consider:

- Caller ID—enables you to see the telephone number of your caller so that you can choose not to answer the telephone.
- Call Block or Call Rejection—enables you to block undesirable numbers from getting through.
- Call Trace—enables the telephone company to note the phone number, date, and time of specific calls made on your line once you enter an access code.
- Call Return—enables you to "call back" your caller by dialing a number such as *69.

Telephone Surveys

The use of the telephone for sales purposes, often through a survey, is not illegal. There are other types of "surveyors," though, who gather intelligence information for illegal purposes, so you should never give confidential information over the phone unless you absolutely have confirmed the other party on the call. Do not answer questions concerning where you work, what you look like, your income, any items of value you may have in your home, your sexual habits, or anything else of a personal nature. A good tactic is to say that the caller has reached an answering service and that she may leave a name and number. If the caller is illegitimate, she will most likely hang up. If an unwanted call continues, simply hang up yourself. You may wish to respond to legitimate surveys, but do so only after you have determined that their objectives are worthwhile and beneficial. (See chapter 24 for information on telephone fraud.)

Telemarketing Calls

Unsolicited phone calls from telemarketing firms can be highly intrusive. If you want your name removed from telemarketing (and promotional mailing) lists, contact the Direct Marketing Association at www.the-dma.org.

You can also avoid calls from telemarketers by registering your home and cell phone numbers with the National Do Not Call Registry.

Registration is free and effective for five years. Placing your phone number on the National Do Not Call Registry will stop most, but not all, calls from telemarketers. You may still receive phone calls from political organizations, charities, companies with which you've done business, and telephone surveyors. The registry is designed to prevent you from receiving calls that solicit the sales of goods or services; if the purpose of a call is solely to conduct a survey, the call will not be covered by the registry. You can access the National Do Not Call Registry at www.donotcall. gov or 1-888-382-1222.

In addition to the National Do Not Call Registry, each individual organization should have its own "Do Not Call" list. If you want to stop receiving phone calls from a particular company, call the company and ask to be put on their list. Once there, they won't be able to call you anymore.

Placing your phone number on the National Do Not Call Registry will stop most, but not all, calls from telemarketers.

Using Internet-Based Phone Services

Many communications companies now offer Internet-based phone services. While these services may save you money, they could also put you in danger in an emergency. This is because Internet-based phone lines do not connect to 911 in the way that regular phone lines do, making it difficult for 911 operators to pinpoint your exact location. In some cases you may not be able to reach a 911 operator at all. Many Internet-based phone companies do, however, provide you with access to Enhanced 911, which routes your call to a local emergency center where operators can access your location and send help.

Not all Internet-based phone companies have these shortcomings. For example, cable companies sometimes offer Internet-based calling, and they do not have the same problems with 911, because the customer's phone number is linked to an actual address. If you decide to use an Internet-based phone company, make sure the phone line will still directly connect you to a 911 operator and that the operator will be

An Extra Phone Can Save Your Life

Some people use cell phones only when on the go and get into the habit of leaving them in their car. But having an extra phone in the house could save your life. Burglars sometimes cut phone lines or remove a phone from a reciever so homeowners can't call for help. Consider having an extra phone line installed in the bedroom or keeping an extra cell phone hidden somewhere in the house so you'll always know it's available in an emergency.

able to identify your exact location. But keep in mind that an Internet-based phone line won't work if the power goes out or if the user's Internet connection is down, making it impossible to call 911. Therefore, if you decide to have an Internet-based phone line, make certain to also have a cell phone in case of an emergency.

CHAPTER 5

SERVICE EMPLOYEES AND INVITED STRANGERS

Who has access to your home? Delivery people, babysitters, repair workers, pest-control personnel, decorators, carpenters, meter readers, remodelers, housekeepers, and more. And with each comes the possibility of burglary, identity theft—or worse.

All these people have one thing in common: access inside your home. Each has the opportunity to pick up a key ring or leave one of your doors or windows unlatched so they can return later. Many of them may know where items of value are kept in your home. And at least one category, the domestic employee—whether full-time or part-time—may know practically as much about your household habits, idiosyncrasies, income, savings, and many other personal aspects of your family and your family's lives as you do. And with each of them comes the possibility of developing a real or imagined grievance against you, which gives them a rationale greater than greed for jeopardizing your person or property.

RISK PROTECTION

How do you protect yourself against such risks? Learn how to hire people safely and then bond them to protect your possessions.

Check References

Remember this rule of thumb: Do not let anyone into your home unless you know who they are, and always check references completely. If a prospective employee can't provide references, do not hire that person under any circumstances. Even with references, consider a background investigation conducted by a reputable investigative agency, plus a retail credit check and a call to the Better Business Bureau.

If you are left with even the slightest doubts, request a records check from the police departments of areas where the applicant has previously lived. You may encounter some difficulty here because right-of-privacy legislation can prohibit the police from releasing information.

Fidelity Bonds

The bonding of domestic employees is not inexpensive, but the benefits outweigh all other considerations if you are really concerned about security. In simple terms, a fidelity bond is a contract in which a bonding company will protect you against dishonest acts by an employee. A bond differs from insurance in that it covers the acts that the employee has control over, while insurance covers uncontrolled events, such as accidents and natural disasters.

Your insurance carrier can provide you with information on bonding employees. Bonding also gives you a valuable by-product: another investigation into the background of the employee, one independent of your own.

HIRING HELP

Whether you use an employment agency or hire help on your own, you need to follow a few simple rules to stay safe.

Employment Agencies

One word of caution about domestic employment agencies: Some are very good, and some are not. Ask friends and relatives for recommendations of trustworthy agencies. If you deal with an agency, investigate it as thoroughly as you do the individual it recommends. Consult the

Better Business Bureau for complaints. Check past editions of the yellow pages (often available at your local library) to determine which firms have stood the test of time.

Babysitters

Research a babysitter the way you would any domestic employee, and trust your instincts. At the very least, always obtain and check references. Teachers, coaches, and the clergy provide reliable references. Conduct an extensive interview, and be sure to ask your potential babysitter how she disciplines children and what she would do if the child gets angry.

Don't assume you can trust a babysitter just because she's a neighbor—you still need to do your research. You may have known the teenager down the street for years, but you may not know that her boyfriend has a drug problem and that as soon as the children are asleep, he visits your house and stays until just before you are expected home. A little digging on your part may reveal this type of issue.

Regardless of the age or experience of the babysitter, you must leave clear, complete, written instructions, including:

- where you will be and your cell phone number
- the name and phone number of a neighbor to contact in an emergency
- the name of your physician and directions to the nearest hospital emergency room
- phone numbers of fire, police, and poison information hotlines
- medications to be administered and instructions on administering them
- locations of aspirin, bandages, and similar supplies
- names of callers who may stop by (and instructions never to let anyone in).

In some locations a hospital or other organization may offer a babysitting class on the weekends. It is well worth the tuition to send a favorite babysitter to the class to learn emergency first aid and other procedures.

There are commercial agencies that specialize in babysitting. These companies are generally bonded and conduct extensive interviews and thorough background checks of babysitting applicants, in addition to

Safety for Babysitters

If you are a teenager who is asked to baby-sit, accept jobs only from people you know. If you don't know the caller or feel uneasy about a job offer, ask your parents to speak for you. They should ask the caller who recommended you, and then they should contact the reference. Ask a friend to accompany you to the interview. Once you report to the job, lock all doors and windows. Never open the door to anyone except in an emergency when you need assistance. If you go outdoors, neither you nor the children should talk to strangers. Be alert for suspicious persons or happenings. If in doubt, call the police.

When the child's parents return, report to them all suspicious or unusual occurrences or telephone calls. If they plan to take you home but appear intoxicated, insist on calling your own parents for a ride or make other arrangements, such as a taxi, public transportation, or a ride from a friend.

providing training for them. While usually more expensive, such agencies may provide another alternative for babysitting services.

Cleaning Services

Many people hire professional cleaning services, who often work in your home when you're not there. As with any other stranger you welcome into your home, you need to be extremely careful about whom you choose.

- Conduct interviews with potential cleaners, and ask about bonding, insurance, price, workers' compensation, contracts, personal compatibility, schedules, payments, and who will be responsible for providing the cleaning supplies.
- Make sure the service you hire is bonded and insured, in order to protect your home and property from damage or theft, and to protect yourself from liability in case the cleaning person is injured while at your home. Any reputable cleaning service can provide you with a certificate of insurance.
- Ask for references, and follow through in contacting them.
- If possible, hire a service that comes highly recommended by a neighbor or friend.

Some people hire individual cleaning people rather than going through a professional cleaning service. While this strategy may save money, it also comes with several disadvantages.

- An individual cleaner may not have insurance or be bonded, leaving you responsible if she is injured while on your property and providing no assurance that anything stolen will be replaced.
- Taxes are already deducted from the wages of the person who works for the professional cleaning service, but an individual might not pay taxes on their earnings, in which case *you* may be held liable.
- With a professional cleaning service, even if one cleaner cannot do her work due to injury or illness, another cleaner can usually come as a replacement. If something prevents an individual from coming for a scheduled cleaning, you will simply be left with a dirty house.

Even after carefully picking your cleaning service, you need to take several precautions before the cleanings begin. First, lock all of your valuables away in a safe place. Your safest bet is to place them in a locked cabinet or safe. Also, keep in mind that your tangible goods are not the only things that can be stolen—so can your identity. Make certain that your home computer is password-protected in order to keep all your personal information secure, and lock up your various personal and business files.

Be especially careful if a yard worker or other visitor asks to use the bathroom—a popular trick is to unlatch the window so they can return later.

Finally, decide if you want to give the cleaning professionals access to your home when you're not there. The cleaners can more easily do their job when no one is home to get in the way, and most people can't stay home each time the cleaners come. Therefore, many people provide their cleaners with their own set of keys and give them the codes to their security systems. As long as you have done a thorough background check on the professionals you choose to hire, this should be a safe decision, but there is always the chance that you are opening yourself up to be victimized.

Consider giving your cleaning crew a distinct code to the security system to be used only between designated hours. If given a key, it should be stamped DO NOT DUPLICATE and immediately retrieved upon termination of the work arrangement. However, be aware that providing security system codes or dwelling codes carry potential risk for future intrusion.

REPAIRMEN, CONTRACTORS, AND THE LIKE

Don't disclose information about your comings and goings to courier services, service personnel such as mechanical contractors, or delivery personnel who regularly visit your home. Irregular visitors—such as movers, carpenters, painters, decorators, and repairmen—are an even greater security hazard. They are generally employed by others who are providing services to you under some form of contractual arrangement, which means that you have no control over the selection or investigation of the people entering your home. Their work usually creates some confusion and movement of people and commodities. Unless you can be everywhere at once, you are vulnerable. Be especially careful if a yard worker or other visitor asks to use the bathroom—a popular trick is to unlatch the window so they can return later.

Consequently, well before the first worker shows up, you need to do some careful planning. Move jewelry, furs, art objects, valuable documents, and any other portable valuable items to your safety deposit box, security closet (page 23), or other secure place, such as a neighbor's home. Do the same with liquor, wine, medication, firearms, and small appliances. And make sure all house keys have DO NOT DUPLICATE stamped on them. If possible, establish a designated path in and out of the work area and insist that workers use this route.

Deal only with reputable companies or individuals who can furnish ample references, and check those references. Have someone you trust from the company present to check up on the workers. If you plan to monitor the work yourself, don't try to do the job alone; there is much truth in the old saying about safety in numbers. Consider engaging a security officer or patrol service in the evening hours, especially if there are ladders lying around the yard or windows that must remain open to allow paint to dry. If you move out until the

Selling Your House Safely

Anytime strangers come into your home, your security is threatened—especially when selling your house. Burglars have actually gone to open houses pretending to be a buyer but really assessing the valuables to see if it is worth a second visit. It is best not to have any open houses when selling your house. One viable alternative to the in-person open house is the "virtual" open house, where you allow potential buyers to inspect your home via photographs on a website.

work is completed, hire a house sitter or security officer to protect your residence.

Once things get back to normal, make an inventory check, and consider changing your lock cylinders—including window locks.

DEFENSE AGAINST DISGRUNTLED EMPLOYEES

When an unhappy domestic worker leaves your employ, take similar precautions. First, check your home inventory; second, change your locks. Even if you don't have a spare door key somewhere around the house—or if you've never left a key lying around that may have been duplicated—change the locks.

Although you probably keep most of your valuables in a safety deposit box or nonbank depository, you may also have chosen hiding places at home for valuable items you use on a day-to-day basis. Your domestic employee may have found these caches, and an employee who hasn't stolen from you during his or her time of employment may not be so honorable on departure. Periodically changing your hiding places will minimize this risk. Don't simply trade places—change them. Move the good silver from the dining room to a spot in the kitchen or to an upstairs bedroom; transfer the diamond ring from the decorative box in the china cabinet to the toe of an evening shoe in the closet. And make absolutely certain that you change the entry on your home inventory list; otherwise, there's a chance that you will forget the new location. Also, find a new, secure spot for the inventory list itself, unless you want to present a burglar with a nice, neat shopping list.

CHAPTER 6

LIGHTING

Given enough time and determination, an intruder can break into your home regardless of any security measures you might take. And without adequate lighting, you provide burglars with ample opportunity.

EXTERIOR LIGHTING

The lighting outside of your home must be sufficient at all wall openings (doors, windows, exhaust ducts, crawlspaces, and so on) to deny an intruder the cover of darkness.

In a few instances, floodlights on opposite corners of a house can sufficiently illuminate all openings in the walls of a structure. Generally, however, some degree of lighting on all four sides of a house is necessary to light it adequately. In all cases, lighting should be intense enough so that your neighbors can see a suspicious person within 100 feet of the dwelling, but not so strong that it disturbs their peace and privacy.

If your street is adequately lit, so much the better. If it isn't, light your entranceway so that you won't encounter any unpleasant surprises when you arrive home late at night. Light as much of the front part of your property as possible at night—with lampposts, lights over your garage, and so on—and encourage your neighbors to do the same. Report any burned-out streetlights.

Should you leave a light burning in the front part of the house or on a front porch at all times during the night? Yes and no.

The front door should always be adequately lit. On the other hand, a porch light left burning periodically, rather than all the time, signals that you are out but expect to return soon, an indication that might cause a potential intruder to pass you by. The best technique is to alternate time and lighting sources to confuse the would-be intruder.

Shadowed Areas

Trees, heavy shrubbery, bay windows, enclosed porches, and many other natural or constructed features of a house create shadowed areas; these areas should be illuminated. You can often provide adequate light by placing a lamp inside the house close to a window. In many instances, however, windows and doors are hidden from the street and from neighbors as well, irrespective of interior lighting. These are principal areas of vulnerability that definitely should be illuminated.

Alleys

Alleys servicing the rears of homes are invariably hazardous areas. They are usually dark, not particularly well kept, and seldom traveled at night. They often harbor trash containers, which provide convenient cover for intruders. If you are home alone, put off taking out the trash until morning or, alternatively, call a neighbor and ask that she watch you on your errand.

Typically, alleys are separated from houses by solid fences to hide their unsightliness, but fences also prevent residents from seeing what's going on. Adequate illumination of the entire area between the fence and your house is essential for maximum security. You should also light the areas adjacent to the gates of all fences around your property.

Motion-Sensitive Lights

Fortunately, technology is always improving the way we can secure our home. In particular, motion-sensitive lights are extremely useful for outdoor security, turning on only when they detect movement. This lighting serves the dual purposes of helping you see what is happening outside your home at night and scaring off any predator trying to sneak up on the house in the dark. And since motion-sensitive lights turn on only when they sense movement, they are far more economical than permanent floodlights, which stay on all night or until you manually turn them off. In addition, floodlights might annoy your neighbors, who understandably prefer to sleep in the dark.

Motion-sensitive lights serve the dual purpose of helping you see what is happening outside your home at night and scaring off any predator trying to sneak up on the house in the dark.

When considering where to place your motion-sensitive lights, focus your attention on doors and windows and any other possible entryways into your home that might seem attractive to a potential offender. And keep in mind that in addition to providing illumination, motion-sensitive lights can also be hooked up to various alarm systems.

Not only do motion-sensitive lights help protect your home and family from intruders, they also help ensure your personal safety outside your home. Coming home to a dark house may leave you open to victimization before you even put your key in the door. Motion-sensitive lights ensure that an outside light will shine on you when you walk up your front walk.

INTERIOR LIGHTING

Turning lights on and off as you move around your house provides plenty of evidence that you are at home. If you're home and awake and moving around, a burglar is generally going to skip you—so use your lights to burglar-proof your house, as well as to avoid falling over your furniture. But how should you handle the lights when you are not home or after you've gone to bed?

Timers

You can find timers capable of handling four or more separate instructions for less than the price of a shirt. Several of these, distributed throughout your house, may completely confuse a nighttime prowler. These timers are typically equipped with a backup battery, which will keep the memory intact in a power outage. The timer will remember its instructions once the power is restored. (See also "Tune in to Intruders," page 19.)

When You're Out

Before going out for the evening, it's extremely important to set the interior lighting to appear as though you are home. You should always leave lights on in apartments so that light from under the door shows in the hallway. In a freestanding house, however, one look through the window into a well-lit interior can show a potential intruder that the coast is clear. You can—and should—draw the curtains whether you are home at night or not.

The experienced burglar knows that when a room is occupied, an occasional shadow will pass between the light source and the drape when an occupant walks by. He or she won't be deterred by a living-room light, but that's not necessarily true for all burglars. So a general rule of thumb applies: If in doubt, turn on the light.

If you're going to be gone for several hours or even days, use timers that will periodically turn lamps on and off.

When You're Home

When you retire for the evening, do not turn off all the lights. Lighting, remember, is a major enemy of the burglar. But don't leave the same lights on every night, because if your house is being cased, you don't want to give your adversary the advantage of your predictability.

When you get up during the night, make some noise and turn on some lights. A burglar who isn't reasonably sure that you're asleep generally won't try to enter your home. And if he or she does, he will leave the moment he realizes you're awake and moving around. So your best

Hazards of Lighting Up

While it is very important to keep your home well lit in order to deter would-be intruders, you must also keep in mind that lighting comes with certain hazards. Electrical problems are a major source of home fires, and you should therefore be certain to check on the safety of your lights. For example,

- Be sure to use only the lightbulb that the manufacturer recommends in order to avoid overheating.
- Keep a lightbulb in all light fixtures in order to reduce the risk of electric shock—even a burned-out bulb is better than no bulb at all.
- Make sure that none of your wires are cracked or frayed.
- Be careful not to overload your extension cords; this can cause a fire.
- Avoid running electrical wires or cords under rugs or furniture.

bet to discourage burglars is to switch on the lights and open and close some interior doors.

Consider installing a switch in your bedroom and any other well-used room at night to turn on outdoor lights, as well as a second switch that turns on all (or many) inside lights simultaneously. A sneaky thief cannot sneak very well when bathed in light.

LIGHTING FOR PARKING AREAS

Install motion-sensitive lights over your driveway or other parking area, or buy outdoor lights that automatically turn on when it gets dark, to ensure your safety. When you come home at night, be sure to park in a well-lighted area. This is especially important if you return at the same time or at a predictable time each night. If the lights illuminating your garage or parking place aren't burning and you know you left them on, keep right on going and find a police officer or neighbor to accompany you back home.

CHAPTER 7

MAINTAINING SECURITY OUTSIDE

Security is certainly not the prime consideration when you consider your home's outside appearance. A house surrounded by an 8- or 9-foot fence, brilliantly illuminated with high-intensity lighting and with large, vicious dogs roaming the yard, looks more like a prison or a top-secret missile base than a home. Nevertheless, there are various ways to maintain good security without sacrificing curb appeal.

BASIC PRECAUTIONS

Keeping the inside of your home safe means taking special precautions outside. Overgrown hedges, stepladders stored outside, and unlocked tool sheds are just a few of the things that will attract an intruder.

Install Perimeter Fencing

If you'd like a decorative hedge or fence surrounding your property, by all means have it. In fact, a clear delineation of your property line will help establish trespassing if an intruder is caught on your property, even if the intruder was not attempting to break into your house. On the other hand, you don't want a hedge or fence so high that a passerby couldn't see an intruder trying to break in.

For reasons of liability and security, limit access to your property with a minimum number of gates in your fence. Install and use latches with self-closing mechanisms on all gates.

Whether gates should be locked or not is debatable. If the lot is very large, they probably should be, at least after dark. But locking the gates whenever you leave the house is a giveaway to criminals. Instead, lock all gates except those in front, and lock those only at night.

Don't Flaunt Valuables

Outside security means keeping indoor valuables out of sight. If you have valuable art objects, collections, antiques, or similar treasures, place them on inside walls where you and your guests can enjoy them, but don't put them near windows through which they can be removed. At night, draw your drapes.

Don't store firewood near the house, because it can serve as a hiding place for an intruder or as a stepladder up to the windows.

Keep Your Yard Neat

If you let the shrubs outside your house grow high enough to conceal an intruder, you are asking for trouble. The same holds true for large accumulations of limbs, branches, and assorted garden refuse, as well as other piles of waste. You should also knock down and flatten large shipping cartons or other containers before you put them out with the trash.

Don't store firewood near the house, because it can serve as a hiding place for an intruder or as a stepladder up to the windows. Instead, store the firewood some distance away.

An open garage when no one is home, and bicycles and toys lying around the yard, are open invitations to a thief, as well as indications of a careless homeowner—the thief's delight. A lawn in need of cutting or a sidewalk of unshoveled snow—giving the impression that the house is unoccupied—is also likely to catch the burglar's eye.

On the other hand, a beautiful flower bed and an assortment of potted plants lets the burglar know you have taste. And taste indicates there are nice things inside your home.

Go Nameless

Don't post your name on your mailbox—or anywhere else—if you value your security. A thief, walking randomly down the street could see your valuable items through an undraped window and get your name and address from your mailbox and call your house. If you aren't home to answer your phone, you're likely to experience a break-in then and there. If you're home, he might fabricate a story to persuade you to open your door.

Don't Trash Your Identity

One thing people often fail to think of when it comes to safety and security is their garbage. If you are not careful about what you place in the trash, you may be making yourself vulnerable to crime. Do not put in the trash any papers or other items containing personal information, such as your Social Security, credit card, or bank account numbers—information that can be used by an identity thief. Do not throw away old credit card bills, old credit cards, and unused checking-account deposit slips, all of which can be used by an identity thief to "become" you. Shred them first. Do not throw out any credit card applications you receive in the mail; these can be fished out of the garbage, filled out, and submitted by an identity thief under your name. Shred these documents, too, before putting them in the garbage. Be aware of what you place in the garbage during the holidays. Empty boxes signal burglars that you have valuable goods inside.

There are also steps you can take to protect the contents of your trash.

- Keep your garbage cans locked up in a safe place, such as your garage, until just before garbage pickup.
- Take your garbage out early in the morning, just before pickup, rather than leaving the trash out overnight for would-be offenders to sift through.

- When out of town, ask a neighbor to bring your garbage cans out on trash day (ideally, filled with some of their trash) and then bring them back in. Otherwise, potential burglars might notice your empty garbage cans and realize that you are away and your house is empty.

Secure Outside Structures and Swimming Pools

Structures within the yard can draw intruders, whether it is a shed full of valuable tools or a pool that draws uninvited nighttime swimmers. In each case, it is important to keep the structure heavily padlocked and the pool surrounded by a high, sturdy fence.

A pool poses more problems than safety to outsiders, however. Its very presence tells a thief that your home is one of affluence, especially if your neighborhood has few pools. Although lighting around the pool might discourage nocturnal swimmers, it draws interest. A yard dog, a neighborhood patrol service, or a Neighborhood Watch group may enable you to do without attention-drawing lighting. Better yet, install a pool-alarm sensor that detects water motion, which is good for both safety and security. Posting signs prohibiting unauthorized use of the pool may assist in developing a defense regarding liability issues.

Tool sheds, storm cellars, greenhouses, and other outdoor structures should be equipped with strong padlocks and top-quality hinges. If the hinges are exposed, weld them in place or insert screws through the hinges at an unexposed point. Keep garage doors locked. If you use an automatic door opener, consider a key-operated automatic device for tight security.

ARSON

Arson is the intentional or malicious burning, or attempt to burn (with or without intent to defraud), a house, public building, motor vehicle or aircraft, or personal property of another kind. Only fires determined to be intentionally or maliciously started are classified as arson. Fires of suspicious or unknown origin are specifically excluded. But while perpetrators of these crimes may intend merely to destroy property, all too often their crimes result in serious injury or death.

Why Arson Fires Are Set

People deliberately set fires for a number of reasons: personal gain, revenge, mental illness, profit, concealing another crime, vandalism, intimidation, jealousy, spite, and so on.

Arson-for-profit schemes are sometimes carried out by greedy or cash-strapped property owners in a fraudulent attempt to collect insurance proceeds. Unpaid mortgage or property-tax obligations are red flags for such crimes.

Finally, arson cases often involve the destructive act of a bored adolescent looking for excitement. A trash-strewn property with waist-high weeds is an irresistible attraction for a young arsonist. The less you appear to care about your property, the more likely you are to become a victim of arson.

Keep your house and surrounding property well lit, since arson is often committed in isolated and dark areas.

Preventive Measures

You can take several steps to reduce the incidence of arson.

- Work with a community organization to report suspicious-looking individuals, vehicles, and fires.
- Teach your children proper awareness of the dangers of fire, and make them cognizant of the horrible consequences of setting fires.
- Organize neighborhood youths to clean up refuse-strewn lots or deteriorated buildings.
- Encourage civic or business groups to offer rewards for information leading to the arrest of an arsonist.
- Keep your house and surrounding property well lit, since arson is often committed in isolated and dark areas.
- Do not leave containers of motor fuel visible and unsecured.

VANDALISM

Vandalism is the intentional destruction of property. It is usually committed by bored, playful, or vengeful teenagers. A quarter of all vandalism acts are premeditated. Like numerous other offenses, vandalism is a crime of opportunity. Whether you live in an urban, suburban, or rural area, chances are that you have been exposed to some form of vandalism.

Types of Vandalism

Vandalism includes defacing statues and monuments, breaking windows, destroying parking meters, writing on storefronts, tearing pages from school and library books, smashing school furniture, clogging school toilets, knocking over tombstones, and ruining business property.

Vandalism also damages your personal property. You may have experienced tire tracks across your front lawn, gardens and shrubbery maliciously torn up, or automobile antennas missing. Perhaps you have had the unpleasant experience of cleaning raw eggs off your car and house after Halloween.

In general, vandals avoid property that is properly maintained. Allowing anything to lapse into misuse or abuse is an open invitation.

You may have seen a vacant house that remains untouched for months on end. If, however, a single window is broken, almost overnight all of the windows may be shattered and the structure will be broken open. Soon the building gives every indication of having been thoroughly vandalized.

At the extreme, vandalism can become life threatening. Disabled elevators in a college dormitory would be considered by most observers a mild inconvenience. In high-rise apartments for the elderly, the same situation could be tragic. Broken street lighting could lead to rape, robbery, or worse. The offenders rarely consider the consequences of what they often consider harmless pranks.

Combating Vandalism

If the windows of your home are repeatedly broken, replace them with unbreakable plastic or glass. Erect a fence with a locked gate to serve as a further deterrent by delineating your property. Make repairs and remove graffiti as soon as possible to avert continued destruction. And don't forget to ask a Neighborhood Watch or citizen patrol for help.

Defending Yourself in Your Own Home

The law authorizes people to use force—even deadly force—when they reasonably believe that it is necessary in order to defend themselves against imminent bodily harm or injury. Self-defense is technically composed of four elements: 1) an unprovoked attack; 2) an honest and reasonable belief that you are in imminent danger of death or serious bodily injury; 3) an honest and reasonable belief that it is necessary to defend against the attack at that moment; and 4) a reasonable (not excessive) use of force to repel the attack.

As the fourth element states, the amount of force authorized in this circumstance must be proportional to the threat and should be the minimal amount of force required for defense. In addition, most states require you to retreat if escape is at all possible, rather than using force to defend yourself. One exception to this rule is the Castle Doctrine, which states that people should not have to retreat from their own home, or castle. Therefore, when people are threatened on their own property, they have the right to stand their ground and defend themselves rather than flee.

The exact content of the law, including the specific types of property in which the Castle Doctrine can apply, varies from state to state. You should determine the specific statute in your state and whether and under what circumstances you have the right to stand your ground in your home or whether you are required to retreat.

WATCHING OVER THE NEIGHBORHOOD

One aspect of being a good neighbor is getting to know your neighbors and knowing who doesn't belong. A stranger driving around and around the block could well be cause for concern. If in doubt, take down the car's license plate number.

Don't call the police every time you encounter an unfamiliar face, but do take notice, and make it clear that you are taking notice. If you see strangers in your neighborhood taking undue interest in your neighbor's car, be on your guard. You may have to notify police. The same is true if you hear breaking glass or an explosive noise. Remember, a community where neighbors care and watch out for each other is much more secure than one where neighbors hardly know or talk to one another. (See "Don't Fail Your Neighborhood Watch," page 240.)

One aspect of being a good neighbor is getting to know your neighbors and knowing who doesn't belong.

Trespassers

If you see a prowler or trespasser in your yard or a neighbor's after dark, turn on lights—the more, the better. If the prowler takes off running, activate an alarm and phone the police. Don't chase a fleeing suspect. It is better—and safer—to keep him or her in sight than to try to apprehend him. Leave the chasing to law-enforcement officers, who know what they are doing.

Security Patrol Services

A neighborhood security patrol service is a valuable addition to your security arsenal, but it is only a supplement. Capable burglars will see to it that they are working in the patrol officer's wake. Patrol officers should vary the starting point of their route and occasionally double back so that the times of their appearances at your place aren't predictable.

The cost of patrol services varies according to frequency and quality of work. Be sure to investigate the service thoroughly: Check references and determine if the patrol officers are properly licensed if a state requires it.

CHAPTER 8

VACATIONS AND SPECIAL OCCASIONS

Your home is most vulnerable to an intruder when it is empty, and a family vacation increases that risk. Don't make it obvious that you are away.

PREPARING FOR A TRIP

Newspapers piled up on the driveway, unshoveled snow, and lights that go on at precisely the same time every night are red flags to even the inexperienced burglar that no one is home. But you can take specific steps to keep your home safe while you're away.

Don't Cancel the Mail

You should cancel the newspaper and ask the post office to hold your mail for the duration of your vacation because accumulations of these items are dead giveaways to potential intruders, right? Not so fast. If you do this, you will have told five or six people your plans, including how long you will be away. It is far better to let the deliveries continue and ask a friend or neighbor to bring your papers and mail into your home. If no one can do you this favor, then cancel all deliveries.

Also ask neighbors to check daily if any flyers have been stuck in your front door and to remove them promptly. Burglars have been known to leave pizza flyers in doors to see how long it takes an owner to remove it. Any flyers left overnight are an open invitation.

Don't Kennel Your Dog

If possible, ask a friend, neighbor, or a professional dog walker to feed and walk your dog rather than lodge him at a kennel during your vacation. The dog is an extremely valuable deterrent around an otherwise unoccupied house.

Avoid the Second-Car Giveaway

If you're a one-car family and you take that car with you on vacation, there's not much you can do to hide the fact that your car is not parked in the driveway. You're in better shape, of course, if you customarily keep your car in a closed garage. If you're a two-car family on a motor vacation, your second car, parked in the same spot day after day, signals that you're away from home. Ask your neighbor to move it every day or so.

Avoid Pretrip Publicity

If you are prominent in your community and news of your trip might be included in your newspaper, make certain the news doesn't run in the paper until after you return. Professional thieves and burglars read newspapers, and if they know you will be out of town for your daughter's wedding, they may come calling. If for some reason you can't delay this news, arrange for the protection of your home. If you can't find a trustworthy house sitter, hire an on-premises security officer.

Burglars have been known to leave pizza flyers in doors to see how long it takes an owner to remove it. Any flyers left overnight are an open invitation.

Don't Forget the Smaller Details

You've taken care of deliveries, the dog, and the car before your vacation, but you need to think about the smaller details, too.

- Use your safety deposit box or nonbank depository for valuables, or give them to a friend or relative while you're away.
- Pay your bills before you go, or leave checks with a friend or a neighbor who can pick up your mail and pay the bills soon after they arrive.
- Have your intrusion and fire alarms inspected before you leave, remembering that you don't need to tell the service representative why you want it checked. Check auxiliary power supplies, too.
- Leave an itinerary with a friend, neighbor, or relative who can reach you in the event of an emergency.
- Scatter a few toys or garden tools in the yard to make it look like the house is occupied. Ask a neighbor to change and rearrange your bait. Otherwise, an experienced thief will see through your ruse.
- If you normally leave your curtains open, don't draw them just because you're going away. If you open them during the day and close them at night, ask your neighbor to do the same for you.

Notify Neighbors and the Police

Tell the police that you will be away so that they can pay additional attention to your property while you are gone. If you've arranged for a house sitter or the assistance of a neighbor, give her name to the police to avoid an unpleasant incident. Also give the police the names of any other friends or relatives who have keys to your house. It will be helpful if you furnish law enforcement with information about the make and model of vehicles that will be used by the friends or relatives.

Don't Pack the Car the Night Before

Don't try to get an early start on your vacation by packing your car the night before. It's not worth it when you consider the risk of awakening to find everything, car included, gone from your driveway or garage. And even if all is intact, a burglar may be watching you pull away, waiting to get at all the goodies you didn't take along. Just before departure, confirm that all doors and windows are locked and that you have taken all extra keys.

WHILE YOU ARE AWAY

Although the assistance of a friend or neighbor is the best means for protecting your property while you're away, this can become too much of an imposition. Here are other ways to make your house look occupied.

Lighting

An experienced burglar will notice if the lights go on and off at precisely the same time every night. You can buy inexpensive timers that vary on-off times continuously, including a timer that activates a lamp (or any electric appliance) each time the compression motor of a refrigerator activates.

If a timer isn't available, leave some lights on when you go. They will probably go unnoticed during the daytime, but the total absence of lights will be apparent at night. Turn down the volume control of your telephone so a passerby won't hear the continued ringing of an unanswered telephone. Better yet, use an answering machine.

> Turn down the volume control of your telephone so a passerby won't hear the continued ringing of an unanswered telephone.

Air-Conditioning Advantage

An added benefit of putting your air conditioner on a timer is that air-conditioning removes the humidity from your house, helping to preserve your furniture, floors, books, drapes, and whatever else could be warped or damaged by dampness while you're away.

Air-Conditioning

Don't shut down air-conditioning or heating equipment. A still heat pump on a muggy night is proof that the house is unoccupied. Ensure that the thermostats on window air conditioners are functioning. To

Handy Vacationer's Safety Checklist

Before you leave home for any extended period of time, it's best to take steps to keep your home safe while you are away. Use the list below as a last-minute checklist.

- ☐ Arrange for a friend or neighbor to retrieve mail and newspapers during your absence.
- ☐ Arrange to have your dog fed, and walked at home rather than kept at a kennel.
- ☐ If you have a second car, arrange to have it moved occasionally in your absence.
- ☐ Avoid publicity about your impending trip.
- ☐ Leave an itinerary with someone so you can be notified in case of emergency.
- ☐ Consider using a neighborhood patrol service during your absence.
- ☐ Notify police of your absence, providing them with the names of house sitters or neighbors who will be assisting you, and the names of others who have keys to your house.
- ☐ Don't pack your car the night before departure; load it quickly in the morning.
- ☐ As a last effort before departure, check to see that all doors and windows are locked and that you have taken all necessary keys.
- ☐ Arrange for secure storage outside your home of furs, jewelry, and other valuables while you are away.
- ☐ Prepay bills that will come due in your absence, and arrange for the payment of others that may arrive while you're away.
- ☐ If you have a home security system, have it checked before you leave.
- ☐ Leave shades and curtains in the positions they would normally be in if you were home, arranging, if possible, to have someone raise and lower them routinely while you are away.
- ☐ Use variable on-off timers to turn lamps on at night.
- ☐ Set thermostats or utilize timers for air conditioner/heating operation that fits weather conditions.
- ☐ Turn down the volume control on telephones. Install an answering machine, preferably one that allows you to retrieve messages from wherever you happen to be.

conserve energy, cut back on the cooling level of heat pumps and air conditioners, but leave the fan motor running. Make certain that timers and related wiring are of sufficient capacity and voltage to handle the power requirements of your window air-conditioning units.

Lawn Care and Snow Removal

Keeping your lawn cut or the snow shoveled is essential when you're away from home, and you want everything to appear normal. Either hire a lawn and snow-removal service or entrust vacation mowing or snow shoveling to a neighborhood child. Pristine snow is a certain giveaway that you're not at home, so at the very least, have someone put footprints in the snow on your walk and driveway.

Gates

While a locked gate will deter a burglar, one locked at noon will signal that you're not home. If you don't have a neighbor who will lock your gate in the evening and unlock it in the morning while you're away, lock the gate and hope that a burglar will think twice about lifting items over the fence, particularly in broad daylight.

Trash Pickup

It is rare for an occupied home to have no trash for two weeks. Ask your neighbor to put out some trash in front of your house on pickup days. If your pickup is not regularly scheduled, consider leaving a trash container at a visible location adjacent to the house.

House Sitters

Consider engaging a house sitter who will live in your house while you're away. A friend, relative, or domestic employee whom you completely trust is ideal. You might also be able to find a house sitter through college placement offices. Mature students and even faculty members often make themselves available for house-sitting duties. Other trustworthy house sitters include people you work with, members of your church or synagogue, or people referred by neighbors.

Maintaining Safe Food and Water

Whether on special occasions or in your daily living, how can you protect yourself against contamination of your food and water?

- Purify your water before you drink it.
- Keep a supply of bottled water in your home in the event of an emergency. Glass bottles are preferable, as plastic may contain carcinogens.
- In an emergency, follow the authorities' instructions about water purification ("boil orders") or use other water supplies until instructed that you can safely consume the public water again.
- Examine the packaging of the food you buy to make sure it hasn't been torn, damaged, opened, or tampered with in any other way.
- If the plastic seal on a container has been broken, do not eat the contents.
- Check the "sell by" dates on any food you buy.
- Once you have brought food home, make sure that it looks right before consuming it—do not consume anything that looks discolored or moldy or has a strange smell.
- If any sort of liquid or foam spurts out when the container is opened, bring it back to the store and report the tampering to your state department of agriculture.
- Cook your foods at proper temperatures to ensure that bacteria are killed.
- Refrigerate your foods as soon as you get home from the grocery store, since the cold temperatures prevent bacteria from multiplying.

HAZARDS OF SPECIAL OCCASIONS

Special occasions can also be the source of special security problems. Any occasions covered in the local newspapers present problems, as do social get-togethers. Holidays are also a time of increased risk of crime.

Holidays

Holidays are a time of celebration, but danger and crime can quickly bring all the fun to an end. Around Christmastime, burglaries and thefts tend to increase. Cash and gifts are more abundant than at any other time throughout the year. Try to shop for gifts early, and don't carry too many packages. An overburdened shopper is an easy mark for a crook. Be sure to keep packages in your car out of sight, placing them in your trunk or under a car seat. Many shoppers have been surprised to find a broken car window or door lock after leaving "for only a minute." (See chapter 12 for more tips on security while shopping.)

Scams are also rampant during the holiday season. While shopping, don't believe anyone who approaches you with an unbelievable price—even in a store. (Crooks have posed as sales clerks.) Never buy expensive items on the street. The goods are likely to be either stolen or counterfeit. For similar reasons, never buy tickets for holiday shows (or any other show) from scalpers.

Always confirm that the charity collecting holiday donations is legitimate. (Many fraudulent Santas will collect your donations for themselves.) If you receive a telephone solicitation, ask the caller to mail you materials about the organization. Never give out your credit card number over the phone unless you are positive the person is legitimate—whether or not you placed the call. Sending a check or money order is a lot safer. (See chapters 22–24 for additional tips on protection from scams.)

New Year's Eve presents yet another opportunity for burglars, who don't take holidays off. If you leave home, make sure your residence appears occupied; leave a light and/or a radio or television turned on.

Exercise extra caution on Halloween as well. Be sure to secure your residence and your car. If you have a garage, by all means use it. In addition, always check to see who's calling at your door before you open it. Don't just assume that the caller is another trick-or-treater. (*See also* "Halloween Hazards," page 210.)

Funerals and Weddings

A death in the family typically is followed by an obituary in the press, listing the time and place of the funeral service. Every member of the deceased's household will probably attend the service, and burglars know it. Arrange for a friend or neighbor, or a contract security officer, to house-sit while you are attending the service.

A wedding is a joyous occasion, so make certain it's not spoiled by a burglary during the ceremony. Criminals can be tipped off by a wedding notice in the newspaper, a band hired to play at the reception, a notice of marriage published at your church, or an employee of your caterer, florist, jeweler, or someone else providing services or goods who happens to double as a "bird dog" for a burglary ring. Take extra precautions and hire a house sitter or guard.

Parties

If you're having a big party at home, your planning should include some commonsense security, especially if you don't know all your guests well. Resist the impulse to show off your collection of gold coins. Put away any important papers or documents, especially those containing financial information. Safeguard small, easily portable valuables. Check out any help you hire by requiring references, contacting the Better Business Bureau, and conducting personal interviews prior to hiring.

Thieves attending gatherings such as an author luncheon or political fundraiser are on the lookout to steal small, easily concealed items. They may also rifle through guests' handbags. Furs, too, are highly sought-after items and can be removed by concealing them under other garments.

In addition, don't store your guests's property in a room easily accessible from outside. A thief could drop items through a window or fire escape to an accomplice waiting below. Don't use your bedroom to store property. If you're like most people, you keep your valuables there. Instead, use a spare bedroom or that of a youngster.

A Friendly Game of Chance

You may host other events at your home, such as a weekly poker game. But at what point does your friendly Friday night poker game become a professional gambling operation? More than a few poker games will be raided by robbers this year, and some will be raided by the police as well. High-stakes poker games constitute gambling and are an attraction to robbers. The potential for trouble increases if one player has gotten in over his or her head and might find non-sporting ways to get even.

Avoid high-stakes games. But if you'd rather not, at least take some precautions, such as using chips rather than currency and settling at the end of the game by check instead of cash.

You also have to pay attention to gamblers with gambling problems. Recognizing compulsive gamblers in the early phase of their problem is not easy. Yet a number of indicators, in combination with one another, suggest a gambling problem:

- **The amount of time spent gambling.** Note any increase in the amount of time spent gambling, especially if you notice a surge in activities away from home, such as spending time in other cities.
- **Growing size of bets.** Be aware of any sharp increase in the amount of bets. If $5 to $20 bets increase to $50 or $100, you can be sure that compulsiveness is imminent.
- **An intensity of emphasis on gambling.** The compulsive gambler finds it exciting to talk endlessly about gambling, and searches out special occasions for gambling, like sporting events, parties, and junkets.
- **Loss of interest in other activities.** Gambling becomes the most important event in the gambler's life. Be wary if your gambling spouse starts to lose interest in you and your children.
- **Suspicious absences from home and work.** Strong indicators of compulsive gambling are absences from work and home without explanation or with only suspicious explanations.
- **Shifts in personality structure.** The stress associated with gambling often produces belligerent behavior, impatience, and irritability.
- **Siphoning off family funds.** When the compulsive gambler begins cashing in insurance policies, redeeming securities or savings bonds, pawning family valuables, and draining the family savings account, you can be sure that gambling has reached the addictive stage.

If you suspect gambling has become a problem in your family, look in your telephone directory for the local chapter of Gamblers Anonymous, or contact their national hotline at 1-888-GA-HELPS (1-888-424-3577). You can also search for branches by state at www.gamblersanonymous. org/mtgdirTOP. You can also try to find a treatment center for compulsive gamblers in your area. Contact the nationwide helpline of the National Council on Problem Gambling at 1-800-522-4700.

CHAPTER 9

TIPS FOR APARTMENT AND CONDO DWELLERS

There are many home-security issues that are of exclusive concern to the occupants of an apartment, co-op, or condominium. It is important to recognize which features will keep you safest.

SECURITY FEATURES TO LOOK FOR

When seeking out an apartment, there are a number of security features you should look for before you decide to sign a lease. Some apartment complexes boast maximum security; others, on a more limited budget, offer more basic safety measures. If the apartment complex does not offer even the simplest safety features, you should request that the land-lord provide them.

Maximum Security

At a minimum, an apartment building with maximum security should have around-the-clock features:

- Here are some other features you should look for: doorman or security officer who announces all guests and requires proper identi-fication of all visitors and callers.

- Fire stairs equipped with one-way doors, which should open only from inside the fire stairwell on the ground floor and roof and only from outside the fire stairwell on all other floors.
- Garages equipped with self-closing outside doors, or a security officer, or both.
- Controlled access into the building from the attached garage.

Minimum Security

Few apartment complexes have the resources to supply maximum security. But even a small, limited-budget building can follow good security measures, which should include the following:

- Door-opening systems, equipped with an intercom system or closed-circuit television, with every tenant trained to use the system properly.
- Self-service elevators with small mirrors that permit a view of the entire interior of the car before boarding.
- Entrance into attached or basement garages controlled by key or electronic access card, and automatic closure of these doors.
- Adequate lighting throughout the common spaces of the building.
- Light fixtures located or protected so that an intruder can't tamper with them.
- Roof doors operable only from the inside.
- Well-lit alcoves or other blind spots in corridors, with mirrors to prevent them from being used as hiding places.

In apartment buildings, most crimes result from the failure to use existing locks, or from their inadequacy or vulnerability.

Keys and Locks

In apartment buildings most crimes result from the failure to use existing locks, or from their inadequacy or vulnerability. For your own peace of mind, change the locks when you move into an apartment.

Your building superintendent may insist on having a key to your apartment. If he does, try to dissuade him by pointing out that a burglar breaking into his apartment would then have access to every apartment in the building. If fire codes require the superintendent to have a key, put yours in a sealed envelope with your name signed across the flap. If you don't have to give the super your key, leave it with a friend. And of course, don't hide your key near your door.

Consider adding a lock of your own—preferably a deadbolt—to your apartment door. You would be protected even if a passkey fell into the wrong hands. Your landlord may object, but your possessions, even your life, might be on the line. One caveat: In the event of an emergency, police or fire personnel would be unable to save your life or protect your belongings without forcibly opening your door.

Doors and Windows

Be sure to install chain locks and peepholes on outside or corridor doors. Lock outside or corridor doors at all times, whether you're home or not. (See chapter 1 for more about doors and windows.)

Doorplates (and mailboxes) should not indicate the gender of the occupant. "M. Jones," for example, is preferable to "Ms. Mary Jones."

Don't leave notes on doors indicating when you'll return to your apartment or that you'll be returning alone.

In an apartment, you will probably have fewer windows to protect than in a house, and perhaps only one or two walls will have windows at all. Some of these windows, though, may open onto fire escapes, which offer access from your apartment to the ground and vice versa. These windows must be protected by foldable, lockable metal accordion screens to keep intruders out but still allow you to exit. (If this violates building codes, shatterproof glass serves the same purpose.) In addition, the keys to these grilles must be kept close by to enable you to get out if there is a fire. A word of caution: Don't position emergency keys so close that they could be reached from outside the building. Store them out of sight from anyone on the fire escape.

PROPER SECURITY PRACTICES

One of the most important security measures for any apartment is to make the communal home more secure—and this is largely up to the tenants. Know your neighbors and work with them to make your building safe. Here are a few basic rules by which you should all abide:

- Report anything not operating properly: doors, burned-out lights, inoperative locks, rotted fire hoses, and so forth.
- Report any unusual incidents to the landlord and to the police.
- Don't open the exterior door to anyone that you don't recognize or expect to arrive.
- Don't open the exterior door for someone who claims to be visiting or delivering a package to a neighbor. He or she may know your neighbor isn't home and, once inside, can go about his mission relatively safe from detection.

Lobbies

Draperies on lobby windows denote an air of privacy, but you don't want privacy in the lobby. An intruder who gains entry into the building can hide behind the protective curtains to prey on residents.

Intruders often position themselves near lobby mailboxes. Why? A tenant who pays more attention to the mail than her surroundings may have left her apartment door open for the trip downstairs, providing a thief with a golden opportunity. Thieves may also hang around mailboxes on days when Social Security or public-assistance checks are delivered. Anyone who receives checks in the mail on a regular and predictable basis must change to direct bank-deposit services for protection against thieves.

The most desirable security features at an apartment complex are closed-circuit TV, an abundance of lighting both inside and outside the building, and quality locks, including deadbolt locks.

The mailbox area should be well lit. If a stranger is loitering near the mailbox area, wait until he leaves or return later. Ask the building manager to install a surveillance camera for extra protection, and encourage your neighbors to do the same.

Finally, the lobby—as well as the outside of the building—should be adequately lit: You should be able to read your wristwatch by it.

Elevators

Most elevator crimes occur in residential buildings, most likely because, unlike a business elevator, the traffic is sporadic, tenants often return home late at night, and it is less likely to be monitored by a professional service. Here are a few tips to help you avoid becoming a victim.

- Don't ride in an elevator alone with a stranger. Wait for someone you recognize to accompany you.
- Never board if the interior lights are off.
- Stand near the control panel and locate the alarm. If a suspicious person gets on, get off at the next floor.
- Do not press your floor number until all strangers have pressed theirs. A criminal will be most interested in your destination and make it appear that he lives on the same floor.
- Always try to position yourself with your back against one of the elevator walls so that you minimize your exposure to muggers and pickpockets.
- When you arrive at your floor, check the corridor before you leave the elevator. If you see a stranger in the hallway, don't get off.
- If you are attacked, activate the alarm, press several floor buttons so the elevator will open up sooner, and yell loudly.

Basements

As a general rule, the basement is the most hazardous location in an apartment building. Basement parking may increase the possibility of an intruder entering the building by driving in behind a car that arrives legitimately to park. Once there, the intruder is free to enter every floor in the building (unless tenants have keys to the elevator on the basement level or a doorman in the lobby monitors a video camera in the basement).

Basement laundry rooms are equally hazardous, mainly because they are used less frequently than most other areas of the building. For this reason, they are favorite areas for attacks. To the criminal, especially the sexual predator, the lack of activity is beneficial. He can wait for the right moment and the right victim, and once he zeros in, he will likely have the time he needs to commit his crime.

If you find yourself on an elevator mistakenly descending to the basement, punch the "door open" button on the elevator, then get off on the first available floor and wait to board an elevator that is headed in your direction.

Don't use indoor emergency exits (fire stairs) except for emergencies. These stairs are built to withstand a fire, and the fireproof doors deaden all sounds on the stairs. Your cries for help may be inaudible outside the staircase.

Remember the saying about safety in numbers. It is far safer—and much more sociable—to go to the mailbox area or the basement laundry room with a neighbor. If you must go alone, trust your instincts and keep moving if you are at all uncomfortable with your surroundings.

Health Clubs and Solariums

More and more new apartment buildings, especially co-ops and condominiums, include health clubs and solariums. Many of these feature indoor or outdoor swimming pools, saunas, steam rooms, heated whirlpools, restrooms, showers, lockers, gyms, and even a play area stocked with toys for children. The solarium, often situated on or near the roof, may be equipped with expensive chaises, chairs, and tables. All this paraphernalia may provide easy relaxation for hardworking residents, but it also presents security issues.

For protection in these areas, these basic security principles should be adhered to:

- All doors to all rooms, storerooms, and utility closets shuld be locked with a deadbolt when not in use.
- Rooms with expensive equipment should be alarmed.
- An attendant and a lifeguard should be on duty during scheduled hours at the club and swimming pool.
- Closed-circuit television should monitor strategic points in all rooms, hallways, and corridors.
- Panic buttons should be available in each room to patrons who feel threatened or physically ill.

- The solarium should be equally equipped, especially if it is situated far from the rest of the club.
- Anything of value should not be taken with you to the health club; leave them securely locked in your apartment.
- If you choose not to leave your purse or wallet in your home, keep them and all other personal belongings in a locked locker while you exercise or swim. Use your own combination lock.
- The children's play area should be kept neat and orderly, with all toys secured in a locked closet when not in use.
- Do not enter the playroom if you see a suspicious person. Report the person in question to the doorman and ask them to check this person's identity and reason for being in the playroom.

Terraces

A terrace offers relaxation and privacy, but it may also attract burglars, who see it as a way into your apartment. Even a terrace on a high floor is accessible to burglars, who may reach it from an unsecured hallway door leading to the outside or through a neighbor's apartment that they forcibly entered. Your apartment is the next target.

Secure all windows and doors leading to your terrace, particularly sliding glass doors. Install shatterproof glass or other impact-resistant glazing, insert a broom handle (cut to size) in the track on which the doors slide, and attach locks with vertical barrel bolts to fit into holes in the top and bottom tracks.

SECURITY AT DIFFERENT TIMES OF DAY

Many times complexes scale back on the level of security at certain times of the day when they believe there is less risk of crime. Before you accept this, consider the possible consequences. If your condo board or tenants' association wants to switch from two guards at night to only one in the morning, check your local laws. A court, questioning why certain shifts are covered by only one security guard, might attribute negligence to the building management during these hours. For help in determining high-risk hours, call in a crime expert or your local police department. The police

Tenants' Associations

Tenants' associations vary in their degrees of formality. Some consist of a group of people within a complex who band together to form an official association that develops guidelines for protection and harmony. For example, they may ask the local police to teach them how to better protect themselves, form patrols to provide security for the apartment complex, hold crime-prevention meetings, copy Neighborhood Watch activities, or contact management with suggestions to enhance security measures.

Other complexes have more casual associations. Their guidelines might consist of asking a neighbor to look after an apartment if someone plans to be away for a few days. Some neighbors even install buzzers between their apartments for quick response in case of an emergency.

are often willing to provide this expert advice without charge. Taking such reasonable measures could constitute a strong defense in a lawsuit.

RENTING OUT YOUR APARTMENT OR CONDO

All security equipment, such as locks, bolts, and alarms, should be in proper working condition for your protection, but if you rent your condo or co-op, you must also be concerned for your tenant's safety.

A female who rented a condo in California was abducted from the condo's parking lot, robbed, and assaulted. Citing fraud and negligence, she sued the condo association for her injuries. She argued that the owner of the apartment had assured her that the private parking lot was protected by a modern key-entry security gate, but her attackers entered through a defective gate. The court ruled in her favor because condominium owners are required to take reasonable measures to safeguard tenants, and defective gates abrogated this responsibility.

Generally, property owners are considered liable for dangerous or defective conditions with respect to the property they own. This is also true for condo owners, not only for their individual condo units but also for the common areas of the residence.

PART TWO

SECURITY AWAY FROM HOME

CHAPTER 10

CAR SAFETY

Motor-vehicle theft has touched more than 2 percent of the nation's households, according to the Bureau of Justice Statistics. And the FBI notes that owners of one car have a 9 percent risk of having their car stolen during a 10-year period. This figure increases to 17 percent with two cars. With carjacking still very much a problem, car owners are finding that they are at risk even while driving.

SIMPLE TIPS TO PREVENT THEFT

A motor vehicle is probably the second-largest investment you'll make, and there are a number of things you can do to protect your investment, including the obvious: Don't leave keys in the ignition, lock car doors, and park in a safe location. As basic as these precautions are, most car thefts would be eliminated if drivers followed these simple tips. About 50 percent of stolen cars were left unlocked, and nearly 20 percent had keys in the ignition.

Nearly one half of stolen cars wind up in "chop shops"—garages that dismantle stolen vehicles. A thief can get as much as five times the value of a car by selling parts to chop shops. Engrave your Vehicle Identification

Number (VIN) on various parts and panels of your vehicle to make it less attractive to car thieves who dismantle it for parts, and easier to identify if parts are recovered.

Cars with an outside hood-release mechanism are particularly vulnerable. Thieves can open the hood, cut battery cables with a bolt cutter, and get away in seconds. Key-operated hood locks are available at auto accessory stores, and heavy chains and padlocks can sometimes be used to prevent a hood from being raised. This method, while effective, is inconvenient when you need to open the hood for routine maintenance.

SAFEGUARDING ACCESSORIES

Sometimes thieves don't want your entire car—instead, they only want to steal particular items and accessories. You must therefore take steps to protect not only the car itself but also what you keep inside.

Never store your driver's license and automobile registration in your car. Carry these documents on your person, and handle them as you would any valuable papers. If keeping the registration on you is impractical (as would be the case if a number of drivers used the same car frequently), keep it in the trunk or make a copy for each driver. The glove compartment and the area above the sun visor are among the first places searched by a thief.

If your car is equipped with mushroom-shaped inside door locks, replace them with straight or tapered ones. The older kinds allow a crook to gain entry with a coat hanger.

The glove compartment and the area above the sun visor are among the first places searched by a thief.

Protect your various car accessories, such as a radar detector or GPS (Global Positioning System) unit. Do not tempt a thief by leaving these devices in plain view. More and more thieves want the computer, or Electronic Control Module (ECM), in the dashboard. These computers are the vehicle's operating center, controlling everything from power door locks to the flow of fuel to the engine. It takes an experienced thief only about 30 seconds to steal the ECM, which may be resold for several hundred dollars. Increase your protection by purchasing a metal cage that can be bolted (not welded) to the metal interior of your car.

Airbag thefts are increasing, especially in large cities. More than 75,000 airbags are stolen nationally each year. To minimize the issue, ensure that the car is always locked and in a visible location.

FAST LANE Transponders

FAST LANE transponders are electronic toll-collection devices that let you progress through highway toll plazas without having to stop. The transponder attaches to the inside of the windshield. Each time you drive through the designated lane, the toll transaction takes place electronically and is recorded to your account. If you have a positive balance on your account, you'll see a green light as you drive through the plaza to show that your transaction has gone through. You have different payment options, such as keeping a balance on your account, from which the toll fees get deducted, or having tolls deducted directly from your checking account or designated credit card by using automated toll payment services such as FAST LANE or E-ZPass.

The FAST LANE transponder is small and portable, making it easy for you to transfer it from one car to another. Unfortunately, the transponder's size and portability also makes it a very attractive target for thieves. Be sure to detach your transponder from the windshield and keep it out of plain sight (preferably in the trunk rather than the glove compartment) when the car is not in use.

Global Positioning Systems

Perhaps the most valuable accessory you can have in your car these days is a Global Positioning Systems (GPS). A GPS not only helps you figure out where you are located should you get lost, but it can also figure out the best route for you to take to a designated location. A GPS can also alert you via phone or e-mail if your car alarm has been triggered, and it can aid in locating the vehicle. Unfortunately, the GPS units themselves are small and portable and can be easily stolen.

Be careful not to leave them out in plain sight when your car is not in use—even if you're leaving the car for only a few minutes to go into a gas station. However, simply removing the GPS unit from its holder is not enough, because if you leave the holder (usually attached to the windshield) in place, any would-be thief knows that you have a GPS unit. Therefore, you should remove both the unit and its holder from the windshield when you leave your car. If you can't take them with you, lock them in your trunk rather than in the glove compartment, because that is one of the first places thieves look.

Removable Car Stereo Faceplates

If you have audio systems or other attractive electronic components, such as a CD player, satellite radio, GPS unit, or a citizen's band (CB) radio in your car, you are displaying desirable goods to a thief. If practical, detach the system and take it with you when you leave the car. Many should fit in your pocket. If carrying the device with you is not feasible, lock it in your truck.

MP3 Players

People are increasingly bringing their home music libraries into their cars via MP3 players. An easy way to do this is to simply hook up your portable MP3 player to the car stereo. There are several devices designed specifically for making this connection; oftentimes, you simply need to plug your iPod into a device that fits into the car's cigarette lighter. This type of setup is ideal because you are likely to take your iPod with you when you leave the car, thus protecting it from being stolen from the vehicle. However, it is still a good idea to remove any iPod accessory devices and hide them so that would-be thieves won't be alerted that you own an MP3 player and be tempted to look for it in your glove compartment.

Another option is to simply burn your MP3 songs onto a CD, which most car stereos can read. You can also have MP3 hard-drive systems installed in your car rather than use a portable player. The system is usually installed in your trunk, and you transfer your home music onto it via the unit's removable storage device. You can then access the music through your car radio, which will enable to you to search by genre, artist, or playlist. The advantage of this setup is that the system is hidden in the trunk and therefore not visible to thieves.

HATCHBACKS, CONVERTIBLES, AND SUVs

Popular styles of cars, such as hatchbacks, convertibles, and SUVs, come with extra security risks. The hatchback does not have a trunk. Instead, it has an integrated cargo area behind the second row of seats, which is accessed from behind the vehicle by the tailgate, or hatch. The rear cargo area is visible through the car's rear window.

To discourage thieves, cover valuables in the back with a tarp. Some think this method will invite break-ins because thieves will believe the tarp indicates that something valuable is hidden underneath, but the thief will actually be taking a greater risk because he or she doesn't know exactly what the payoff will be.

The convertible is defined by its retractable or collapsible roof. Regardless of whether or not you leave the top down, these cars are highly susceptible to theft; soft tops can easily be sliced open. Never keep anything valuable in your convertible. Hide any accessories in the trunk, such as MP3 players and GPS systems, and get a stereo with a removable faceplate. Even your sunglasses are likely to get nabbed if you leave them sitting in an open convertible!

ALARMS AND OTHER SECURITY DEVICES

If you must carry items of value in your car, frequently test your alarm system. However, some car-alarm systems are subject to false alarms, and like most alarm systems, they can be circumvented. Despite these disadvantages, a car alarm is useful for security.

Alarms that require the ignition key for deactivation are less effective, because a thief can disarm the alarm by altering under-the-dash wiring. Alarms that require a code to be entered on a pad may also be disabled. Remote alarms are the most effective, and the most expensive. Alarm systems that go off immediately after entry are better than those that go off after 30 seconds or more. This may be all the time a thief needs to take off with your car. An expert should install your alarm since expert-installed alarms are harder for a crook to defeat than self-installed systems. The newest alarms on the market are portable and activated by air pressure; they emit a piercing sound when a door or window is opened.

As with home alarms, car-alarm decals may help, particularly if the person trying to steal the auto isn't very sophisticated. The practiced thief, however, will be able to distinguish between alarmed and unalarmed cars.

An expert should install your alarm since expert-installed alarms are harder for a crook to defeat than self-installed systems.

One common and highly visible antitheft device is the steering-wheel locking mechanism, which prevents the steering wheel from turning. However, even this can be compromised by a resourceful thief. There are also locks that encompass the steering wheel and hinder accessibility to the ignition. You can also find various types of "passive systems" that immobilize the vehicle. Here are examples of what's available:

- **A hidden "kill switch,"** which prevents your car from being started until it is set in the proper position.
- **An ignition cutoff switch,** which shuts off the car engine automatically seconds after it is started.
- **A fuel switch,** which cuts off the gasoline supply automatically. (A gas cap lock is also a good idea—a thief will be able to go only as far as the amount of gas in the tank allows.)

Stolen Vehicle Recovery Systems (SVRS), such as LoJack, are also effective. These devices send out signals that help police locate your car. However, the distance from which these signals can be detected can be quite short (usually from 2 to 5 miles but also as short as 5 blocks in areas with radio disturbance). SVRS are not available in all areas, and it is not visible to potential thieves, so it fails as a deterrent. It also does not prevent vandalism, unless the car is equipped with an alarm. Nevertheless, LoJack boasts a 90 percent vehicle recovery rate. It's prudent to inquire at your vehicle dealership about available options. Vehicle add-on security is often expensive and may not be covered by dealer warranty.

Also effective is a Global Positioning Satellite (GPS) anti-theft/duress system, which allows a vehicle to be tracked and sends out a silent duress signal. Alternatively, the Safe & Sound option for the OnStar auto system provides several antitheft features, including stolen vehicle location.

Ask your local police department if it has a car-theft program, such as New York City's Combat Auto Theft (CAT), Philadelphia's Stolen Auto Verification Effort (SAVE), and Stop Cleveland Auto Theft (SCAT). For a small fee, you will receive decals for your car window, and the police will stop your vehicle during late-night or early-morning hours to make sure the driver has authorized use of the car. These programs and devices may even entitle you to receive a discount on your vehicle insurance.

HAZARDS WHILE ON THE ROAD

Car theft is always a concern, but even more alarming is how vulnerable you are when driving alone at night or walking to your car in a dark parking garage.

Before Entering Your Car

As you approach your car, check for flat tires and obstructions near the wheels and for any suspicious shadow lines that may indicate that a person is hiding underneath. Before getting in, check for illegal entry. If you think your car has been broken into, don't disturb fingerprints or any other evidence that may assist the police.

Next, look in the window and check inside your car front and back. (Use a small penlight during hours of darkness to examine the interior.) Do this even if the car has been in an attended garage or a parking attendant delivered it to you. Again, you may discover evidence that you shouldn't disturb. You might also discover someone crouching on the floor. If all appears in order, unlock the door. If the door isn't locked and you are reasonably certain that you locked it when you left, be cautious. Before you get into the car, make sure your radio and other electronics are still there and the glove compartment door is closed.

From a security standpoint, a citizens band radio or a cell phone is an excellent item for a well-equipped auto. You should even consider having both devices. There are gaps in the coverage of cellular phones when you leave populated areas. In this circumstance, your CB might help you through an emergency. CB Channel 9 is monitored continuously for emergency radio traffic throughout most of the United States.

Before you get into the car, make sure your electronics are there and the glove compartment door is closed.

After Entering Your Car

Once you're in the car, lock all the doors, fasten your seat belt, and start the car. But what if it won't start?

If the car is parked in your driveway or in front of the house in daylight, the problem is probably a mechanical malfunction. If it is late at night and you are parked in an unfamiliar or high-crime neighborhood, the car's disability might have been caused deliberately. Look around. If you observe persons acting suspiciously or out of place but the area is well lit and there are witnesses around, get out of the car, lock the door, and seek assistance. A potential place for safety is to return to the place you just left, returning to your vehicle only after obtaining assistance of your own choosing or the next day during daylight hours. If, on the other hand, you believe robbery or assault seems likely, and if you are not on a brightly lit or heavily traveled thoroughfare, an alternative may be to lock the car and stay inside, calling for police assistance and blowing the horn if you are threatened.

Whatever you do, don't accept a stranger's offer of assistance. This may be the person who disabled your car. Tell the stranger through a barely opened window that you have already called for assistance and the police are on their way. Don't accept anyone's offer to call a service station for you; an accomplice may be standing by to act as a service station employee. If you're inside your car and a would-be benefactor tries to get you to unlock the door, blow the horn and keep blowing it until your "friend" leaves or until someone in the neighborhood gets disturbed enough to call the police. In such situations, be suspicious of females as well as males.

If You Are Being Followed

. . . on the road. If you think someone is following you when you are driving, ask yourself if you have given anyone reason to do so. Did you flash a roll of money in a store? Did you just cash a check? Were you just in an altercation? Did you just cut someone off? If you think it's likely that someone is following you, don't panic. Here's how to take action:

- If your follower persists, call 911 on your cell phone.
- Drive toward a busy intersection, activate your flashers, double-check that your doors are locked, and safely park by an intersection curb.
- Request assistance from law enforcement and remain at the location until a uniformed police officer arrives.
- If in doubt about the officer's legitimacy, proceed to a public area, such as a nearby police station, where the officer's identity can be determined.

. . . into your driveway. When entering a driveway or a garage, make sure no one is following you. If the garage has automatic doors, confirm that there are no suspicious-looking people or vehicles inside. If there are, don't go in. Find out who they are or wait until they leave. If they don't leave, call the police. In addition, make sure the garage door is closed and that nobody has followed you in before you get out of your car.

If You Have Car Trouble

If you are driving along the expressway and your car stalls, steer it completely off the roadway. Get all passengers out of the car and away from the road. Signal for assistance. Attempt repairs if you are qualified, but do so away from traffic.

Keep in mind that you can drive on a flat tire if you find yourself in an undesirable or remote area. The tire may be ruined, but your safety is more important.

Signal that you need assistance by displaying a flag or white cloth tied to the radio antenna. Leave lights on at night, using emergency blinkers

Tips for a Safer Towing Experience

Make sure the towing company is licensed. If the truck arrives and the company's name, address, telephone number, tow rates, and license (where required) are not visible on the truck, be suspicious. Most vehicle manufacturers have 24-hour 800 numbers and will dispatch reliable tow services at your request. The 800 number is located in manufacturers booklets, usually contained in the glove compartment of the vehicle or on a side-window decal.

Inspect your vehicle for damage, and remove all valuables before it is towed. Countless complaints of damage and theft have been made against towing companies.

Contact your repair shop. If this is not practical, do not sign an "Authorization to Repair" unless you are satisfied with the expertise and integrity of the repair shop chosen by the towing company.

Request a repair estimate and an itemized bill. You will need this if you decide to challenge the charges. (You'll also need an itemized bill if your vehicle is covered by a warranty or for insurance reimbursement.)

Pay by credit card. If it's possible, this is always the best way to pay. Credit card companies will protect you in case you contest repair charges.

or turn signals to warn oncoming traffic. Raise the hood to signify that caution is in order and you need assistance.

Learn how to change a tire on the car you drive. Use your driveway or another safe location to practice changing it. Keep in mind that you can drive on a flat tire if you find yourself in an undesirable or remote area. Slow the car down and proceed cautiously to a public area. The tire may be ruined, but your safety is more important. And driving on the flat may attract the attention of law enforcement.

TOWING TIPS

Okay, your day was going just fine until your car died. Don't panic. Lock your doors, take out your cell phone, and make a call to roadside assistance. But first gather the following information:

- license plate number

- your present location—an address or intersection and a landmark
- the year, make, and model of your car
- if your vehicle is a front-wheel drive, rear-wheel drive, 2-wheel drive, 4-wheel drive, or all-wheel drive
- the address of where you wish to be towed.

CARJACKING

Carjacking is a popular (and brazen) crime. Your car is stolen while you're still in it, or just as you're getting in or out. With new and better alarms and protective devices for cars, it is becoming increasingly difficult for thieves to steal an uninhabited vehicle, a development that has made carjacking more appealing to the criminal element.

Techniques

The most widespread carjacking technique is the "bump and rob," in which you are rear-ended by a driver. Although your first instinct after getting bumped is to immediately get out of your car, *don't!* Getting out leaves you extremely vulnerable, especially if you are alone. If you are bumped, stay in your vehicle; through your rearview mirror, gather information about the car that hit you. If the circumstance is suspicious or you are in a remote location, roll down the window slightly and tell the other driver to follow you to a public place. If their vehicle is disabled, wait for the police to arrive.

You may also be followed home from a mall, an ATM, or any other place that involves goods or money. Carjackers have even been known to establish fake valet parking setups, where you literally hand your car keys to them.

Carjackers also impersonate police officers to make you pull over. Make sure the police car is really a law-enforcement vehicle or, if the car is unmarked, try to determine if the officer is wearing an authentic uniform. Assess what the officer says as he approaches your car. An authorized law officer will tell you why you've been pulled over and immediately request your license and registration. Roll the windows down only an inch or two and ask to see the officer's badge or ID. If still

Places That Pose the Greatest Carjacking Risk

Carjacking incidents take place at all times and in all places, but you may be at a greater risk under these circumstances:

- When stopped in traffic, especially at red lights and stop signs in the curb lane
- In parking lots and garages
- When getting on or off a highway
- At a self-service or late-night full-service gas station, carwash, or convenience store
- At an automated teller machine (ATM)
- When getting into or out of your car

suspicious, advise the person to follow you to a public place, activate your vehicle flashers, and drive slowly to a visible public location.

Increasing Your Odds against a Carjacker

Statistics show that a weapon is used in a greater percentage of all carjackings. Experts say that if you get into the car with an armed carjacker, there is an increased chance you will not survive the incident. If you refuse to go with the carjacker and run away, there is a reasonable chance you will not be injured. If you're in the car, distract the carjacker with your credit card, ATM card, or money; throw them out the window, get out. and run. Most likely the carjacker will go after the valuables. If you can't run, lie flat on the ground—it's too hard for the assailant to force you to go with him. If your child is in the car when you are attacked, throw your keys and pocketbook out of the car and tell the assailant that he can have the car but not your child. Grab your child and run.

Distract the carjacker with your credit card, ATM card, or money; throw them out the window, get out, and run. Most likely the carjacker will go after the valuables.

Try to get a description of the assailant. Report the incident to the police, giving them a description of the carjacker, along with any evidence you have and information about your vehicle. Tell them the direction the carjacker was heading in your car.

Below are a few tips to follow to avoid a carjacking incident.

Always keep your windows rolled up when driving. If the weather is hot and you don't have air-conditioning, keep them at least three-quarters of the way up.

Always lock your doors as soon as you enter your vehicle. Carjackers most frequently get into cars when doors are not locked. Use the "panic button" (if your car has one) that automatically locks all doors and windows in the event of an emergency. As a rule, vehicle door locks should be unlocked only when entering or exiting the vehicle, including when parked inside your own garage or on your property.

No idle waiting. Do not wait in a car for a companion with the engine running and the doors unlocked.

Keep your purse and other valuables out of sight. These should be kept in the glove compartment or under the seat as you drive.

Don't be reckless or foolhardy. If another driver appears to need assistance, stop, roll down the window slightly, and ask if you can send help. Don't allow yourself to be talked into giving assistance. Go for help.

Get away, even if it risks a collision. If someone other than a uniformed or plainclothes police officer in a squad car or another clearly

Key Safety

Keep your car keys on a different key chain from your house keys, and keep your house keys in your pocket. If your car keys are stolen, the thief will not have access to your home, and you will still have your house keys even if your purse is stolen. (If your house keys are stolen, however, change your locks immediately.)

It's also a good idea to keep an extra set of car keys, and remote if you use a remote, separate from your first set of car keys in case you accidentally lock your keys in your car.

identifiable department vehicle attempts to force you to the curb, try to get away, even if it means a collision. Sound the horn and drive to a service station, a well-lit house, or anywhere else you might reasonably expect to find assistance, and from there report the matter to the police.

If someone tries to enter your car at a stop sign or a stoplight, drive away. Consider running a red light if there is no risk of collision. Sound your horn, activate your flashing lights, and attract as much attention as possible.

Know your surroundings. If you must travel alone on a regular basis, consider these two rules: First, learn the location of police and fire stations or other locations that may be frequented by the police, including all-night restaurants. Second, travel familiar streets and find out as much as possible about the areas through which you pass.

The following are a few additional quick tips to keep you on guard:

- Always carry your cell phone with you when you travel so that you can summon assistance quickly if you need it. Consider having more than one cell phone with you in case one fails. Also carry an extra cell battery.
- Park in well-lit, busy, and open areas. Try to find parking lots with attendants or security patrols.
- Leave enough room in a parallel parking space between the car in front of you and your car so that you can drive away if threatened.
- Drive slowly toward a red light on an isolated street so that by the time you reach the intersection, the light will be about to change. This way you will not be a "sitting duck" while waiting for the light to change.
- Don't turn the car on to heat up in cold weather and leave it running while you're in the house.
- Do not leave children and babies alone in your car, even for a moment.
- Avoid driving a car that may be identified as rented. Carjackers are especially tempted by tourists.
- Be wary if someone tries to sell you merchandise when you are in your car. They may be distracting you from an accomplice approaching from another direction.

- Stay calm while driving. Suppress your need to tell off other drivers or to gesture to them. Such behavior may provoke an incident. "Road rage" has resulted in injuries and even death.

POINTERS FOR SAFE PARKING

Many things can happen if you don't take the time to find a proper place to park or you forget to lock your car doors. Often, people are in a hurry to get to where they are going and lose all common sense. From being accosted in a remote, dark lot to having your valuables stolen, the risks are very real. However, these incidents can easily be avoided if you use good judgment. For instance:

Park where passersby may serve as a deterrent to someone who might steal, or steal from, your car. If it's daylight, ask yourself if it will still be light when you return. Try to park near a storefront that will be brightly lit, on a main thoroughfare, under a street lamp, or somewhere you anticipate heavy traffic (either vehicular or pedestrian). In a driveway, park with the front of your vehicle facing passersby who may witness a thief tampering with your engine. Avoid remote, unlit areas.

Don't park in the same location at the same time every day. To make it more difficult for your vehicle to be towed, turn your wheels toward the curb and put on your emergency brake. If you have automatic transmission, leave it in park. If it's manual, leave the gear in first or reverse.

Once parked, roll up your windows and always lock your car. This is important even if you will be away for only a few minutes. Always take your key with you when you exit your automobile, and always double-check to be sure that all car doors are locked and all windows closed.

Be particularly careful when parking in public lots. The chances of your car being stolen from an unattended lot are five times greater than from the street or an attended lot. (See chapter 12 for information on car safety when shopping.) At an attended garage, leave only your ignition key. And don't use a magnetic holder with a spare ignition key that attaches to the car's frame. It is an open invitation to car thieves. In self-parking garages, park facing out if possible.

BUYING AND SELLING A USED CAR

Selling anything through a classified ad can put yourself at risk to strangers, because you must provide contact information. But when it comes to buying or selling a car, safety extends far beyond the advertisement.

Selling

There are so many avenues you can take to sell a car nowadays—from Craigslist to posting signs at your local market. But when it comes to safety, the old rules still apply. Below are the most vital.

- Never disclose if you are a male or female by revealing your first name when placing an ad.
- Never let the prospective buyer know where you live or where you usually park your car.
- Agree to meet with prospective buyers only in a safe public location.
- Ask to see a valid driver's license and proof of insurance before letting anyone test-drive your car, and make sure that the driver is over 18 years of age (otherwise, be sure to have their parent come along for the ride). Make a mental note of their description.

> If you let someone test-drive your car alone, he or she could make a copy of your keys and come back later to steal the car—or they may simply drive off with the car.

- Let the buyer do the test-driving, but you do the navigating, taking him or her along a preplanned route that allows them to see how the car drives under different conditions.
- Bring along a friend for your own security.
- Keep something of value behind as the buyer's collateral.
- Keep an eye on your keys; if you let someone test-drive your car alone, he or she could make a copy of your keys and come back later to steal the car—or they may simply drive off with the car.
- If someone buys your car, insist on payment by certified check, and make sure you cancel your insurance immediately.
- Be sure to remove your license plates and registration decal before turning over the car to its new owner.

Buying

You are as much at risk when buying a used car. Here are some tips to make sure you don't get swindled.

- Use a reputable dealer.
- Shop during the day, and inspect the vehicle carefully.
- Pay special attention to the VIN (Vehicle Identification Number); you may be sold a stolen car. Make sure that the VIN matches the title and that it hasn't been tampered with. Check the VIN on the national registry website www.vehicleidentificationnumber.com or www.dmv.org, or request law enforcement to check the VIN.
- Be sure the license plate and inspection and emission decals are valid.
- Be wary if the car has had a recent paint job or there is suspicion that the interior has been wet.
- Check for proper wheel alignment, rust, leaks, and worn brakes, and look for signs of tampering with the odometer.
- Start the car, listen carefully, and look for excessive exhaust.
- Take the vehicle for a test drive with a mechanic or other knowledgeable person to examine the vehicle before you make any commitment.
- Find out if your state has a "lemon law" that allows you to return a used vehicle to a dealer within a specified period of time if there are mechanical issues.

SECURITY FOR OTHER TYPES OF VEHICLES

Owners of recreational vehicles, such as motorhomes, motorcycles, and bikes need to consider issues specific to them.

Motor Homes, Recreational Vehicles, and Vans

You can protect motor homes and recreational vehicles (RVs) by employing the same measures as for automobiles. There are, however, a few areas of particular concern. Motor homes are especially vulnerable at times of seasonal change, when thieves might steal them for sale to vacationers or for transportation to another climate.

Elaborately styled and personalized vans are another consideration. The individualized nature of many of these vans makes them less attractive to the local thief but more attractive to the organized career criminal, who transports them to another part of the country, where an outlet can sell them quickly.

Motorcycles, Mopeds, and Bicycles

Motorcycles and mopeds need to be locked up to discourage theft. No lock is 100 percent theft-proof, but there are devices that discourage or delay a thief considerably. Invest in a lock that lets you link your motorcycle to a pole or street sign when it's not in use. Among the locks available today are Kryptonite U-shaped bars, braided and plastic-covered steel cables, and old-fashioned chains and padlocks. A beeper that sounds when someone tampers with your motorcycle is also available; it is audible for up to one-half mile. Don't rely on the automatic steering lock built into a motorcycle. This will prevent the wheels from turning but will not keep the motorcycle from being lifted onto a truck and spirited away.

A bicycle is easily stolen and extremely difficult to trace, so bicycle security demands your vigilance. One way to discourage bicycle thieves is to buy the bicycle secondhand. Since your "like-new" transportation will not have the resale potential of the pacesetting models, you're less likely to be ripped off.

Safeguard against bicycle theft by recording your bike's serial number and registering it with your local police department.

You also need to protect your bike from theft with a good padlock. Many bicycle locks are available: heavy shackle locks, chain-and-key padlocks, horseshoe-shaped clamps, and cable combination locks. Assault-resistant cable or U-shaped locks and the superheated steel chain are your best bets—but perhaps more important is the way the bike is secured and where. Secure the bike through the frame or through both the frame and tire, rather than just the tire. Secure it to a lamppost, tree, or other object that is large enough to prevent the object from being removed along with the bike. The object should be tall enough so that the whole assembly—bike, chain, lock and all—cannot be slipped off the top.

Further safeguard against bicycle theft by recording your bike's serial number and registering it with your local police department. When you are not riding the bicycle, put it in a locked room, basement, or garage, not in your backyard or driveway where it can be seen from the street. And remember to lock the bike, even if it's in the locked garage.

PROTECTING YOUR BOAT

Protecting a boat is, in many ways, similar to protecting your home (see Part 1). You need good deadbolt locks, protective lighting, and alarm systems, including local alarms for all hatches, to protect your property. You will also need to maintain up-to-date inventory lists (see chapter 2) and should etch or otherwise identify items that are part of your maritime home. Compasses, sextants, depth-sounding gear, radar, radios, and life-preserving equipment should all bear your identification marks.

Secure your boat to a mooring with a steel chain in addition to a line. Be sure to moor or anchor your boat in a secure marina, especially during months when anchorages are crowded. Secure mooring is a safety and security procedure and anticipates weather conditions that may dislodge your boat from its location.

Cooperate with your neighbors at marinas or anchorages for common security. Ideally, you should make use of continuously staffed mooring facilities. Never leave containers of gasoline on your boat.

When you leave your boat, secure the outboard motor with padlocks and chains. Install a secret ignition cutoff switch to prevent a thief from stealing your craft. Most important, when you leave the boat, don't leave the registration papers behind. The availability of a registration may allow someone to sell your boat.

You will most likely be required to display craft registration numbers on your hull unless the vessel is documented by the U.S. Coast Guard. You should also place vessel-identifying numbers in remote locations on the boat. Placement should be at a location within the bilge area of the hold or other area not normally accessible. The identifying numbers should be permanently attached.

CHAPTER 11

SECURITY
ON THE STREETS

More crimes against people are committed on the streets than in any other place. Staying safe requires a combination of common sense and proven security guidelines. Follow these tips to protect yourself.

BASIC PRECAUTIONS

Taking mass transportation, jogging, or inline skating all come with special risks if you're not equipped with the proper knowledge of what criminals are looking for. A few precautions will greatly reduce your chances of being victimized.

Don't Carry Large Amounts of Cash

The first rule is to limit your losses. Don't carry more than you can easily afford to lose. If you carry little cash, the robber's take won't break you, but it should be enough to satisfy him. Carry only credit cards that you think you are likely to need, and don't carry keys in your purse along with identification. If your purse is stolen, you might find that your home has been robbed before you have even finished filing the police report.

If you need to carry more cash than you're comfortable with, consider traveler's checks.

Surrender Your Valuables

The second rule is simple. Remain calm, obey all commands, and surrender your valuables. But don't make any sudden moves. Tell your assailant that you're reaching for your wallet; then do it very slowly. You may be risking a fair amount of money, but the robber, who is risking a minimum of 10 years in jail, will be as nervous as you are. Don't let your attacker move you into an alley, doorway, or other secluded place. Explain that there's no need to do so and that you are perfectly willing to cooperate.

Regardless of how accommodating you are, you may still be attacked. In this case, you have little choice but to defend yourself. What's your best defense? Scream for help and run away. Don't fight. The robber is probably better equipped for combat than you are and is likely to be armed with a gun or knife.

Do not carry cash in your handbag. Purses are too easily stolen. A coat pocket (particularly an inside one) or an old-fashioned money belt is more secure.

WHAT TO DO IF YOU'RE BEING FOLLOWED

The third protective rule is, when possible, walk in the middle of the sidewalk facing oncoming car traffic. This eliminates the possibility of someone's sneaking up behind you in a car. If you're accosted, an oncoming motorist might see you and send assistance.

If you are being followed on a well-traveled street, slow down, speed up, reverse direction—in other words, let your pursuer know that you're aware you are being followed. Then go straight for help. If you are being followed on a deserted street, don't play games. Walk as fast as you can until you find police officer or other responsible person to help you. Look ahead for the presence of other people.

Most important, don't go straight home if you're being followed, especially if no one is there to assist you. You are safer on the street than you are inside your empty home or in an elevator alone with your assailant. If your empty dwelling is the only option you have, then address the immediate problem at hand—your personal safety—and go to your residence.

DEFENSE WEAPONS

Self-defense products, such as spray, mace, stun guns, and tasers, effectively provide some degree of leverage over an attacker. But they are completely useless if lost at the bottom of your person or left in a drawer at home. (To learn about defense tactics and some nontraditional defense weapons, see page 318.)

Self-Defense Sprays

Many Americans carry defensive sprays, which, when directed into the face of an attacker, causes extreme pain and burning of the eyes and skin. These sprays are effective up to a distance of about 10 feet (3 m). Some defensive sprays may be less effective against a severely emotionally disturbed person or intoxicated assailant, who may not respond normally to pain.

Many people carry a red-pepper (capsicum) spray. It works faster than tear gas or Mace and has been used to ward off attacking animals. However, pepper spray often has a shorter range than Mace or tear gas because of the spray mist. Certain types of pepper sprays are combined with Mace, offering the advantages of both in a single spray. These sprays incapacitate an attacker for as long as 20 minutes, but the sprays may take anywhere from 3 seconds to a minute to take effect. Some sprays are equipped with an ultraviolet or orange-red dye that can mark an attacker for up to a week, aiding in detection and identification. These sprays are also fairly inexpensive, ranging anywhere from $10 to $50.

Caution: Sprays are ineffectual beyond their expiration date and may be ruined by extreme hot or cold temperatures. Do not leave them in your car in direct sunlight, especially during the summer months, because the canisters can explode at temperatures above 130°F (54°C). And realize that given the short range of spray, depending on wind conditions, the

Defending Yourself against a Mugger

Most muggings take place on the street. Thus, the best protection is to be alert and cautious at all times. Be suspicious of strangers, and never trust anyone you don't know. Avoid walking alone at night, especially in dangerous or unfamiliar neighborhoods. If you must go out at night, walk on well-lit main thoroughfares. It is useful to carry a small amount of money, say $50, to appease the potential mugger, but large sums should be avoided. Walk next to the curb, and stay away from buildings, alleys, doorways, shrubbery, trees, and benches. Walk at a determined speed, and appear in a hurry to reach a destination. Cross the street if you spot someone suspicious walking toward you or following you.

If confronted by a robber, use your common sense; maintain your cool and follow the mugger's instructions precisely. After the robbery, call the police. Bear in mind that robbers or muggers initially are after your valuables, but if they should feel threatened by you, it could be very dangerous. Let the robbers or muggers have whatever they ask for, and remember that your primary objective is to survive.

red-pepper spray could blow into the victim's face. Always conduct an initial test of a new spray to ensure that it functions properly.

Self-defense weapons are effective only if carried in your hand or in an easily accessible place, such as a pocket or on your belt. When driving alone, place your weapon on the passenger seat next to you.

If you are attacked, there is the possibility that your device may be grabbed and used against you, or the wind could blow the chemicals in your face as well as your attacker's. Unfortunately, this is especially true of mist sprays. In case of inadvertent contact, remain outdoors (or get there) and flush the eyes, nose, and mouth with water. Seek medical attention. You can guard against accidental discharge by activating the safety switch on the device, but it must be disengaged before use. Practice using your spray before you need it, instead of trying to figure it out at the moment of attack. Test it outdoors every month with a short blast. Replace sprays every year. In addition, use a spray only against an unarmed attacker—spraying a person holding a weapon could subject you to retaliation or an accidental shooting. If attacked, use your spray only as a means of escape; don't attempt to battle your opponent. Run away immediately and seek assistance.

And finally, never buy sprays or weapons from the street. Your local law-enforcement agency can refer you to a legitimate dealer.

Stun Guns and Tasers

A more expensive defensive alternative is a stun gun. Although we don't recommend this form of defense—the use of any shock device on a person with severe medical conditions can have very serious, if not fatal, consequences—stun guns are accepted as a legal form of self-defense in most areas; some states and cities place restrictions on these types of weapons. Check with local law enforcement regarding the laws in your area.

Stun guns transmit a high-voltage electric shock that can incapacitate an assailant for as long as five minutes. Besides fatality, there are other risks of using a shock device: Some require direct physical contact with an attacker and must be applied for several seconds to be effective. Momentary contact may only result in causing enough pain to provoke your assailant toward even greater violence. Older models are virtually ineffective if the battery is weak or the attacker is wearing thick clothing (see box below).

One popular type of stun gun is the Taser. A Taser is a type of stun gun that fires a wire-tethered projectile that delivers an electric shock, ultimately incapacitating an assailant. Modern-day Tasers shoot out small dartlike electrodes that are attached to the Taser through metal wires. The maximum range is up to 30 feet (9 m), which means that you can

Old vs. New Tasers

Older Taser models required the electrodes to have direct contact with the skin in order to be effective and had difficulty penetrating thick clothing. Newer models, however, use a shaped pulse of electricity that can deliver the shock without the need for metal prongs to penetrate the skin, so thicker clothing may no longer be an issue.

defend yourself before your assailant gets too close to you. Once the electrode is fired from the gun, you will have to replace the used cartridge. Many Tasers now come equipped with stun-gun electrodes as well, so you can use the gun itself to deliver a shock if the assailant gets close enough to you.

Whistles and Personal Alarms

Wear a whistle capable of a piercing sound strapped to the wrist for protection—don't carry it in your purse or pocket. Be circumspect about wearing a whistle on a substantial chain around your neck. An assailant might attempt to strangle you with your chain.

More sophisticated than whistles are personal alarms. You can purchase a handheld shrieker, often for under $25, at discount chains, sporting goods stores or police supply outlets. When squeezed, the device activates an ear-shattering and disorienting 120-decibel distress signal, which is turned off by entering a code. Another personal alarm, which you can buy for under $30, clips on like a pager and is activated by pulling a pin that triggers a blasting, shrieking siren. Or you can acquire a battery-powered or pressurized-gas alarm that emits a screeching sound; this type of alarm costs anywhere from a few dollars to over $100.

Personal alarms are easy to conceal and carry, they do not involve contact with the criminal, and unlike a weapon, they can't be turned against you.

Personal alarms might distract your attacker for the second or two you need to escape. They are easy to conceal and carry; they do not involve contact with the criminal; and, unlike a weapon, they can't be turned against you. However, if you live in a large city, don't expect help when the alarm goes off, because people are inured to the many false alarms that constantly sound. Also, personal alarms offer virtually no help in secluded areas. And finally, there is always a danger that the alarm might enrage the attacker.

PURSE SNATCHERS AND PICKPOCKETS

Always be on the lookout for purse and briefcase snatchers. To avoid drive-by snatchers, walk some distance from the curb, and with your purse or briefcase on the side of your body away from the street.

Carry your purse with the strap over one shoulder so that it hangs straight down, and clutch the bag between your arm and body. If your handbag strap is too short to carry this way, put your arm through the strap and cradle the purse in your arm, like a football. The same goes for strapless bags.

A pickpocket works best in a crowd and generally has an extremely light touch. You may feel only a slight pressure if a pickpocket is removing your wallet from your purse or your inside coat pocket.

NIGHTTIME WALKS

If you must walk at night, avoid the curb, whether or not vehicles are parked on the street. An attacker could hide between two parked cars and ambush you. Or someone driving by could reach through the car window and snatch your purse or briefcase. Don't walk too far from the curb, either. Pay particular attention to doorways and shrubbery abutting the sidewalk, either of which provides an excellent ambush point.

If your late-night walks are regular and predictable, vary your route, particularly on paydays, Social Security–check days, or other times when you might carry more than your usual amount of cash.

Stay in touch with others. Ask friends or relatives to call you when they reach their destination so you know they have arrived safely. In turn, call them when you arrive at your destination. Another note of caution: Do not talk unnecessarily on your cell phone (see sidebar, opposite) as you walk or wear earphones listening to music. Be alert and aware at all times and in all places, even if there is no apparent threat.

JOGGING AND INLINE SKATING

You may feel invigorated and confident while jogging or running, but beware: Runners, particularly female runners, are a prime target for criminals. The rules below apply to inline skaters as well.

Be especially careful when jogging alone, after dark, and on deserted paths. These are the times when you are most at risk. Run with a friend

On Your Cell Phone

You are especially vulnerable when using your cell phone. Engrossed in conversation, you become a prime target for pickpockets, muggers, and rapists. What can you do to avoid being a target while on the phone? Keep your purse, briefcase, or other personal belongings within grasp. Never stand with your back to the street. This way, you can observe any suspicious-looking characters that may approach you.

You may also want to program an In Case of Emergency contact (ICE) into your phone to assist emergency responders should you become incapacitated.

---

or a dog. Ask a runners organization, such as the Road Runners Club of America (RRCA), to provide safety tips for running in your area. Stay on well-traveled routes you know, and avoid trails with shrubbery or alleyways where attackers can hide. Know places along the way you can go for help in the event of an attack. Vary the routes you take and the time you run, and try to let a friend or relative know the path you will be taking.

Don't wear earphones. Even though music makes your workout more enjoyable, it inhibits your ability to hear what's going on around you. As with the prevention of other crimes, awareness is key. Take note of your surroundings and run facing oncoming traffic. Be aware that a friendly fellow jogger may be a criminal in disguise. If someone asks you for directions or the time, don't stop. Ignore lewd comments.

Don't wear jewelry or an expensive watch. Wearing something flashy or seemingly valuable may make you a target for thieves.

Carry identification and bring along your cell phone. Having an ID on you may be necessary if you suffer an injury or other medical emergency. You can use your cell phone to call for help if you are injured or sense a dangerous situation.

Bring along a whistle or handheld alarm. If Mace or other self-defense sprays are legal in your area, take these along. Keep them in an easily accessible place, such as in your hand or on your waistband, be prepared to use them, and don't be afraid to scream if you are attacked.

Learn self-defense tactics and practice them. If you're an experienced runner, you have a great amount of power in your legs, so kick sensitive areas to escape your attacker. If your assailant is unarmed, do everything you can to flee. If he is armed, surrender any money or valuables at his request. Never get into a car—you're unlikely to return.

Don't let speed lull you into a false sense of security. The speed of inline skates may make you feel more in control, because an assailant on foot can't keep up with your pace, but it takes only one blow to knock an unsuspecting skater off balance. And once you've lost your stride, your skates become a hindrance; you'll have trouble getting up, keeping your balance, and using any self-defense techniques with inline skates on your feet. Follow the guidelines above for jogging for maximum security while rollerblading.

A special word of caution: Whether you are skating, jogging, or walking, be careful when crossing bridges, because there are likely only two avenues of escape. Never use a bridge or pedestrian walkway when alone at night; have a friend accompany you. Try to take your walks during daylight hours when other pedestrians use the walkway. Make sure the bridge pathway is well lit and frequently patrolled by police.

MASS TRANSPORTATION

Public transportation is an economical and quick way to get around, but transit crimes—robbery, rape, purse snatching, pickpocketing, indecent exposure, assault, and even homicide—call for extra precautions when you travel.

Put your fare or token in your hand when you leave home. This way, you won't have to open your wallet or purse in public.

Know where you're going and the safest way to get there before leaving home. Call the place you are going or your local transit company for directions. If possible, travel with a companion when using mass transportation in more dangerous locales. Put your fare or token in your

Mass Transit Travel Checklist

- [ ] Know where you're going and the safest way to get there before leaving home.
- [ ] Keep your fare or token in your hand to avoid opening your wallet or purse.
- [ ] Do not carry more cash or credit cards than you need.
- [ ] Sit as close as possible to the bus driver or, in a subway car, near the conductor, and avoid empty sections.
- [ ] Be wary of anyone who bumps into you for no reason.
- [ ] Leave as soon as possible if trouble starts or if a fight breaks out.
- [ ] While waiting for a bus, stand back from the curb until you are ready to board.
- [ ] Never stand at the edge of a train platform.
- [ ] Avoid isolated or poorly lit platforms.
- [ ] Be aware of anyone appearing inebriated.
- [ ] Don't get off at a deserted stop or go directly home if you suspect you're being followed.
- [ ] Remain alert: Don't get so engrossed in magazines or music that you lose touch with your surroundings, and never close your eyes to relax.

hand when you leave home. This way, you won't have to open your wallet or purse in public.

Do not carry more cash or credit cards than you need; you should, however, carry a little extra cash in case of an emergency. Separate your money, keeping portions in your purse, pockets, and on your person—if you are the victim of a purse-snatcher or pickpocket, your losses will be minimized.

Sit as close as possible to the bus driver or, in a subway car, near the conductor, and avoid empty sections. Don't sit near an exit or an open window; a purse-snatcher could grab your belongings and be gone before you get out of your seat.

Be wary of anyone who bumps into you for no reason. Look around and take note of who is beside and in back of you. If you can't find a seat, try to stand where you are not crowded by other people. Keep your arms close to your body. Thieves can snatch a wristwatch off your arm, particularly one held by an expansion band.

Leave as soon as possible if trouble starts or if a fight breaks out. If someone harasses or insults you, remain calm and ignore the insult. If the person persists, tell the driver or conductor and move to another seat.

While waiting for a bus, stand back from the curb until you are ready to board. Never stand near the edge of a train platform—commuters have been pushed off platforms into the paths of oncoming trains and had purses snatched by thieves standing between two cars. Avoid isolated or poorly lit platforms, especially at night. If your train or bus runs on a schedule, plan to arrive just a few minutes before its arrival. If there is a delay, wait in a local well-frequented business or restaurant until departure. Numerous stations have mirrors that enable you to see around corners and determine if anyone is loitering. If you observe a suspicious-looking person, leave immediately and alert an attendant or police officer.

Protect yourself from chain snatchings by not wearing a chain. Turn your rings around so that the stones don't show. Dress in a manner that does not attract attention. Never take out your wallet or display money. If you wish to give money to a panhandler, keep spare change in a pocket separate from your wallet.

If you suspect you're being followed, don't get off at a deserted stop, and never go home. Ride on to a busy stop, and take a taxi or call for help. Make sure nobody follows you out of the station or away from the bus stop. Remember, subways and buses are equipped with two-way radios. In an emergency situation go to the driver, motorman, conductor, or to a police officer.

Be aware of your surroundings. Books, magazines, and earphones are distracting. Never become so engrossed that you do not realize who and what are around you. Even closing your eyes to relax will signal a lack of awareness. Keep your eyes open, and remain alert throughout your entire trip.

GOING OUT ON THE TOWN

Safety is probably the last thing on your mind when you head out on the town with your friends and loved ones. Unfortunately, this lack of precaution can have some serious consequences, as there are many ways you can be victimized while you're having fun.

Restaurants

Your credit card information is more likely to get stolen at a restaurant than at any other establishment. And while you might assume that a restaurant employee is to blame, this is not always the case. A likely culprit may be a hacker who breaks into the restaurant's computer system and downloads customers' credit card information. Ensure that your information is masked on any printed receipts to prevent identity theft. If you receive a receipt that lists your full credit card number, shred it as soon as you get home, and use cash at that particular restaurant the next time you go.

Be particularly careful when eating at fast-food restaurants. This is especially true now that many major fast-food chains have introduced late-night hours. Whenever you go to a fast-food restaurant, keep your wits about you and avoid going alone. Use the drive-thru window (with your car doors locked) rather than going inside the building late at night.

Movies

When you go to the movies, don't just choose the film you want to see; also make sure that the movie theater is in a safe neighborhood. Don't

Online Ticket Sellers/Auctions

These days, more and more sports and concert fans buy their tickets from online sellers and auctions. Some official ticket-selling websites, such as Ticketmaster, allow you to buy tickets safely and securely. Many venues also have their own websites from which you can buy event tickets.

People use the Internet to resell tickets they have already bought so you can also find tickets online to events that have sold out. When buying tickets from unknown people online via an auction site like eBay, do your research first. Sellers at online auctions usually have feedback ratings from people who have previously done business with them. Read these reviews and see what people had to say. Keep in mind that anytime you buy a ticket through an on-line auction, you run the risk of being scammed. Your tickets may never get delivered, or they may be in a different section than what you were told. Be sure to get as much information as possible about the tickets before buying them. And even if the ticket is legitimate, you should find out if you can get your money back if the event is canceled.

sit near boisterous or suspicious individuals, and never talk to another moviegoer about rude behavior; tell an usher instead.

Sporting Events and Concerts

Since pickpockets work best in a crowd, you need to be particularly careful at sporting events and concerts. If you carry a wallet, keep it in a secure pocket. If you carry a purse, lock it up tight and keep it close to your body. You can also hide your money in a money belt underneath your clothing. Since pickpockets often work in teams of two, avoid being sandwiched between two people.

Sporting events and concerts are also breeding grounds for scammers and frauds. If you want to buy souvenirs, buy them from a salesperson at the event itself rather than at an outside vendor, who may be peddling fraudulent merchandise. And be wary of buying your sporting events or concert tickets from a scalper or online (see box above), as you are far more likely to be the victim of a scam.

Help by Getting Help

If you're a witness to a crime on the streets, don't help by getting immediately involved personally. Do so only if you're positive that there is no danger to you, and request help by calling the police or an ambulance. Only then should you offer any personal assistance.

Don't forget that you may encounter frenzied, volatile fans who may be quick to get in an altercation at a sporting event. Even parents at their children's sports events have been known to get so heated that they get into fights. Avoid these people as much as possible.

It is always a good idea in these situations to note the location of the emergency exits. And finally, designate a meeting place for after the concert or sporting event in case you become separated from your friends, and carry a cell phone with you at all times.

Clubs

Heading out for a night of dancing and socializing at a local club? These dark, crowded places are ideal for criminals, especially when patrons have had a few drinks. Here are valuable steps you should take to ensure that your night of fun is a safe one.

Before entering any nightclub, make sure that the main entrance is wide enough to allow for easy exit in case of an emergency. Locate emergency exits once you're inside the building.

It is very easy to become separated from friends in a crowded nightclub. Carry your cell phone and designate a place to meet at the end of the night in case you lose your friends. Bring as few valuables with you to the club as possible, carrying only enough money to get you through the night. Leave your credit cards at home.

Although dancing and talking with strangers can be fun, you must always be on your guard. Don't leave the club alone with someone you've just met. And never leave your drink unattended or accept a drink from a stranger. If you do, you run the risk of being drugged and assaulted.

CHAPTER 12

SECURITY WHILE SHOPPING

Shopping can be a social time with friends and family, but if you're caught unawares, it can bring forth a wealth of opportunities for thieves, rapists, child abductors, and so on, from the time you park to the minute you return to the car with your packages. Paying special attention to things like how you dress and what time you shop can make all the difference.

PARKING PERILS

Many parking lots are large, have inadequate lighting, and lack reliable security. They are opportune places to commit a crime. Whether they are outdoor areas remote from main buildings or multilevel garages connected to an indoor mall or department store, such areas contain hidden spots that provide hiding places for criminals. You can easily be accosted in a wide-open space where there are few people and help is far away, or in the more confined isolated space of a multilevel garage. Customers who are confused about their car's location, carrying packages, or concentrating on the search for their car keys are perfect crime victims.

Safe-Parking Rules

Choose your parking place with care. In a downtown area, for example, try to use an attended parking garage, but remember to remove any personal-identification items from the car and to leave only your ignition key with the attendant. If you're parking in an outdoor shopping center lot, select a spot in the interior. Many parking-lot crimes occur on the lot perimeter because this usually presents a better escape route for the thief. Choose a space near a mall entrance or elevator if you park in a multilevel garage. If your shopping excursion will extend through sundown, park near a source of light. Avoid parking near extensive shrubbery, as it provides a perfect cover for a criminal. Do not park next to an occupied car or near suspicious individuals. (*See also* chapter 10 for more on car safety.)

Many parking-lot crimes occur on the lot perimeter because this usually presents a better escape route for the thief.

Never show cash or valuables in a lot (or, for that matter, at any time while shopping), and never leave valuables visible inside your car. Never leave a child or animal inside your car, no matter how quickly you expect to return. Stay alert as you walk through the parking lot, and walk confidently.

When reentering the parking area, carry only a reasonable number of packages. Have your car keys ready. If you feel uncomfortable or see suspicious people, ask a security officer to accompany you to your vehicle. If you think you are being followed, move quickly to a populated area, and find a security or police officer. Report any crime or suspicious incident occurring in the lot. Before you reach your vehicle, look under the vehicle, check the backseat before getting in, and lock your doors immediately on entry.

Be wary of strangers who approach you in a lot, and never accept their help should your vehicle fail to start. If anyone tells you before you enter your vehicle that there is something wrong with your car, find a security officer or call the police immediately.

Proper Parking Procedure Checklist

- ☐ Don't park on the perimeter of an outside lot.
- ☐ In a garage, park near the elevators or mall entrance.
- ☐ If you plan to shop through sundown, park near a source of light.
- ☐ Be wary of strangers who approach you in a lot.
- ☐ Remember where you parked your car and walk confidently and quickly to it.
- ☐ Have your keys ready before you leave the store.
- ☐ Never accept any help from a stranger if your vehicle fails to start.
- ☐ Carry only a reasonable number of packages.
- ☐ Do not leave any valuables visible in your car.
- ☐ Lock all car doors.
- ☐ Check in the backseat and under your car when you return.

Follow the locking and checking procedures mentioned in chapter 10 when you park your car and when you return. If all shoppers took the split second required to lock all doors when exiting and entering cars, a great deal of crime could be avoided.

PROTECTING YOUR PURCHASES

If your shopping trip takes you to more than one store and you must carry your parcels home yourself, store them in the trunk, not on the backseat. Remember, though, that while the trunk of your car is considerably more secure than the passenger section, it is by no means impregnable. Therefore, arrange your shopping itinerary so that you acquire the most expensive items last.

Keep a close eye on your packages if you stop along the way, but don't think that it is only your property that is at risk while you are shopping or visiting a coffee shop or restaurant. You should also be concerned about your personal safety. Make sure that upon leaving a restaurant or store, you keep your guard up. Relaxation and friendly conversation are fine while dining, but continued vigilance is prudent.

MALL SAFETY

Even with the growing popularity of online shopping, many people still prefer to shop at malls and shopping centers. Attractive as they are, however, malls can be dangerous. The shoppers' state of unawareness, the wide variety of potential victims, and the larger-than-usual amount of cash carried by shoppers attract criminals to shopping malls. Follow these guidelines below to stay safe.

Always pay attention to what and who is around you. While some crimes at malls—auto theft, petty theft, and abduction—occur in parking areas, you need to be aware of swindlers and pickpockets in stores and hallways. If you are daydreaming, distracted, or intensely focused on store windows, you are a prime target for criminals. In addition, before entering a store, check to see who's inside. Don't go in if you see a group of suspicious people together, people unknown to you are staring at you, or if cash registers are left unstaffed. Trust your instincts. If you feel uncomfortable, leave the area immediately.

Always keep an eye on your purse or bag. Straps are easily cut, and you may not feel your purse being stolen. Keep your bag or purse tucked under your arm. When paying for a purchase, do not place your purse or wallet on the counter where thieves—aware that you're distracted—can grab them. Try not to place purchases or bags on the floor of store dressing rooms, especially near a door, where they may be easily snatched. Don't leave your purse or bags in your dressing room, even for a moment—a moment is all a thief needs.

Carry as little cash as possible. And, of course, don't let anyone see how much money you have. Use credit cards and checks, as these may be canceled if stolen. Never place your wallet where it is visible or easily accessible in your purse or pockets. If anyone brushes against you, check for your purse and wallet immediately. Try to see who bumped you. Pickpockets usually pass a wallet to an accomplice.

Always check your purchases before leaving a store. Oftentimes an item you paid for doesn't make it into your bag. Beware, too, of a "deal" too good to be true. Criminals posing as store employees may offer you a break on a stereo or DVD player. When you get home, you may find that your fantastic purchase is a piece of wood in a box.

Avoid groups of teens at malls. They sometimes menace shoppers or are disruptive. Report immediately to a guard or police officer any teen causing trouble or engaging in illegal activities. Do not allow your youngsters to spend excessive time "hanging out." They may be influenced by the negative environment.

Be careful in the restrooms. Restroom crime commonly involves women's purses. A thief will wait until a purse is on the floor inside a stall, then reach under, snatch the purse and flee. Loop your purse over your arm or place it on a shelf, if the stall has one. Do not hang it on the clothes hook mounted on the stall door. Brazen thieves reach over and lift coats and pocketbooks off the hooks. When washing your hands, do not select the sink nearest the door. A thief can snatch your bag and be out the door before you can react.

Keep a close eye on your children. Child abduction is a huge concern at malls. Crowds of people provide cover for the kidnapper, who can target and accost a child who has strayed from parents. Know where

Laundromats

You should never go alone to a self-service Laundromat at night. A Laundromat may be dangerous after dark because typically there are few people using it, and there likely is only one way in and out. Criminals know that whoever goes into a Laundromat will have some cash with them and will be attentive to what they are doing instead of to their environment.

your children are at all times. Child molesters wait in public or family restrooms for children who enter alone. Instruct your children to go to a security officer or a store clerk to ask for help if they become separated from you. (*See also* chapter 16 for more about child abduction.)

NIGHTTIME SHOPPING

All elements of concern during daytime shopping are also present at night; darkness is the ally of the thief, because visibility is impaired at night, so you must be even more alert.

If you are on foot, you will be less able to discern someone approaching. An intruder crouched in the back of your car will be more difficult to spot, and a thief who grabs your belongings will find it easier to disappear under the cover of darkness. Moreover, the composition of nighttime crowds is different—more muggers, pickpockets, and robbers are cruising the streets. Most retail establishments have fewer personnel on the job at night, so you will be less protected in the places where you shop. At night there also tend to be more intoxicated shoppers, who are subject to irrational behavior. If a person's sobriety is in question, leave the area.

HAZARDS OF CREDIT CARDS

Credit and debit cards are popular—and so is credit card fraud.

There are two ways a credit card thief can rip you off—by stealing your individual cards or buying stolen card numbers in bulk from other criminals to use for his gain.

Merchants and/or their employees may abet the frauds. Their contribution is primarily apathy and carelessness rather than duplicity. Ask

The Supermarket

Supermarkets are often crime locations where thieves can easily steal purses or remove wallets from inside purses. Never set your purse on a shopping cart. Keep it on your arm.

If you lose a purse or wallet in a supermarket, report it at once and demand that store personnel help you try to find it. A robber will often remove the cash and credit cards and then discard the wallet, so it is worth looking for.

If your purse is nabbed and it contains identification and the keys to your home, change the locks on your home and car.

yourself this question: When was the last time your card's signature was compared with that on the receipt you just signed? Merchants also often fail to check the list of canceled credit cards or bank retrieval notices.

In other cases, merchants may be cheats. They may print extra charges using your card or violate authorization limits. Still other merchants are outright crooks. They will buy stolen cards or borrow or steal lists of valid credit card numbers and run the credit card numbers through as legitimate transactions.

Make sure that the clerk servicing you processes only your charges. It isn't uncommon for a salesclerk to validate two or more charge tickets, then trace your signature from one of the receipts, filling in additional items later. This is a particular hazard in a service station, where an attendant takes your card inside to complete the paperwork. Always try to stay with your card to avoid the effort of having to prove forgery later.

Avoid revealing personal information such as your address and telephone number on credit card receipts. If you are using your credit card as identification for cashing a check, make sure the clerk does not write your credit card number on the check.

Develop the habit of checking the name on your card each time it is returned to you. If you are victimized by a switch and discover it immediately, talk to the manager, not the salesperson or waiter involved. The clerk or waiter could simply claim an error and quickly retrieve your card.

Con artists may try to steal from you by representing themselves as "security officers" checking into illegal use of credit cards over the phone. They will ask you for your credit card number in order to "verify" it. Do not give your credit card number over the phone unless you initiate a purchase and are confident to whom you are talking and doing business with. Needless to say, if anyone calls and asks for your credit card number, hang up. Even a representative from your issuing bank or credit card company will not request this information. Call the issuing bank and credit card company immediately.

So what should you do to protect yourself from credit card fraud?

- Examine all receipts before you sign them. This way, you can prevent errors or fraud before they become fact.
- Personally destroy all carbons of your receipts if you run across a merchant still using the old carbon devices. Do not allow the clerk to do this for you.
- Retain your receipts and compare them to charges on your statement to protect yourself from fraudulent charges.
- Don't leave your credit cards lying around your home, office, or especially your car.
- Destroy unneeded duplicate cards.
- Shred all credit card statements before throwing them away.

Protecting Your Cards

Some banks offer to imprint your picture and signature on your credit card. Provided the vendor checks, a picture and signature offer extra protection against the use of the card by an unauthorized person. The best recourse, though, is to leave your credit cards at home; take them with you only if you plan to use them.

Keep credit cards in one secure place. That way, if they are lost or stolen, you will know right away. To protect yourself, compile the following information for each credit card in your possession:

- Card name (American Express, Visa, MasterCard, and so on).
- Issuing organization (such as a bank or other financial institution).
- Your account number (and the security code on the front or back of the card).
- Telephone number for reporting lost or stolen cards. (The number may be displayed on the back of the card.)

If You Lose a Card

Report the loss as soon you realize it has occurred. Follow the instructions you receive from the credit card company. File a report with the police within 24 hours of the loss or theft. You will probably be issued a new card by your credit card company. (If you discover that you haven't lost your card at all but merely misplaced it, destroy the old one and begin using the new one.) You may be contacted by the security department of the issuer, particularly if a number of bogus charges are made to your card. Of course, you should cooperate.

Finally, when you get your bill, look for unfamiliar charges. Bring these to your credit card company's attention, but pay only the charges you legally owe. Federal law allows you to challenge charges for which you are not responsible, but you still must pay your just debts.

You can register your cards with a service that notifies issuers of your credit cards that they have been lost or stolen.

IDENTITY THEFT

Even your reports of a lost or stolen card to the issuing bank, the credit card company, and the police may not be enough to protect you from a rapidly increasing type of fraud known as identity theft. (See also chapter 18 to learn more about identity theft and cybercrimes.) This occurs when a criminal uses the personal information from your stolen credit cards and/or identification to impersonate you in order to open lines of credit under your name. To prevent this, call all three major credit agencies and ask them to add a fraud statement to your file immediately. This will prevent anyone from using your lost or stolen card to open a new line of credit. Continue the requests every four months and you will receive three free credit reports per year. You should keep checking your credit reports regularly for any fraudulent activity. Here's how to contact the three major credit agencies:

- Experian Consumer Assistance: (888) 397-3742 or www.experian.com
- TransUnion: (800) 888-4213 or www.transunion.com
- Equifax: (800) 685-1111 or www.equifax.com

Secrets of the Identity Thief

As many as 10 million people a year in the United States were victims of identity theft last year, and this number is expected to increase. While the two largest groups of victims are young adults, especially college kids who share computers in libraries and dorm rooms, and small-business owners, who tend to make sizeable financial transactions over the Internet, everyone is a potential target. In fact, it is estimated that 1 in 20 Americans are at risk of becoming a victim. Here are some tricks identity thieves don't want you to know:

- Your Facebook page offers a wealth of information. Thieves comb profiles to find out which charities you support or which organizations you're involved in. This way they can call you and ask for a donation to be charged to your credit card.

- The red flag on your mailbox that tells the postal worker there's outgoing mail is a red flag for identity thieves as well. It means there's probably credit card numbers or a check in there.

- Holding out your card when paying at a register is a great way for thieves to get hold of your number. They simply pretend they are checking messages on their phone and snap a picture of your card.

- Thieves can do a lot of damage to your credit card account in a 30-day period; they hope you don't check your bank account on a weekly basis.

- Thieves can duplicate the data on the magnetic strip of your credit card using a $50 device.

- Trash left out overnight is a virtual goldmine of information. It's filled with preapproved credit card applications, old bills, checking deposit slips, and expired credit cards.

- Skimmers can easily be attached to ATMs to capture credit card and PIN information. The most likely machines to be invaded are kiosks.

- A simple call to 888-5-OPTOUT will stop preapproved credit card offers from being sent to you, making you less valuable to the identity thief.

- Thieves can call the electric company posing as you and coax them into giving out your Visa or Mastercard number by pretending you were confused if you paid your bill the previous month.

You can register your cards with a service that helps you if your cards are stolen. You simply call the service's 24-hour toll-free number, and the service immediately notifies all issuers of your credit cards of the loss. All liability is ended as soon as you report the loss. Related services are also available, including emergency cash and prepaid airline tickets for a stranded traveler, as well as requests for replacements of stolen cards. There is no limit on the number of cards covered by these services, so the more cards you carry, the more advantageous the service is to you.

ATM MACHINES

Twenty-four-hour automatic teller machines (ATMs) can be extremely hazardous. Some thieves force customers at gunpoint to withdraw money or steal their money after withdrawal; others watch as you enter your Personal Identification Number (PIN), then steal your card and take the money out themselves. Still others rig fake ATMs that copy customers' PINs. The thieves then make counterfeit cards using these secret codes.

ATM Safety Features

Not all ATMs are created equally. Here's what you should look for:

- Untinted glass doors so passersby can see inside and call for assistance in the event of an attack
- Entry limited to ATM cardholders, with a door that locks behind you
- A well-lit vestibule
- A well-lit parking area outside of the ATM
- Surveillance cameras
- A screen and data-entry pad that only you can see, so that others can't learn your PIN
- Mirrors at the machine that allow you to see who's behind you
- Telephones with an operator, not a recording, who will answer when you pick up the receiver or push a "panic button" to summon assistance
- A security officer

Safe ATM Protocol

ATMs are certainly convenient, but making these transactions on your own can put you at risk. Here are a few tips to maintain safety at the machine.

- Bring a friend along to watch your back while you are at the machine. You are most vulnerable when you're alone. Nearly all attacks—over 95 percent—involve a single victim.
- Use a familiar machine.
- Avoid ATMs on the street. If possible, choose an indoor machine with a vestibule door that locks behind you.
- Never let a stranger in.
- Steer clear of facilities with panhandlers operating as ATM doormen. Even if they're harmless, they might let in somebody behind you who is not.
- Stay away from ATMs near accessible hiding places or bushes.
- Don't use the same ATM at the same time every day. Criminals are on the lookout for routines.
- If you feel you are being menaced while operating an ATM, protect yourself by entering an incorrect number three times in succession. If you do this, many machines will not only lock you out but also keep your card; that might avert a robbery.
- Do your banking during daylight hours.
- Never lend your card to anyone or use it to help someone else with a transaction.
- Do not accept assistance from anyone when using your card.
- Never disclose your PIN.
- Be wary of con artists who try to persuade you to hand over your card. A thief may pose as a bank security officer attempting to repair a malfunctioning machine, then ask for your card and PIN to test the it.

Lost or Stolen ATM Cards

You should treat your bank card like cash. If it is lost or stolen, report that fact to the bank immediately. They will deactivate the card and issue you a new one. If someone has used your card, your loss is limited to $50 if it is reported within two days; beyond that, your loss limit is $500. Check your monthly statement for unauthorized usage. If you fail to report an unauthorized use of your card within 60 days, you can be held accountable for an unlimited amount. Send a letter noting the unauthorized charges to your bank via certified mail.

Drive-Up ATMs

When using drive-up teller machines, lock all doors and keep all windows rolled up, except the driver's. Keep your engine running and remain observant. As with walk-up machines, don't use those in isolated and poorly lit locations.

Nighttime ATM Safety

If you must go to the bank at night and cannot arrange for someone to accompany you, be cautious.

- Park as close as possible to the cash machine.
- Do not leave your keys in the car with the engine running, and lock all your doors.
- Look around for suspicious people loitering outside the bank or waiting in a nearby car.
- Check for loiterers inside the banking area as well.
- Have your card ready so that you don't have to fumble for it.
- Don't waste time. Complete your transaction, and leave as quickly as possible.
- Put your money, your bank card, and your receipt into your pocket, wallet, or handbag quickly; take the time to arrange everything later.
- Make sure no one is following you; if someone is, go directly to a police station or any public place to ask for assistance. (Many banks have now installed red panic buttons that can be used to summon emergency assistance.)

Protecting Your PIN

Plenty of criminals would love to learn the PIN number to your ATM card so they can access your account. You must take precautionary steps to protect this number.

- Make sure no one is standing near you when you enter your PIN number at the ATM.
- Cover your hand as you enter the PIN number so that even a hidden camera cannot see it; same with a telephone calling card PIN.

- If the ATM doesn't appear to be working, immediately remove your card and go elsewhere.
- Don't accept help from someone—scammers frequently pass themselves off as Good Samaritans. Conversely, don't offer to assist someone who appears to have a problem accessing an ATM.
- Change your PIN on a minimum annual basis.

Bank employees will never request your PIN. A thief who has stolen your purse or wallet may call you and impersonate a police officer or bank employee. The caller will claim to have caught your purse snatcher and request your PIN to determine if any cash has been withdrawn from your bank account. Don't fall for this scam. Report suspicious events to the bank security office or to the police.

In selecting an identification number, do not use a sequence of numbers from your phone number, date of birth, Social Security number, street address, or any other numbers found among identification papers you carry.

In selecting an identification number, do not use a sequence of numbers from your phone number, date of birth, Social Security number, street address, or any other numbers found among identification papers you carry. If you carry several ATM-type cards, select different ID numbers for each. If someone guesses (or observes) one number, you may limit your losses to assets available through the use of that one compromised card. If you must record your PIN, store the record securely. Better still, memorize the number.

CHAPTER 13

SECURITY WHEN YOU TRAVEL

Travelers should practice heightened awareness on the road, because they are likely to be carrying more money than usual, feel jet-lagged and less self-confident, have fewer places to turn to for assistance, and are less able to find the help that is available. And because of dress or speech, a traveler may be easily identifiable as being out of their element.

In other words, travelers are often easy "marks," and everybody knows it—unless, of course, the traveler takes the trouble to dress to blend into the surroundings, behave in a manner that doesn't attract attention, avoid overindulgence in drink, and partake in safe and secure activities.

GETTING THERE BY AIR

Traveling by plane has become more complicated due to incomprehensible fares, extra luggage fees, and stricter security measures. You don't have control over those issues—but you do have control over your personal security both to and from the airport and at the airport itself.

At the Airport

If you're traveling by air, have a friend or relative drive you to the airport. If this isn't possible, take a taxi or an airport limousine service. If you drive yourself instead, decide where to park based on what time you'll be returning. For example, if you're arriving late at night, park under a light and avoid isolated areas, or park in an off-airport secured parking facility that provides a shuttle to and from the airport.

Leave yourself plenty of time before departure, and take as little luggage as possible to avoid lost, stolen, or damaged property.

Security checkpoint procedures require you to place carry-on bags, laptops, coats, and shoes on a conveyer belt for X-ray screening while you walk through a metal detector. Keep a watchful eye on your property, particularly valuables such as computers and handbags, as it awaits screening and then passes through to the other side of security. Another traveler—on purpose or by mistake—can easily grab your possessions in the rush and confusion at the security checkpoint.

Safeguarding Your Luggage

Few things are worse than losing your luggage when you travel. Whether it's by accident or due to a thief, there are ways to avoid it if you follow these guidelines.

- Don't pack your luggage too full. An overpacked bag may pop open if dropped. Dishonest baggage handlers may drop bags deliberately and rifle through them.
- Pack cash, jewelry, and other expensive items in your carry-on.
- Avoid expensive luggage.
- Label your bags with your name and address. However, instead of your home address, use a work address or the place you'll be staying so thieves won't learn the location of your empty home.
- Make your luggage distinctive so that you don't get it mixed up with another traveler's.
- Proceed directly to the baggage-claim location as soon as you deplane. It is far too easy for someone to walk off with your bags, especially if they cycle several times on the luggage conveyor belt, appearing unguarded.

- Report lost or stolen luggage and fill out a certificate of loss immediately. Liability limits for lost or damaged luggage are fairly restrictive, so see if your homeowner's insurance policy covers valuables lost or stolen during your trip.

If you have several packages or pieces of luggage and a long layover in an air terminal, use a coin-operated locker (if available), preferably near your departure gate, to store your belongings. When storing or retrieving your packages, be extremely careful about accepting offers of assistance from anyone other than air-carrier station personnel or skycaps.

Taxis and Drivers

Try to establish taxi fares from the airport to your destination (and vice versa) in advance. Unscrupulous drivers will often overcharge an unwitting visitor. Before you enter a cab, ask the dispatcher or driver how much the ride will cost. If you don't settle on a fare but instead pay per mile or by time and feel you are being taken to your destination in a roundabout way, let the driver know immediately and tell him you won't pay for the extra traveling. If you've settled on a fare up front but the final fare is more than originally stated, sparking an argument, note the cab number, driver's name, and time. Do not give a tip. Ask for a receipt, and report the incident to the company and/or taxi commission and the police.

Be sure the cab you are using has a legitimate medallion and that the driver identification is clearly visible.

Beware of drivers standing in or near the terminal—but not in the official taxi line—offering "taxi rides." These drivers will often take you to their Town Car for an expensive ride. Besides overcharging, the potential for assault or robbery by the driver always remains a possibility. Unless dealing with a reputable car service, always seek out official taxi lines or even less costly shuttle services arranged at a service desk in the terminal.

If you have luggage with you, be certain the driver puts all your baggage into the trunk and takes all your belongings out when you are dropped off. The driver may leave your suitcase behind for an accomplice to grab.

Be sure the cab you are using has a legitimate medallion and that the driver identification is clearly visible. Do not ride in unlicensed cabs. They are dangerous and illegal and are not covered by insurance in the event of an accident.

If the driver is operating the vehicle recklessly, tell him so and threaten to file a report. Never sit in the front seat next to the driver if you are alone. Do not respond to personal questions or offer information about yourself, and never accept any food or candy a driver offers you. If you don't want the driver to know where you live or work, have him drop you off a block away from your destination.

If you are traveling by train, keep your luggage close. Before selecting a seat, quickly survey the passengers already seated. Do not select a seat beside or close to someone acting erratically, or someone whose sobriety is in question.

WHEN YOU'RE THE STRANGER IN TOWN

You are considerably more likely to encounter crimes against your person, especially assault and robbery, when you're away from home. You need to know how to protect yourself while on the road.

Hotels or Motels

When choosing a hotel or motel, be aware that a lower price may attract an undesirable element and that surrounding areas may be dangerous.

Review the selected hotel or motel website prior to arrival. Make sure it is not a hangout and that people are not loitering in the parking lot. Try to avoid motels that have outside entrances to rooms from the parking lot. A criminal can wait in a car and attack you as you are about to enter your room. Use hotels that have indoor entrances in which access is strictly limited to guests and hotel employees. Hotel employees and/or security officers should be visible throughout the facility. Some travel experts recommend smaller hotels because strangers can be more readily detected.

Request a room near places of activity, such as the front desk, hotel offices, or room-service stations. Rooms near the elevator are much safer than those at the end of the corridor. Any extra noise is well worth the added security. The room you stay in should be equipped with a peep-hole on the door and double-bolt locks. Electronic card locks provide enhanced security.

Ideally, you should select a hotel room on the fourth through seventh floors. Aerial ladders used by fire departments rarely reach heights higher than the seventh floor.

Most important, consider the construction of the building. Fire escapes should let you out but no one else in, and doors and windows should be secure against undesired entry. Ideally, you should select a hotel room on the fourth through seventh floors. In the event of fire, your only means of escape could be out the window of your room. The aerial ladders used by fire departments rarely reach heights higher than the seventh floor of a new hotel. In older structures with high ceilings, the fifth or sixth floor might be safer.

Security inside Your Hotel Room

You might think the best way to avoid being victimized in an unfamiliar city is to retreat to the safety and security of your hotel room. However, thousands of travelers are victims of crimes that take place inside their hotels.

When you check into a hotel or motel, make sure the desk clerk does not loudly announce your room number. If this happens, request another room and tell the clerk to write down the number and show it to you. Check in using your last name and only your first initial, and tell the clerk not to disclose your name to anyone. Request that you be notified if someone asks about you.

Use all locking devices when you are in the room. Your key or electronic key card isn't the only one that will open your door. Most hotel rooms provide some backup device, such as a door chain or a deadbolt operated by a thumb turn, the additional turn of a key, or a button that, when pushed, prevents all keys from opening the door. Never leave your door open, even if you're just running out for ice or a soft drink.

Improvise protective measures of your own. A chair wedged under a doorknob can be an effective additional "lock," as can a furniture barricade. Inserting a simple rubber wedge in the crack under the door will prevent the door from being opened. You can bring along a doorstop that emits an alarm when the door is opened or an alarm that you can hang from the doorknob that sounds if the knob is turned. You can opt for an inexpensive beeper-size motion alarm for detecting intruders. You might even want to consider carrying your own portable travel lock; when this lock is attached to the room entry door, it is very difficult to open the door without breaking it down.

Lock all windows and doors to balconies accessible from the outside. Often these are left unlocked. It is easy for someone from an adjacent room or from a rooftop below to gain access to your room. Many hotels post signs requesting that you lock balcony doors.

Don't open your room door unless you determine the identity of the caller. Call the front desk if you are in doubt about room service, a bellhop, a housekeeper, or other hotel personnel.

If you are a woman traveling alone, request that a bellhop escort you to your room to check for intruders before you enter. Don't be embarrassed to request this service when returning to your room by yourself, especially at night. Use only the main entrance to the hotel.

Be on the lookout for suspicious people loitering in the hallway. Needless to say, never invite strangers to your room, even for business purposes. Always have your key or access card in hand before you get to your room. Once inside, look out the peephole before exiting your room.

Do not leave keys, money, or valuables in your room. Use the safe in your room or the hotel safe. The amount the hotel is responsible for varies and can be quite low. The best policy is to leave your valuables in a secure spot at home. If you do leave your valuables in the hotel safe, seal them in a manila envelope as if they were business documents, and be sure to get a detailed receipt for them. You may also purchase portable "safes" that look just like cans of shaving cream or other toiletries and are indistinguishable from them.

Or you can make your own book safe by cutting out a square in the inside pages of a thick paperback or hardcover. Put valuables inside and place the book among others in your room. When you put your belongings in drawers or closets, arrange them so that you will notice if something is missing.

Park only in well-lit areas, or try to frequent hotels with valet parking services (but give the attendant your ignition key only). Never leave anything behind in the trunk, even if you are staying for only one night.

Make sure the credit card imprint is destroyed. Even if you pay in cash upon checking out, the clerk may have made an imprint of your credit card when you checked in. Employees have been known to put the bill on your credit card and keep the cash. Always keep your hotel card key upon checkout from the hotel. Some card keys imprint your credit card information on the magnetic strip on the backside of the card key. Destroy the card key upon your return home by cutting it into several pieces or, better yet, by shredding it.

Hotel Fires

The risk of fire in a hotel—large or small—is significant. Review carefully all fire instructions provided by the hotel. These are usually posted on your room door; if not, request a set of instructions from the front desk. Determine whether the fire signal is a bell or other audible signal, and ascertain what to do if the alarm is activated.

> Count the number of doors between your room and the emergency exit. If smoke engulfs your floor, you should still be able to locate the fire exit—by counting doors.

Before retiring for the night, step into the corridor outside your room and locate the nearest fire exit. It will usually be easy to find, because it will probably be illuminated and bear the word EXIT. Next, count the number of doors between your room and the emergency exit. If smoke engulfs your floor, you should still be able to locate the fire exit—by counting doors—even if your vision is completely obscured.

In the event of fire, try to leave as soon as you see or smell smoke. But first be sure to take your room key or card in the event that you have to retreat to your room and carefully touch your room door. Only if it is not hot should you slowly open it, just a little and, while holding your breath, examine the passageway. If all appears in order, return to your room, get your key and a wet towel, and fill your lungs with air. Head toward the emergency exit, either upright or on all fours, depending on air quality. The wet towel could literally be a lifesaver. Use it to wipe your face and eyes, to cool and filter the air you breathe, and to cool and protect exposed skin surfaces. If you encounter smoke outside your room, drop to your knees, since the air near the floor is less likely to be filled with volatile, toxic substances. Do not use the elevator; elevator shafts usually fill with smoke during a fire. Proceed to the nearest fire exit and determine the location of the fire. If it is above you, go down the stairs; if it is below, go up the stairs to the roof.

Always travel with a small roll of duct tape. It can be used to attach wet towels to air vents, seal doors from smoke, or spell HELP on a window.

You may not be able to escape a fire that has spread to a number of floors. You may be forced to return to your room to wait out the fire. In this event, close the door. It offers protection against the spread of the fire into your room. Fill the tub with water—immersing yourself may save you from serious burns. Put dampened towels around the door to help prevent the spread of noxious gases into the room. Try to maintain an attitude of optimism. Most occupants survive hotel fires. Above all, do not panic. Your chances of surviving are greater if you maintain your composure.

Always travel with a small roll of duct tape. The tape can be used to attach wet towels to air vents, seal doors from smoke entering around the frame, or spell HELP on a window to alert the fire department. (Duct tape is also handy to make emergency luggage repairs.)

CAR TRIPS

If you are traveling by car, you could run into a few safety issues, especially if your car has a large decal on it exclaiming that it's a rental. The

Souvenir Shopping

Shopping is almost invariably a part of any trip. When it comes time to pay, keep in mind that you probably won't be able to pay by check. However, traveler's checks are almost always a suitable substitute for cash, and stores worldwide generally accept credit cards. Carry your purse or briefcase and your most valuable purchases closest to your body for added protection.

following are some additional concerns for which you should take note.

- Consult a service such as the American Automobile Association (AAA) or a travel agency for advice about speed traps or other hazards, motel recommendations, and so forth.
- Take time to learn the local traffic rules and regulations.
- Confirm that your car insurance is adequate for your trip.
- Shield your license plate from prying eyes by parking between two cars. (Your out-of-state or rental-car license plate distinguishes you as a "mark.") Be especially careful if you are driving a car with vanity plates or a decal identifying the vehicle as a rental. This only advertises your vulnerability.
- Take all your bags and packages into your room with you if you are stopping for the night.

CAMPING OR WILDERNESS VACATIONS

If you are taking a trip using a camper or motor home, be sure all the doors and windows are locked while you're on the road. Just as you don't want to stop for hitchhikers, you also don't want to harbor a stowaway.

Maybe your vacation is going to involve a return to nature. Fine, but be careful: A bear rummaging through your food isn't the only hazard you might encounter. Another threat to your safety and security could be your fellow camper. Every year, reports surface of rapes, assaults, robberies, and other crimes in isolated camping areas. You can best protect yourself by checking in with ranger stations or park police and by camping at sites they suggest. At least let them know where you plan to be. Take the time to find out how to reach help on foot in the unlikely event that you might need to. Introduce yourself to friendly family campers nearby; you may need their assistance. Before the trip, activate your cell phone GPS.

If you are threatened and your car is nearby, get to it and honk your horn. It will carry a long distance in still mountain air. You can also carry an air horn.

RESORT AREAS

Your taste in vacation spots may run more to the bright lights and constant activity of a resort than the isolation of a campsite. At resorts, marauding bears may be a rarity on the beach, but human wolves and jackals are not. Pimps, hustlers, robbers, con artists, addicts, shakedown artists, pickpockets, and all types of hoodlums haunt these areas. Always ask yourself why any stranger is going out of his way to be friendly and accommodating. If you can't come up with a non-threatening answer, beware.

If you are going to devote an evening to a round of nightclubbing or a day to shopping, take the suggestions of the hotel manager or desk clerk rather than those of a taxi driver or the local cocktail waitress in a bar. If at all possible, go with a crowd of your choosing. It is usually the lone, lost sheep that falls victim to the wolf pack. Stay on the beaten path, especially at night. See the quaint out-of-the-way places during the day, when the light is better, preferably in the company of a reliable guide.

OVERSEAS TRAVEL

Increases in terrorism, violence, and crime dictate that you must be prepared for any contingency when you travel overseas. Careful preparation and common sense are your most important weapons.

Consular information sheets and travel warnings published by the U.S. Department of State contain useful information for travelers. For instance, they include names of countries dangerous for Americans, the location of the U.S. embassy or consulate in the subject country, and information on crime, security, drug penalties, minor political disturbances, passports, currency, medicines, and what to do if you get into trouble in a foreign country.

You can get this information from the Bureau of Consular Affairs, either by visiting http://travel.state.gov or by calling Overseas Citizens

Services at 1-888-407-4747. For the State Department's general tips for traveling abroad, go to http://travel.state.gov/travel/tips/safety/safety_1747.html.

A travel agency or airline can provide additional information, but it may not be precise or up to date. Along with avoiding known trouble spots, get familiar with any problems in a particular region. Try to determine the frequency of terrorist acts against U.S. installations or businesses in the country you plan to visit, whether American travelers have been attacked or threatened, and whether an active propaganda campaign exists in the underground press by contacting the country state department desk or the security representative at the respective embassy or counsel. Talk to travelers who have recently returned from the area, and ask about demonstrations, strikes, and threats.

Bring along a copy of your birth certificate and make at least one color copy of the inside front cover of the passport with photo and personal information. Keep it separate from your passport during travel.

After registration at the hotel, safeguard your passport and other valuables in the safe in your hotel room. Do not carry your passport during your tours and individual sightseeing unless advised to the contrary by your tour guide or the concierge at the hotel. In lieu of the passport, carry the passport copy made before departure and one piece of identification (driver's license).

If you are a Canadian citizen or a citizen of the United Kingdom, take the same precautions as applicable for Canadian or U.K. overseas travel.

Language Barriers

Don't assume that wherever you travel, someone will be able to communicate with you in your own language. Learn at least enough of the local language to be able to ask for assistance, report a crime, and find out if your language is spoken. Besides a portable dual-language dictionary, take along a country guidebook, as you may need to show a destination to a non-English-speaking police officer or taxi driver. You may also want to bring a picture book of everyday items to further help with communication. Also helpful will be copies of pertinent information from reliable websites concerning your hotels, selected restaurants, local medical facilities, and the respective U.S. embassy or consulate.

If you need help with the language, be sure you get it from a trustworthy individual referred by a local state department representative. Some of the people you encounter, though quite fluent in your language, will act as if they have no idea what you are saying. They may be pretending in order to lull you into falsely believing that when you speak English, you won't be understood. If you are bargaining with a foreign shopkeeper and at the same time discussing prices in English with a companion, you may be undermining your bargaining position. You almost certainly will end up paying more than you should.

Cars and Driving Regulations

Driving regulations and traffic laws in other countries often differ substantially from those in the United States. Find out as much as possible about local traffic rules and regulations, and call AAA to get an international driver's license. Then check with your insurance company to see if you are covered in a foreign country and make sure you have all the correct papers. Border-crossing guards can be particularly helpful with this kind of information.

Request an inconspicuous rental car, and do not display any identifying information such as corporate names or distinctive license plates.

Money

Whenever you travel, and especially when going overseas, you may need to carry more cash than you feel comfortable with. Be sure to use traveler's checks or credit cards, and don't keep all your money in one place. It's a good idea to keep your money and important papers in at least a couple of safe places so that if one stash is wiped out, you are not completely helpless. When you have to carry cash on your person, wear a money belt under your clothes to thwart a pickpocket. You can also use a large safety pin to secure money inside your clothing or pockets. Also, a nylon wallet with a Velcro closure is more secure and less attractive to thieves than leather. Be aware that pickpockets can slice your purse, purse strap, or pocket with a knife and remove its contents. Wear purse straps under a coat or jacket, always keep bags and fanny packs in front of you, and wear a sweater or shirt over your purse or fanny pack. Remove extra credit cards and business cards from your purse before departing on your trip. Make a copy of all credit cards and identification and personal papers, and keep this info at your residence. You might also carry a handheld shrill alarm to sound in case of robbery or in an emergency.

Be familiar with the exchange rates and the appearance of all foreign money you are likely to handle. Also, don't exchange your money for local currency on the street or at your hotel. Go to a bank instead.

The Business Traveler

Business travelers, especially executives, must practice all the general tips for the typical overseas traveler; in addition, they must take special precautions because businesspeople are particular targets for criminals and terrorists (see chapter 29), especially if the traveler is a high-profile person.

Here's the best way to handle yourself:

- Maintain a low profile. Do not broadcast your travel plans and itinerary. Provide information about your schedule only on a need-to-know basis.
- Consider traveling under an assumed or modified name and make reservations in several hotels when visiting a hostile country.
- Avoid repetitious patterns, and vary the days and hours of travel and the routes you take.
- Minimize the time you spend in a foreign country.
- Prepare your itinerary carefully, and give it to a trusted colleague or to a member of your family. In case of an emergency, this information will be helpful in locating you, and it may even save your life.
- Avoid seedy establishments, including hotels and restaurants.

Choosing a Hotel Abroad

Your hotel can be a citadel when you're away from home, but it can also be a trap. Look for accommodations in the middle of your destination, where you can blend into your surroundings, particularly when you are in a foreign country. The size of the hotel is important, too—in general, bigger is better, certainly for anonymity.

Avoid Criminal Activity in a Foreign Country

Obviously, it is imperative to uphold the law wherever you are, but doing so is absolutely essential in foreign countries, where penalties for committing a crime can be extremely harsh. Drug laws overseas are particularly severe. Avoid drugs, addicts, and pushers at all costs. Keep in mind that you might not be able to recognize a law-enforcement officer when you see one. Uniforms vary widely from country to country, and even within a single community.

The best way to avoid potential legal problems is to be aware of the laws in the countries you visit that may prohibit behavior ordinarily considered acceptable in the United States.

- Do not leave valuable papers unattended in your hotel room; deposit them in the room or hotel safe or a safety deposit box.
- Avoid rooms on the first floor or those accessible from the outside.
- Try your best not to be paged.
- Avoid traveling alone, especially at nighttime, unless absolutely necessary; a group is preferred.
- Do not display your name, home address, or company logo on your luggage, although the company address is usually all right.
- Do not display large sums of money or expensive jewelry.
- Ensure that the hotel does not have the traveler's name or the company name on the hotel marquee.

Getting Help

Once you have settled in, register with the nearest American embassy or consulate. If there is no American representation, contact the embassy or consulate of the country designated to handle U.S. interests. In the event of an emergency, such as a sudden evacuation, riot, or terrorist threat (see chapter 29), these contacts could be vital; commonplace assistance includes replacement of a lost passport, contacting your home and family in case of illness, or resolution of minor communication problems.

Ordinarily, American government representatives will not make travel arrangements, replace airline tickets, lend funds to stranded travelers, or more significantly, intervene with local law-enforcement officials. You

Shopping Overseas

While overseas, avoid shops in airports and train stations because of high prices. Haggling is not only acceptable but is expected in certain regions. In most of the Caribbean and in parts of Europe, shoppers almost never pay the ticketed price. Be extremely careful in native marketplaces. What is professed to be genuine gold or silver, an antique, or an artifact is often not.

must abide by the laws of the host country, and if you get into trouble, you will be judged according to local law. Your U.S. representatives will be limited in power and influence, but they can arrange for representation by a local attorney, and they will notify your family of your plight.

Special Considerations in Third World Countries

Third World countries can be especially difficult for the traveler. There may be customs officials or local police who like to throw their weight around. The best advice is to be careful and use common sense. Be aware of the proud nationalism of most Third World officials, and assume that they are going to be more sensitive than many Americans would be in similar circumstances.

CHAPTER 14

MOVING TO ANOTHER COMMUNITY

Anyone who has moved to a new community can tell you that this complicated process requires careful planning. Do your homework: Crime statistics should be your top priority when choosing a new community and school for your children.

RESEARCHING A NEW AREA

Determine the incidence of crime, including the levels of violence and theft, in your prospective new neighborhood. Go to the library, or online at www.fbi.gov, and look up the *Uniform Crime Reports,* published annually by the FBI. This publication contains useful and interesting information on the levels of crime and the number of police officers for most cities and towns in the United States. For your city or town, look up how many homicides, rapes, aggravated assaults, robberies, burglaries, and auto thefts occurred during the previous year. Then compare the numbers with similar crimes in nearby cities of comparable size.

Do Your Homework

Before you rent or buy a house, walk or drive around your prospective new neighborhood, especially at night or on weekends, and look for signs of crime. Keep an eye out for gang members, drug addicts, prostitutes, panhandlers, and drunks. Beware of outdoor gambling, like three-card monte or other forms of street betting. Also, determine if there are bars, saloons, drug dens, "smoke shops," or similar crime hazards in your new neighborhood.

Try to determine whether people routinely use the streets during the day and night or if they are afraid to venture outside. Are the streets deserted and isolated? Ask the same questions about nearby parks. Next, check the lighting in the neighborhood. Is it adequate for the night-time? Is there sufficient lighting outside your proposed new home? Also, examine the exterior of your new house or apartment building to see if it is surrounded by untrimmed shrubbery or foliage, which provide excellent hiding places for criminals.

Make sure there is convenient and efficient mass transportation if you plan to use it. You do not want to walk a mile through deserted streets to the bus stop and then wait an hour for the bus, especially late at night or very early in the morning.

Schools

Check the level of safety in your youngsters' prospective new school, including statistics on the presence of weapons. (*See also* chapter 20 for more information on safety in schools.) Be certain also to check the incidence of racial and religious hate crimes on school property. Newspaper accounts and the annual report by the local police often provide this information. You might even contact the public-relations unit of the local police for information on these highly dangerous crimes. The school system representative can also furnish security and safety information.

Once you have chosen a community and a school, familiarize your children with the safest and shortest route to their new school if they walk. Review the bus or subway routes several times, until they are thoroughly knowledgeable and can avoid getting lost or ending up in a dangerous area. Tell them never to get off at an unfamiliar stop or to explore strange neighborhoods. Discuss with your family the security and safety measures needed to ensure maximum protection at school, such as reporting to parents or school officials the threats of bullying.

Medical Care

When you move to a new community, you need to quickly locate the nearest hospital in case of an emergency. You may also need to find new doctors and dentists for everyone in your family. You should do this right away rather than waiting until someone becomes ill or injured and needs immediate assistance. And don't forget about your pets! Once you've moved, locate the nearest animal hospital that offers emergency service. You should also find a local veterinarian for regular checkups. Be sure to have copies of all of your family's and pet's medical records and prescriptions to show the new doctors and veterinarians.

MOVING DAY

You need to plan your move ahead of time. A reliable moving company is of critical importance because of the chances of thievery when movers and packers roam around your house. Also, reliable companies are less likely to experience robberies from moving vans. Make sure your moving company is authorized by the appropriate state regulatory agency, usually in the public utilities commission. Make sure the same principal driver handles the move; sometimes drivers switch off and the property can be compromised. Also, confirm that the moving company has appropriate insurance. Remember to put all agreements with the moving company in writing.

Don't forget to notify your post office, banks, relatives, friends, business acquaintances, and credit card companies of your change in address. The United States Postal Service (USPS) accepts online changes of address at https://moversguide.usps.com/?referral=USPS.

Security experts recommend the following simple rules when moving.

- Never leave valuable items in plain view.
- Pack your computer, printer, CD player, DVD player, and other electronics in their original packaging, but mask identifying icons and words so that the boxes become nondescript. This way, no one will know you have expensive electronic equipment.

- Don't label your boxes with the contents after they're packed. Mark your boxes "Fragile" and add a code number; indicate in which room they belong so that bystanders will not be aware of their contents.
- Ask friends or family members to watch your possessions while you load or unload.
- If you live alone, ask a friend to stay with you when utilities are connected in your new home, so that no one is aware that you reside by yourself.
- Make certain your previous landlord (or anyone else) does not give out your new address unless you specifically authorize it in writing.
- On the day you move, have new locks installed in your new residence so that anyone with access to the old locks will be out of luck.
- Install a high-quality deadbolt on all your doors.
- Cover all windows immediately with curtains, shades, or blinds. If you haven't had a chance to order coverings, block your windows with blankets or sheets. They will prevent the unwanted from observing anything of value, eliminating an opportunity for crime.
- On moving day, carry in a backpack your purse, wallet, jewelry, checkbooks, cash, change, keys, important telephone numbers, and anything else that may aggravate you if lost, like special family photographs.
- Keep a change of clothes with you for emergencies, along with any medicines you may need.

SETTLING OVERSEAS

When moving overseas, you must first deal with your initial residence. If being relocated for work, discuss with your company the possibility of financial help in selling your home, although such opportunities are rapidly fading. Many companies are tightening their belts and are reluctant to participate in the high costs associated with selling a residence.

Even without your company's help, the best strategy may be to sell your residence. Renting out your house may be more trouble than it's worth. As an absentee landlord, you are much more likely to experience problems than one who is on the scene. Also, rental-management programs are expensive and may be unreliable. The worst thing you can do is leave the house empty. Word quickly spreads about an empty house, not only to neighbors but also to burglars, vandals, squatters, and/or arsonists.

Essential Community Information

As soon as possible, obtain the following information about your new community. These phone numbers may save your life or the life of a loved one. If you can't obtain these numbers before you move, make sure you record them as soon as you arrive at your destination. Photocopy this page and use the space to enter the proper telephone numbers. Post the information near a telephone in your new residence so it is easy to access.

Police Department _____

Fire Department _____

Poison Center _____

Suicide-Crisis Hotline _____

Emergency Medical Service or Ambulance _____

Rape Hotline _____

Arson Hotline _____

Child Abuse or Neglect Hotline _____

Elderly Abuse or Neglect Hotline _____

Spousal Abuse Crisis Center _____

Runaway House _____

Drug Abuse Referral _____

Alcoholics Anonymous _____

Alcohol and Drug Council _____

Toxic Waste Hotline _____

Physician _____

If you decide to rent anyway, make certain your lawn and shrubbery are neatly maintained and that all repairs are conducted immediately. Properties with a shabby appearance have a way of catching the attention of criminals. If feasible, you might consider retaining a professional lawn-mowing service, landscaping company, or gardener. Also, make certain your tenant or property manager has the phone numbers of reliable repair services before you move. Otherwise, you may be the victim of a repair ripoff while you are abroad and not in a position to protect your property. Be sure to check references involving the selected moving company.

PART THREE

FAMILY SECURITY

CHAPTER 15

FAMILY VIOLENCE

The family unit encompasses a wide constellation of relationships, many of which are linked by bloodlines. Understandably yet tragically, the around-the-clock opportunity for conflict and discord within families often causes that same blood to spill. According to the U.S. Department of Justice, about 15 percent of homicides are intrafamilial. The most frequent victims are spouses, followed by children murdered by their parents.

SPOUSAL ABUSE

Spousal abuse involves physical, emotional, and/or sexual abuse. The majority of the victims of spousal abuse are female, commonly referred to as "battered women."

Certain circumstances or certain jurisdictions may preclude an arrest, but spousal abuse is generally a criminal assault that can be diligently prosecuted—if it's reported to the police. However, spousal abuse, like child abuse, is an underreported crime.

Battering is not limited to any age bracket, race, religious background, or education and income level. Don't let the fear of being alone keep

Weekend Violence

Spouse battering tends to cluster more often on weekends and during vacations or holiday seasons. In addition to the emotional stress that holidays and vacations can provoke, spouses are together more frequently during these times (and on weekends), and alcohol is usually present. Most domestic violence occurs between 9:00 P.M. and midnight, partly for the same reasons.

you with a man who abuses you. Do not marry an abusive man no matter how much he promises to change. He almost certainly won't. You will become more isolated and dependent, and it will be much harder for you to escape.

60 to 80 percent of male batterers were exposed to abuse as children, either having been beaten themselves or having seen one of their parents constantly beaten.

Cycle of Violence

The cycle of violence, according to experts, begins with a buildup of tension and anxiety. Then violence erupts and continues either sporadically or steadily over a period of several months or years. As the violence escalates, the woman may seek help from friends or relatives or call the police. Although many men are enraged further by a police response, most will become contrite and beg forgiveness for their behavior.

During this phase, the batterer is kind, compassionate, attentive, loving, and totally cooperative. But soon the violent behavior returns. During this phase, the woman may decide to leave or seek out a new partner for support. Unfortunately, leaving or finding a new partner usually infuriates the angry and jealous batterer even more. It is during this highly volatile and dangerous phase that a woman is at highest risk of critical injury or even murder.

Characteristics of the Batterer

Men who attack and beat women tend to be insecure, frustrated, possessive, and extremely jealous. Unable to manage these feelings, abusers use
violence as a means to control the people in their lives. Abuse is rarely a
one-time occurrence. Unless the batterer gets help and learns to express
his feelings in an alternative way, he will continue to be violent.

Batterers come from all walks of life, and most are not mentally ill. It
has been estimated that 60 to 80 percent of male batterers were exposed
to abuse as children, either having been beaten themselves or having
seen one of their parents constantly beaten.

Several experts have identified risk factors for abuse; the occurrence
of 2 or more of these factors makes violence in the home twice as likely to
occur. Identifying with 7 or more increases one's risk by 40 times. Below
are some of the most common.

- The male is unemployed.
- If employed, the male has a blue-collar job.
- The male does not have a high school diploma.
- The male is between the ages of 18 and 30.
- The male has a history of bullying behavior.
- The male witnessed violence in the home in which he was raised.
- Illicit drugs are used by either partner at least once a year.
- Partners have different religious affiliations.
- Partners share a residence but are not legally married.
- The family has an income below the poverty line.
- There may be alcohol abuse or instances of binge drinking.

Additional warning signs that a partner is or may become abusive
include the following:

- One partner is extremely jealous and possessive.
- The male exhibits hypermasculine behavior, such as declaring the
  male and female roles, and makes all household decisions.
- The male tries to isolate and prevent the woman from spending time
  with her family and friends, especially when he is not there.
- He tries to control her financially—for example, concealing income,
  preventing her from getting a job, and refusing to give her money.

- He is unable to discuss his feelings calmly and rationally.
- He is continually critical of the way she looks or what she says and does.
- He gets angry easily or insults her.
- He threatens her with violence, displays weapons, abuses pets, or destroys her property.
- He has an explosive temper and exhibits controlling behavior.
- The best indicator of all: He has previously hit or injured her (or someone else) in some way.

Domestic violence tends to increase in frequency and intensity with time. The best way to protect yourself is to avoid being in the position in the first place.

Try to open lines of communication with a battered woman—give her the phone number of a battered women's shelter or make the call for her.

How to Recognize a Battered Woman

Psychologists and sociologists have not been able to pinpoint exact characteristics of battered women. However, victims of repeated spousal abuse often have low self-esteem—sometimes as a direct result of the mistreatment—and a heightened need for approval and affection.

Many are passive, non-combative, dependent, powerless, and socially isolated, and have been brought up to accept traditional values, such as the idea that the man is unquestionably the head of the household. Often, these women exhibit physical symptoms, like headaches, difficulty sleeping, anxiety, and stomach pains. Being young, unemployed, poor, and having a history of alcohol and drug abuse increase the chances of being abused. Many battered women are abused while they are pregnant.

When should you be concerned about abuse?

- If a woman interrupts her regular routine, such as missing days at work or not attending social functions she used to enjoy.
- If a woman has mysterious cuts and bruises, puts on heavy makeup, and often wears out-of-season clothes (for example, long-sleeved shirts

Why Don't Battered Women Just Leave?

Battered women are routinely asked why they don't just abandon their situation and seek help. Although getting far away from the violence is their best option, the reasons for their hesitation are comprehensible:

- Many abused women are emotionally and financially dependent on their male partners and often believe the beatings are their own fault.
- Abused women may not know where to turn for help.
- Seeking help in a shelter may prove difficult for an abused woman. Many abused women get turned away from domestic-violence shelters because they are already overcrowded. Abused women with children may have an even harder time, both due to overcrowding issues and because many domestic-violence shelters do not accept male children over the age of 12.
- If a woman walks out on her husband and leaves her children behind, she risks losing custody of them. She may also worry that he'll abuse them.
- Many battered women are afraid their abusers will retaliate or have them arrested.

during the summer months). She may be covering up the evidence of abuse out of fear and embarrassment.

- If a woman makes excuses for cuts, bruises, or injuries.
- If a woman seems to fear the man in her life, or if her behavior becomes drastically more inhibited or controlled around him.

If you believe a neighbor or friend is being hurt, do not hesitate to call the police if it's an emergency situation. The battered spouse may be unable to get to the phone. In a non-emergency situation, try to open lines of communication with the battered woman. For instance, give her the phone number of a battered women's shelter or make the call for her.

IF YOU ARE BATTERED

The very first thing you should do if you are a battered woman is to admit to yourself that you are abused. Then you must plan and act.

- Put money, important documents, and car keys in a secure hiding place so that you will have access to them in a hurry if you need to leave.
- Find out the location of an emergency shelter, or make arrangements to go to the home of a trusted friend or relative before you are beaten again.
- Plan how to escape with your children—don't leave them behind and risk your chances for custody.
- If you do not manage to escape before the next attack, defend yourself to the best of your ability. After the assault, call the police and seek medical help. Make sure color photographs are taken of cuts and bruises.
- If the beating results in hospitalization, get the names of attending doctors, nurses, police officers, and witnesses, as well as copies of X-rays and medical reports. Those listed above can be called to give testimony, and the photos and documents can be used as evidence if the incident results in a court appearance.

The Salvation Army helps people of all faiths and backgrounds and can refer you to people who can assist you.

Shelters, Assistance, and Hotlines

As a battered woman, you may find the most immediate and useful help at a woman's shelter. These shelters can provide a place to stay, food, clothing, financial and legal advice, emotional support, and counseling for you and your children. Staff members, often victims of domestic violence themselves, will accompany you to court if you wish to press charges and will help you with job interviews, apartment hunts, and welfare benefits if you need financial aid. Women's shelters are not exclusively for poor women. They are for any woman who needs help. These shelters are in secret locations, so your abuser will not be able to find you. If you do not know of the nearest women's shelter, call the police to take you there, or call the National Center for Victims of Crime at (800) FYI-CALL. Go online to www.ncvc.org for more information.

Positive Thoughts

Domestic-abuse experts urge victims to always keep the following in mind:

- You are not the cause of the batterer's violent behavior; he is.
- You should not tolerate abuse.
- You are a worthwhile and important human being who deserves love and respect.
- You can have power and control over your life.
- You are not alone; others are there to help.
- You deserve a life of safety, security, and happiness.

Other sources of assistance include your church or synagogue or a psychological counselor or therapist. If you have to go to the hospital as a result of a beating, tell the doctor or nurse how the injury really occurred. The hospital staff can connect you with a source of assistance. The Salvation Army helps people of all faiths and backgrounds and can refer you to people who can assist you. In addition, you can look up crisis intervention services in the telephone book. Lastly, friends and family can be a great source of help by providing a temporary place to stay or emotional support.

If you feel more comfortable talking to someone who doesn't know you, consult the National Coalition Against Domestic Violence at www.ncadv. org/resources/StateCoalitionList_73. They can help you find local agencies or shelters in your state. In addition, you can call the National Domestic Violence Hotline at (800) 799-7233 (SAFE) for information and assistance. Don't be afraid to tell these people everything. They are specially trained and have heard it all. All information given is strictly confidential.

Restraining Orders and Orders of Protection

If you are battered, you need to remove yourself from the abusive situation by getting yourself and your children to a shelter or the home of a friend or relative. However, there is still a chance that your abuser will come after you. One legal step you can take to try to prevent future abuse, no matter where you are, is to obtain a restraining order or order of protection. Both are legal documents issued by a judge, telling the abuser that he must stay away from you. It may take a few weeks to obtain a full order of protection, and you may have to spend several hours in court. However, if the judge determines that you are in immediate danger, a temporary order of protection can be issued, which goes into effect immediately and lasts up to two weeks.

The punishment for violating an order of protection is more serious than for violating a restraining order, with the former usually being handled in a criminal court and possibly resulting in jail time.

Keep in mind, however, that restraining orders and orders of protection are just pieces of paper. In and of themselves, they cannot protect you. The police can only take action once an order has been violated. And before obtaining a restraining order or order of protection, you should find out how the police will respond to an order violation. This response can vary: In some states the abuser can be arrested and brought to jail, while in others he may only be given a citation. If a citation is the only punishment for an order violation, then it might not be wise to get one at all, since this will not deter the abuser from violating the order again, and may only serve to make him angrier and more determined. Generally speaking, the punishment for violating an order of protection is more serious than for violating a restraining order, with the former usually being handled in a criminal court and possibly resulting in jail time, and the latter being handled in a civil court without any jail sentence.

CHILD ABUSE

Perhaps the most despicable crimes are those committed against children by adults. The saddest of all may be child abuse, because it is so often inflicted by parents, whom the child loves the most and on whom the child is most dependent for his or her very life. Unfortunately, physical, psychological, and sexual abuse of children by their parents, caretakers, and other trusted individuals is widespread.

What Is Child Abuse?

The law describes a child as a person under age 18. The abused child may be assaulted with weapons or with the abuser's hands; sexually assaulted; held in close confinement, as when locked in a closet or tied up; emotionally or verbally abused; or otherwise mistreated. Another aspect of child abuse is neglect. A neglected child does not receive necessary care, lacks adequate supervision or medical assistance, and most important, receives inadequate nurturing and affection. A parent must provide a safe environment for the child, including taking measures to prevent accidental harm or injury, such as swallowing poison or falling out an open window.

Children who have run away from home or children born without homes are particularly vulnerable to attack from pedophiles—adults who are sexually attracted to children. These children may be coerced into becoming prostitutes or taking part in child pornography.

Child abuse is an underreported crime. Most children never tell. Adolescents are less likely to report abuse than younger children. And many adults have forgotten about the abuse they experienced when they were children, only to have delayed remembrances in later life.

Child Abusers and Pedophiles

Child abusers do not fit a single profile. They come from all walks of life, from all races, ethnic backgrounds, religions, age brackets, and income levels. They may be gay or straight. Children of wealthy parents are often as abused as children from poor families.

Most child abusers were battered children themselves or witnessed violence in the home in which they were raised. They have been led to believe that this type of interaction is acceptable. Similarly, many molesters were victims of sexual abuse as children. Many people who assault children have a hard time controlling their emotions; they lash out at the child, the one thing they can control.

Child abuse is an underreported crime. Most children never tell.

Most people would like to think that child sexual abuse is perpetrated only by sick strangers, because then one could "see them coming," but this is only rarely the case. In about 80 percent of sexual abuse cases, the abuser is a person the child knows. Often it is a parent, brother or sister, neighbor, babysitter, daycare employee, teacher, coach, minister, or someone else who is surrounded by children. Molesters usually find ways to spend a large amount of time with children.

Recognizing an Abused Child

A seriously abused child shows signs of battering and neglect—for example, frequent, unexplained injuries, such as bruises, welts, cuts, burns, and even bites. Some injuries may even appear not to have been accidentally caused, such as a bruise or a welt with the shape of an object like a coat hanger, an iron, or a belt buckle. A neglected child may be left alone for many hours or be outside in cold weather without a coat. A neglected child may be continually tired and listless or constantly hungry. The child may roam the streets after dark. He may seem excessively fearful of being touched, shying away from a hug or a pat on the head.

Other warning signs include:

- Withdrawal from adults, including parents.
- Unexplained aggressive behavior.
- Demonstration of anxiety when around certain people.
- Behavior that is age inappropriate as observed in playacting or language.
- Short attention span.
- Expression or demonstration of feelings of shame or guilt.
- Inability to concentrate in school or other structured situations.
- Behavioral problems, perhaps associated with poor hygiene.
- Involvement in petty theft.
- Involvement in substance abuse.
- Periods of observable anxiety for no apparent reason.
- Behavioral tendencies that may be associated with depression.

Even if only one or two signs are observed, the child may be abused. It is a good idea to investigate, via a therapist or family doctor, any of these tendencies in a child (whether yours or someone else's)—especially if they represent changes from his routine behavior.

Assisting an Abused Child

Neighbors often know of abuse but are reluctant to report the parents to a child protection agency. This fear of involvement is unfounded. If a child needs immediate medical attention, you can safely phone the police. You do not have to give your name.

> If a child (yours or any other) comes to you to report abuse, you should listen and pay attention.

You can also place a call (anonymously if you wish) to your local child welfare bureau. Do not inform anyone that you have taken action. Abusive parents have been known to coach a child so that when an investigator shows up, everything seems normal.

If a child (yours or any other) comes to you to report abuse, you should believe him or her. Children rarely lie about sexual abuse. Tell the child you are glad she told you. Make sure the child knows you will protect her and tell her that the abuse is not her fault.

If there is any physical evidence of abuse, take pictures and make copies of any X-rays or medical or psychological reports. Put these away in a safe place, and clearly label each item. Give the evidence to the police or the child protective agency when you make your report, and get a receipt.

Do not confront the person or organization suspected of abuse. Call the police or an appropriate social service agency. The only evidence needed is what the child has told you. It is absolutely essential that you report the abuse immediately to prevent the abuser from victimizing more children.

Seek out professional therapists and doctors who specialize in the treatment of child assault cases. Use the help they can provide for you and your child. For nationwide assistance, you can call the National Child Abuse Hotline at (800) 4A-CHILD or (800) 422-4453 and speak to a trained professional.

Teach a child that no one should touch any area that is covered by his or her swimsuit.

Protecting Your Children from Abuse

Here are some tactics you can use to help protect your child from abuse.

- Warn your child to be wary of strangers.
- Make certain your child knows it's important to tell you (or, if at school, a teacher) about any incidents of improper touching by adults or older children.
- Make sure your child knows he can tell you anything, even if it makes the child or you feel awkward and uncomfortable. Also tell the child he won't get in trouble for telling.
- Teach your child to use the telephone. Make sure she knows how to reach you at home or at work.
- Teach your child when to scream for help and run away.
- Respect your child's feelings. For example, if the child doesn't want to kiss Grandma now, do not resort to force. Coercion teaches

children that they must do what adults ask, even if it makes them uncomfortable.

- Teach your child appropriate names for the private parts of the body. Avoid secretive names or euphemisms, as these terms make these areas seem forbidden and may make it more difficult for the child to discuss them with you.
- Teach your child that his body belongs to him and that nobody has the right to touch it. Teach a child that no one should touch any area that is covered by his or her swimsuit.
- Play an age-appropriate "what if" game with your child, and see how she responds to different scenarios. For example, ask, "What if a stranger approaches you?" or "What if somebody touched you in a way you did not like?" Correct the child gently if she gives an undesirable answer, and encourage her to ask questions. Be sure not to scare the child.
- Teach your child that it's okay to say no to adults if he does not like what is going on. When children say no and leave immediately, most abusers will not pursue them.
- Find out if your child's school has programs that teach children about abuse and specialists on site who may be able to recognize the signs of child abuse.
- Determine the screening procedures under which teachers are hired in your community. Be sure that people with police records and poor character are screened out.
- Consider self-defense classes for older children, including karate, and personal electronic alarms to carry in the event of an assault.

What can you tell your children to help them protect themselves? You don't want to weigh the child down with an exhaustive list of things to do, to avoid, and to think about. This list is short and to the point:

- Remember that police officers are your friends; they will help you.
- Go to school with your friends; come home with your friends.
- Tell your parents where you're going whenever you leave home.
- Ask a friend to go with you to the restroom if you're not at home or at school.
- Play where other kids play: friends' houses, playgrounds, or at home.

- Never play in empty buildings.
- Never get in an automobile with anyone you don't know.
- Never talk to people you don't know.
- Tell your parents, your teacher, or a police officer if a grown-up does something bad to you.

Remember that the consequences of child abuse are lifelong. The best solution is to prevent child assault in the first place.

If You're Feeling Angry or Violent

If you're quick to get angry and feel violent, take time to decompress before you confront your child. There are many ways to achieve this:

- Take a short walk or run, but do not drive.
- Take a soothing shower or bath.
- Call someone you can talk to.
- Listen to music or watch TV.
- Leave the room or house for a while.
- Take deep breaths or count slowly until you are calm.
- Try something as simple as making yourself a cup of tea or coffee.

After you calm down and no longer feel angry, call your local division of youth and family services for assistance and support. You may also want to contact the local Parents Anonymous, a nationwide group of adults with abuse problems who meet to give mutual support and to learn ways of dealing with children without resorting to physical violence. Social service agencies can provide local telephone numbers for Parents Anonymous. Additional information can be found on www.parentsanonymous.org.

ELDER ABUSE

Less is known about abuse of the elderly than about spousal and child abuse. Research indicates, however, that slightly more than one quarter of wives are abused by their husbands, while approximately one sixth of the elderly are victimized.

Abused and Abusers

Repugnant cases of mistreatment of the elderly by family members, often by children, unfortunately are not rare events. Victims themselves are often incapable, physically or psychologically, of reporting incidents. Some fear further and more severe punishment or, even worse, abandonment.

Abusive family members sometimes threaten the aged with nursing homes or hospitalization. They may endure the abuse rather than plunge into unknown living arrangements, or they may stay out of fear of living alone. Many aged also hope the abuser's behavior will change.

Others feel embarrassed, ashamed, or guilty about coming forward. Like battered women, elderly victims often have a poor self-image and believe they deserve the brutal punishment. Many senior citizens do not know where or how to find assistance.

Researchers have suggested that middle-class families suffer greater stress as caregivers than lower- and upper-class families.

As with child and spousal abuse, elder abuse occurs at all income levels and afflicts the aged of all races, ethnicities, and religions. However, researchers have suggested that middle-class families suffer greater stress as caregivers than lower- and upper-class families. Affluent families can afford to hire outside help, and lower-class families tend to be more intergenerationally dependent. It is the middle class that, without adequate resources to hire outside help, tends to do more of the burden in caregiving.

Forms of Abuse

Elder abuse has many different faces. Perhaps the most horrible is physical. This includes beating, punching, slapping, bruising, burning, bone breaking, raping, or even killing. Physical abuse may comprise more than one form of violence.

Psychological abuse often can be as severe. This mind abuse frequently includes humiliation, subjugation, denigration, degradation, subordination, domination, and control. Verbal abuse is part of this formula. The vulnerable victims are told they are evil, insane, and unstable. They may be handcuffed to their beds, locked in their rooms, or forced to eat out of a dog's dish.

Yet another form of brutality is financial/material, in which money or some object, such as a bed, is withheld from the victim. Most instances of financial/material abuse involve taking the victim's money and using it for the caretaker's personal needs. This type of abuse is also the most difficult to detect, especially if it occurs little by little.

Neglect is another form of abuse—when food or medication is withheld, or when the helpless victim suffers bedsores from long periods of confinement. This is the most common form of abuse, occurring in about 50 percent of elder-abuse cases. "Granny dumping"—when adult children or other caregivers abandon an aged person in their care—is a form of neglect that has increased in incidence over the years.

Helping to Prevent Elder Abuse

Elder abuse can be prevented if you learn to recognize the typical signs and immediately intervene by notifying the proper authorities. Here are some ways you can help:

- Learn to recognize injuries, bruises, welts, scratches, or bite marks, the origins of which are unknown.
- Watch for long periods of isolation, frequent screams and yells for help, self-reports describing abuse, signs of malnutrition, filth in the home, and unwashed clothes and bodies.
- Be aware of an elderly person's increasing anxiety in the presence of certain people.

Remember, however, that all families argue, complain, and have problems and that not every disagreement or temper tantrum signals elder abuse. Many children manage their parents' finances or attend to their personal needs honestly and intelligently.

Finally, before agreeing to take care of an elderly loved one, you must go through a process of self-evaluation. Assess your own abilities and resources; it's okay to realize that you are incapable of effectively dealing

If You Are Vulnerable to Abuse

Join a community group that educates you about where and how to get assistance and, even more important, emphasizes that seeking help is not shameful or a sign of weakness. Identify an abuse hotline for emergencies and any other situations requiring assistance. Your local social service agencies can provide numbers and addresses of locations. Keep emergency phone numbers by your telephone.

Find out about adult protective services in your community that investigate reports of abuse and where appropriate action can be taken to resolve unbearable situations. Learn about home-care services that will send a companion, visiting nurse, or home health aid to look after an aged citizen part-time or more often as required. If your community has an adult daycare center, visit it and introduce yourself to the people in charge.

Don't hesitate to contact professionals who are concerned with elder abuse, including social workers, nurses, physicians, health-care workers, members of the clergy, and police officers. If you can, join a Neighborhood Watch program and suggest that it expand its responsibilities to include daily checks on individuals who are housebound, infirm, or otherwise vulnerable to abuse and neglect.

with the pressures and responsibilities that go along with caretaking. This does not mean you love the person any less; it means you are concerned about taking on too much and want what is best for your loved one.

If you don't live near an elderly parent, relative, or friend who needs help, call the nationwide toll-free Eldercare Locator telephone number at (800) 677-1116 to find out about services available in their community.

Self-Protection for Seniors

It is important as you age to start thinking about what your long-term needs are going to entail. As a parent, open communication channels with your adult children. You should get together and talk about the increasing requirements for care. The discussions should include sharing responsibilities, budget management, and available community help. Suggest that your adult children take courses on care for the elderly to help them learn what to expect, what to do if the tasks become intolerable, and how to reach out for help. Below are a few ways that will help you stay in control of your future.

Make every effort to maintain your independence. This is especially important if you are being cared for by a friend or relative. Be responsible for your own personal needs, and keep medical, hairdressing, and other personal appointments. Keep your possessions neat and organized, making sure others know that you are aware of where you place your belongings. Have your own telephone line, and open your own mail. Just because someone is helping you does not give them the right to make decisions for you or to invade your privacy.

Thoroughly familiarize yourself with your financial situation. Know how to manage your assets, and determine who will take over for you in an emergency. Put your finances in order. One of the most important things is to prepare a will. Review it annually, but think hard before revising it. Don't deed your house, personal property, or other assets to anyone in exchange for care or other assurances that you will not have to enter a nursing home. Sign nothing before you check with someone you absolutely trust and whose interests are not being served.

Be very careful about allowing an adult child to return home to live with you, especially one who is troubled or who might have a history of drug addiction, alcoholism, compulsive gambling, violence, mental illness, or criminality.

Always have your Social Security checks and other regular payments deposited directly to your bank account. While it is a good idea to have another well-trusted person, such as one of your children, listed on your bank account, this can be extremely risky if you don't know the person well. If at all possible, leave your account in trust for this person instead of listing him or her on a joint account.

Be sure to cultivate new friends and maintain old friends of all ages. You don't want to rely only on your family for social activities and health care. Be very careful about allowing an adult child to return home to live with you, especially one who is troubled or who might have a history of drug addiction, alcoholism, compulsive gambling, violence, mental illness, or criminality. As an alternative, consider helping to support your adult child in a separate residence to preserve everyone's dignity while at the same time protecting yourself.

Make peace with alienated friends or family. Not only will you enjoy the added companionship, but they can assist you in time of need. Plan for later periods of vulnerability by having your attorney advise you about the powers of attorney, conservatorships or guardianships, living wills, and natural-death acts. Appointing several individuals to serve as co-guardians or co-conservators assures that, in case of an emergency, there is always someone responsible and available to manage your affairs.

Remember, once elder abuse starts, it is more than likely to recur unless measures are taken to stop it. Do not wait for a serious injury to occur before you seek help.

CHAPTER 16

SECURITY FOR INFANTS AND YOUNG CHILDREN

Parents must protect young children, whether they are home or in a child-care setting. But the family of the 21st century—a family in which both parents often work and the children are tended by relatives, babysitters, or outside the home in daycare centers—faces safety challenges that earlier families never even had to consider.

DAYCARE CENTERS

If you need a daycare center, you want to find one that is safe and secure. But shocking cases of child abuse and sexual molestation are reported in daycare facilities across the nation.

Of course, some facilities will be better than others, so you'll want to utilize only the best available for your children. If you aren't familiar with the care centers in your area, ask the principal of your school, your physician, neighbors, or your spiritual leader for their recommendations.

Types of Daycare

You have lots of daycare options. You can find public nonprofit centers that charge on a sliding scale depending on income. Private daycare usually is more expensive but may also offer scholarships or discounts based on need. You'll discover highly structured care outside the home, as well as more intimate family-type programs in private homes. You'll find all-day and half-day programs. Many daycare programs have extended hours for school-age children whose parents are still at work.

Only you can judge which program is most suitable for you, your child, and your budget. But whatever form of daycare you choose, be sure it is effective, safe, and wholesome.

How to Recognize Safe Daycare

You won't easily recognize signs of child abuse at daycare by how play activities, toys, games, and equipment are organized. Nor will you detect any indication of child molestation from the quality of food or snacks or the safety precautions against accidents. But several basic signs will alert you to the possibility of danger.

Contact your state or local government organization that monitors daycare centers to determine if the center is properly licensed, certified, or registered to carry out its activities. You can also visit www.daycare.com. Ask if background checks were carried out by the center to determine the fitness of personnel, including the custodial and kitchen staff. Were their references checked carefully? What are the employment qualifications and training for the caregivers? How long have they been in childcare? What procedures are in place if someone other than the parent or designated person comes to pick up the child? Determine if an adequate staff-to-child ratio exists; experts recommend a ratio of about 1 to 4 for children 3 years old and younger, and about 1 to 7 for children 4 years old and older.

When you visit a prospective center or other daycare facility, do so without an appointment.

Find out as much as you can about disciplinary procedures, particularly how misconduct is managed. And don't hesitate to ask the daycare-center administrator questions about strategies for preventing sexual molestation or physical abuse. Make sure the children are never the object of physical punishment, especially beatings.

When you visit a prospective center or other daycare facility, do so without an appointment. You'll get a good idea of what goes on there. Then later, when you sign your child up, make a few occasional spontaneous visits. If you see anything that you don't approve of, you can discuss the problem with the management—or take your child elsewhere. Don't feel strange or embarrassed to visit the center at any time. By observing the children in their routine activities, you will sense what life is really like at the center. No area should be off limits. You will be able to determine whether the children are happy or if there is an air of tension, anxiety, and intimidation.

Be sure that caretakers always receive your written permission to take your child on a trip away from the daycare center. Tell your children in no uncertain terms that they are prohibited from leaving the daycare center without your permission.

When to Find Another Caregiver

Once you find the best care suitable for your child, you still have to assume an active role to make sure that the care does not deteriorate because of staff turnover, changing policies, shifting organizational structure, or general loss of enthusiasm.

Remove your child immediately from a program that does not welcome unannounced visits while the center is open.

Never allow your child to continue in a program that is poorly evaluated by neighbors, friends, or government regulatory agencies or the Better Business Bureau. Remove your child immediately from a program that does not welcome unannounced visits while the center is open. Be especially on your guard if you are required to call before each visit and then are confined to the office or other administrative areas and not allowed into places where children are at play or engaged in other activities. Be suspicious if, after a reasonable period of adjustment, your little one is afraid of the caregivers or resists returning to the center.

What signs are cause for concern at a daycare center?

- A major staff turnover and strange people caring for your child.
- If your child comes home with suspicious injuries or body marks. These are not always signs of abuse, but they at least indicate deteriorating, negligent, and eroding care.
- Your child's complaints about long periods of playing or waiting alone, which may indicate poor supervision, indifference, and a lax attitude on the part of the caregivers.
- Fewer organized activities and outdated or broken toys, which may signify a diminution in the level of supervision.
- Harsh, rude, and irrational behavior by the caregivers toward the children and toward you. They may, for example, become defensive and even angry when you express your concerns.
- Discovering your child has been left alone in a vehicle.

You will know the program is not for you when you begin to worry about your child, lose confidence in the caregivers, and generally feel uncomfortable with the level of care and organization.

PREEMPTING SEXUAL ABUSE

You and your little one can take several steps to prevent sexual abuse in daycare before it occurs. Here's how.

- Teach your children about the body's private parts, and rehearse ways they should react if someone touches them inappropriately.
- Tell them that their body belongs to them and they have the right to tell adults not to touch it.
- Teach your children to say no to adults who try to touch them in places that make them feel uncomfortable.
- Teach them to tell you if anyone touches them where they shouldn't.
- Remind them that it's not their fault if an adult touches them in a private area.
- Teach them to tell you about any pain or punishment or any other dangerous situation they experienced in daycare.

The Sex-Offender Registry

The vast majority of child sexual predators are not strangers but rather people who know their victims. Nevertheless, parents should still be aware of any sex offenders who may be living in their community. All 50 states are required to register sex offenders and notify the community when a sex offender resides there. However, there is a great deal of variation from state to state as to how the community notification is performed, which offenders are required to register, how long the registration lasts, whether the public has access to the registry, and what information is shared.

You can learn more about each state's registry through the FBI's website at www.fbi.gov/hq/cid/cac/states. You can also check out the National Sex Offender Public Registry at www.nsopr.gov, which allows the public to search through the registries of all 50 states and the District of Columbia.

Explain to your child that you can always provide protection. A child will confide in you if she is convinced that you have the power to help. (See chapter 15 for additional information on protecting your child from abuse.)

If your child reports to you any form of physical abuse, follow through as you promised and contact the police or a social service agency. For your child's sake, don't procrastinate, since circumstances are likely to deteriorate further. Remember, the abuser is likely to repeat the behavior either with your child or with another youngster. Also, when your child requires medical or psychological assistance, seek it without delay.

The safety, security, and health of your child depends on you and on the time and energy you spend investigating the best daycare and being alert for danger signs. Don't fail to take all necessary steps to ensure protection.

CHILD ABDUCTION AND MISSING CHILDREN

One of the biggest fears parents have is the possibility that their child may be abducted. The abducted and missing include children kidnapped by strangers, relatives, or parents who do not have custody or legal guardianship.

AMBER Alert

The AMBER Alert is an emergency notification system designed to help in the recovery of abducted children. The alert system was created in response to the 1996 abduction of Amber Hagerman, a 9-year-old girl in Arlington, Texas, who was subsequently raped and murdered. Amber might have been rescued shortly after her abduction if officials had been able to quickly distribute information to people who wanted to help search for her. In 2003 Congress passed legislation establishing national coordination of the various state AMBER alert programs.

AMBER is an acronym for "America's Missing: Broadcasting Emergency Response." The AMBER Alert uses various media outlets to inform the public about child abductions. The decision as to whether to issue an AMBER Alert is left up to the police investigating each particular case. When an alert is issued, the public is informed via the radio, television, Internet, e-mail, and various other media outlets about the name and description of the abductee, the description of the suspected abductor, and information about the abductor's vehicle, if it is known. Since its creation, the AMBER Alert has led to the safe recovery of more than 500 abducted children nationwide.

Abductor Profile

It is a myth that the majority of abductors are strangers lurking in alleyways. Child abductions by strangers are, in fact, quite rare. In the United States, a country with roughly 59 million children, there are only about 3,200 to 4,600 successful child abductions by strangers each year. In reality, most abducted children are taken by a parent or family member during a custody battle. Studies estimate that there are about 350,000 of these cases each year, accounting for 50 percent of all abduction cases.

Child abductions can occur anytime, but the hours of highest risk are from 3:00 to 6:00 P.M., when children are out of school, playing, and less likely to be supervised. Many stranger abductors ask kids for help to search for a lost puppy or kitten or to assist them in crossing the street or going to their car. Many act as if they are disabled. Others tell kids there is an emergency and that they must be escorted home. Still others entice children by inviting them to participate in a television show or a beauty contest. Bribery with candy or ice cream is still surprisingly effective.

Infant Security in Hospitals

Over 100 infants were abducted from hospital nurseries in a recent 20-year period. The typical abductor is a woman of childbearing age who may have previously been employed at the hospital or visited it frequently, so that she is very familiar with the environment. She may attempt to abduct an infant by impersonating a nurse or other hospital staff. Prior to the abduction, she may frequently visit the nursery and ask a lot of detailed questions about hospital procedures and the layout of the maternity ward. She may even try to befriend the hospital staff and the infant's parents.

It is very important that you, as the parent of a newborn, watch out for these warning signs. If you see anyone acting suspiciously, do not hesitate to notify hospital security. Demand to see the ID of any hospital staff member asking to hold or treat your baby. *Never* hand your baby over to a stranger, and *never* leave your baby alone in your room.

Many hospitals now use state-of-the-art technology to enhance the security of newborns. For example, many hospitals use electronic systems to restrict access to maternity wards to authorized personnel only and place security sensors directly on newborns. These sensors will cause an alarm to sound and the exit doors to lock if the newborn is removed from the safety "zone" of the maternity ward. In best-case scenarios all hospital staff wears photo IDs so that imposters are easier to identify, and the maternity ward is under the direct supervision of registered nurses at all times.

Child Security in Daycare

In addition to keeping an eye out for abuse and neglect at daycare, you should also make sure that the center will adequately protect your child from abduction. Daycare personnel must carefully monitor who enters the facility and who has access to the children. They must carefully supervise all pick-ups from the daycare, ensuring that your children leave the facility only with you or adults you have pre-approved.

If you are divorced, let the daycare center know your child's custody status. Be sure to select a daycare facility that performs criminal background checks on all its employees and volunteers. And instruct the daycare center to contact you if your child is absent.

PROTECTING CHILDREN FROM ABDUCTION

You need to teach your children some basic information to protect them from abduction. First, ensure that your child knows his or her full name, your full name, home address, home telephone number, your work and cell phone numbers, how to use the telephone, and how to call the operator or 911/emergency assistance. Teach your child these basics as soon as he or she is ready.

Second, though you may want to tell your kids "Don't talk to strangers," many experts think it won't prevent abductions. Most abductors appear warm and friendly and have no trouble getting the child to trust them. The abductor can cease to be a stranger within a very short time. Teach children that all people with whom they are not acquainted or do not know well are strangers and that they should never go home with them, especially in cars. (Your children, of course, should never hitchhike.)

Ensure that your child knows his or her full name, your full name, home address, home telephone number, your work and cell phone numbers, how to use the telephone, and how to call the operator or 911/emergency assistance.

However, you must be sure not to make your children paranoid about the potential danger of strangers. Most strangers are not harmful and will help in an emergency. Never allow your children's apprehension to escalate to the point where they are fearful of all strangers in every situation. Children should be alert and prepared, not in a constant state of terror.

Finally, teach your children how to respond to adults. Children are commonly taught to be polite and respectful. You need to let them know that you would like them to behave this way, but they also have the right to say no, even to a grown-up, if they are made to feel uncomfortable or are fearful. Teach them to report such concerns without delay. Always encourage your children to tell you about strange events, and assure them that you will always protect them.

Basic Guidelines

Parents must determine the amount of control and supervision necessary for their child in relation to their age and maturity level. Here are other guidelines you should follow to help protect your child from abduction:

- Make sure your children are well supervised. Young children should never be allowed to play or roam outside of adult supervision. It is up to the parents—through their evaluation of their child's maturity level and ability to recognize uncomfortable situations—to determine the age at which they are allowed outside on their own. You must know where children are at all times and how they are going to get to a destination and home again. Know your children's friends and have their telephone numbers and addresses available.

- Do not leave children unattended at home, at the playground, in your car, or in any store while you shop, even for a moment. This is the kind of opportunity the abductor looks for. Also, teach your children to play and go places in groups. Make sure they know they are much safer when not alone.

- Make sure your child knows what to do if the two of you become separated in a store or if she is lost; tell your child to go to a store, security officer, checkout counter, or some other prearranged location. If the child can't find an authority for help, he or she should look for another "mommy" (a woman with children). Wandering around makes it more difficult for you to find each other. Some parents avoid separation from toddlers by using expanding cords to tether them.

- Don't personalize your child's clothing or other personal items so that an offender will not know your child's name. An offender may trick the child into thinking that he is a family friend because he knows the child's name.

- If followed or forced to go somewhere, your child should yell or scream for assistance. Hiding is a dangerous tactic.

- Be certain your children know that they shouldn't answer the door or the phone if circumstances require that they be home alone. They should know to let the answering machine take a message. Such statements as "My mother can't come to the phone right now. May I take a message for her?" is a signal that the child is alone. If someone delivers a package while the child is alone, the package should be left at the door without the child acknowledging the delivery.
- Be careful with whom you leave your children. Trust your instincts about caregivers, teachers, or others who are in contact with your child. Do not leave your child in the care of anyone with whom you are not completely comfortable.

Consider a secret password that only you and your child know that can be used in case you need to send someone to pick up the child.

- Make sure your child's babysitter, school, or daycare facility will not release your child unless you have authorized them to do so first, and then only to those whom you have specifically designated. Ask them to alert you if your child fails to arrive.
- Make sure your child knows not to leave childcare or school with your ex-spouse (if you have one) without your permission. Also, when your child does leave with a non-custodial parent, make sure the adult and child know the agreed-upon place and time of return and that the adult is instructed to call you if late.
- For older children, consider a secret password that only you and your child know that can be used in case you need to send someone to pick up the child. Change the password if you've been separated or divorced. Tell your children never to get into a car with anyone who doesn't know the password, unless you have told them it's okay.
- Play an age-appropriate "What if..." game with children. Present them with situations like, "What would you say to a grown-up you didn't know who asked you to help find his lost dog?" or "What would you do

if a stranger pulled up in a car and wanted to give you toys or candy?" Let the children answer, and gently correct them if the response is not what you want. Don't scare them, and let them ask questions. You can even role-play the situations so that your child can practice yelling "No!" and running away. You and your child can even take turns.

- Be certain your children know you will always love them and want them. Abductors frequently tell children that you don't want them or love them anymore.
- Be wary if you notice an adult paying a lot of attention to your child. Teach your children to tell you or their caregivers or teachers about strangers who want to photograph them.
- Teach your children to tell you if someone asks them to keep a secret or offers them presents.
- Be certain your children know people and places they can go to for help when they are lost or feel threatened. Program their cell phones and home phone with your work numbers, as well as those of neighbors, relatives, and various emergency services.
- Memorize what your child is wearing each day, in case you need to provide a description to the police.

Teach your children these guidelines over a reasonable period of time. Limit what you say to what they need to know at their age, and discuss these issues in a way they can understand. Experts suggest starting when they are old enough to stray from you. You may start by asking them what they already know about or if any of their friends have had experiences they would like to talk about with you. It is very important not to scare children when teaching them these things. Remind them of these guidelines every so often. Children forget things, so telling them once is never enough.

Experts suggest teaching your kids these guidelines as soon as they are old enough to stray from you.

Relying on High-Tech Protection

New high-technology devices to prevent child abduction have appeared on the market. These devices allow you to locate your child utilizing GPS technology. Certain devices will, on activation, sound an alarm to scare off potential abductors. Keep in mind, though, that these products may scare children or reduce the vigilance of a parent or caretaker.

Many daycare facilities have installed Internet-based cameras so parents can use their computers to check on their children throughout the day.

Another alternative is the Internet-based camera. These cameras can be discretely placed throughout the home or directly on your child's computer, allowing you to view what's happening at home while you're away by simply accessing the camera from any Internet-connected computer. Through these cameras, you can find out if the kids are actually at home when they're supposed to be, whose company they are keeping, or if a babysitter is treating them properly. Many daycare facilities have installed Internet-based cameras so parents can use their computers to check on their children throughout the day. But again, while this added precaution might bring you some comfort, it is not enough in and of itself. Technology can assist, but it will never replace good old-fashioned parental supervision and common sense.

Numerous devices for tracking children are also available. You can get an identifying microchip secured to your child's tooth, visible only to a dentist or the police; beepers equipped with alarms that sound if a child goes outside a certain vicinity; and identification bracelets or tags. Of course, extreme measures such as these may not be for every parent, and their constricting nature is more suitable for younger children. As children get older, these devices become related less to security and more to an invasion of privacy. Remember, such equipment won't prevent an abduction in the first place. They are, however, very helpful in the location and identification of your child should an abduction occur.

If you don't want these security items, what can you do to help in the case of an abduction? Keep a current picture or video of your child, a good set of fingerprints, and copies of medical and dental records in a file that could be turned over to the police to aid in search and identification in the event your child is missing.

Studies have also found that children are less creative when they are monitored by their parents. Therefore, you want to be sure to give your child the freedom to play without being constantly under your watchful eye.

Avoid Paranoia

You can easily get carried away when it comes to trying to protect your children from abduction. Try to remember that the chances of your child being abducted by a stranger are very small. If you, as a parent, are overly fearful about abduction, your child may pick up on this and also become fearful, growing to be untrusting and anxious around new people. Restricting a child's outdoor playtime can negatively affect his development. Don't always keep your child indoors where, while he may be safer, he will also be more sedentary and less active.

WHAT TO DO IF YOUR CHILD IS MISSING

If your child is missing or unduly late returning home, remain calm; there is seldom reason for panic. Most missing children return safe, sound, and unscathed, having been so engrossed in what they were doing that they simply lost track of time. If you have been separated from your child in a store or other public place, alert security immediately. Many facilities will page lost children. If your child has not returned home, call the places where she is supposed to be. Call your friends and neighbors. If you still are unable to find your child, call other places that the child is likely to be.

If you still have not located your child, notify the police and give them a complete and detailed description. This should include your child's age, weight, height, hair and eye colors, and unique characteristics, such as birthmarks, moles, eyeglasses, braces, and the clothes she was wearing at the time of disappearance. Make sure the police file a report with the

FBI, or do it yourself. The police must also provide a description of the child to the National Crime Information System. The police in another area may have found your child and may be trying to locate the parents. Ideally, the police will launch an AMBER alert if the criteria are met.

Look for your child yourself, and enlist friends, relatives, and neighbors, as well as the child's friends (and their parents) to help you. Put up posters in your community, and call various organizations for missing children, such as Child Find or the National Center for Missing and Exploited Children (NCMEC) at 1-800-THE-LOST to report your child missing.

NCMEC serves as a clearing-house of information, distributes descriptions and photographs of missing children, does age progression of photographs of long-term missing children, and assists police agencies in the search for serial offenders who prey on children. The Federal Parent Locator Service can help find an ex-spouse who has abducted your child. Visit them at http://www.acf.hhs.gov/programs/cse/newhire/. If efforts to locate the missing youngster are successful or if she turns up, remember to notify the authorities so that the police search is terminated.

CHAPTER 17

SECURITY FOR OLDER CHILDREN AND TEENAGERS

Older children and teenagers are special individuals with special problems. Without adequate experience or judgment and totally without guile, they can become both victims of and accomplices to many security incidents. And young people continue to be at risk during all the years they are growing up.

SAFETY GUIDELINES EVERY CHILD SHOULD KNOW

In addition to the precautions younger children should take (see chapter 16) to prevent abduction, older children need to avoid unnecessary contact with strangers and withhold all personal information from strangers. They should also learn how to reach 911 and which neighbor to go to if they are threatened.

In addition, the FBI suggests older children follow these guidelines:

• Travel in groups or pairs.
• Walk along heavily traveled streets, and avoid isolated areas when possible.
• Refuse automobile rides from strangers, and refuse to accompany strangers anywhere on foot.

- Use play areas where recreational activities are supervised by responsible adults and where police protection is readily available.
- Immediately report to the nearest person of authority anyone who molests or annoys you.
- Never leave home without telling your parents where you will be and who will accompany you.

Your child's school keeps information about him on file as a matter of course. This information should include photographs, personal and medical history, and descriptive information. If any of these items are not included in the school's files, give them to the principal and request that they be placed in your child's file.

Tell the school who is authorized to pick up your children. If you are divorced or separated, provide the school with a copy of the applicable court order. Likewise, tell your children that they should leave school only with people you designate. Make certain your children know exactly who has your approval, and agree upon a special code word for such occasions.

Be sure to tell the school:
- If the safety or life of a family member has been threatened.
- The details of your children's before- and after-school care.
- When your child will not be present.
- The names, addresses, and telephone numbers of people to contact in emergencies. Also, explain the relationship of the emergency contact.

PROTECTION FOR LATCHKEY KIDS

About 77 percent of America's youth carry a key in their backpack so they can unlock their front door once they get home from school. These children remain home, unsupervised, until their parents come home from work. These are referred to as latchkey kids. Latchkey kids are three times more likely to be victims of crime or accidents or get involved in delinquency than children who are well supervised.

The following are a number of things you can do to increase the safety of your latchkey kids after school.

Halloween Hazards

To help ensure that Halloween is safe for both younger and older children, take these precautions.

- Do not let young children go trick-or-treating alone. Make sure there is a responsible person with the group.
- Check your child's costume. It should be flame retardant and have adequate holes for your child's eyes, nose, and mouth. In addition, it should be light enough in color to be seen at night.
- Pin your name, address, and phone number on the costume of a very young child.
- Warn your child not to ring the doorbells of any houses where the lights are out.
- Keep your own house well lighted, and make sure that someone is home.
- Know where your older child is going, and tell him or her to stay in the neighborhood.
- Set and enforce a curfew for your older child, and make certain a responsible person is at home at this prearranged time.
- Inspect all candy that your child brings home. Throw out anything that is unwrapped or looks suspicious.

- Parent associations or community centers may have after-school programs, or you can suggest that they start one your community.
- Confirm with your children the route they should follow when going to or coming from school.
- Remind them that should ride only their assigned school bus and get off only at their assigned stop.

Latchkey kids are three times more likely to be victims of crime or accidents or get involved in delinquency than children who are well supervised.

- Do not permit your children to walk to or from school alone, and tell them to call you or a trusted friend or neighbor when they return home.

- Designate a person who lives nearby who your child can go to in the event of an emergency.
- Make sure your child knows how to carry the key to your home securely, so it will not get lost and will remain out of view. The child may hide the key under his shirt or pinned to the inside of his clothing.
- Tell your children not to answer the door when they are home alone. Teach them how to safely answer the phone. Make sure they don't reveal that you or another adult is not with them.
- Know your children's friends; that way you can anticipate where they might be at any given time.
- Work with your neighbors to establish safe houses on your street for a child who is frightened or in some real or imagined trouble.

Above all, listen to your children. Even more important, take what they say seriously. What they tell you may be the wildest flight of fancy imaginable or it may be a real threat—in which case your belief in your child could avert tragedy. If threats prove baseless, you can allay your child's fears.

INFLUENCE OF VIOLENCE IN THE MEDIA

By the age of 18, the average American child will have seen 200,000 violent acts on television. By the time the average child finishes elementary school, she will have seen 8,000 murders on TV.

As children begin to accept the persistent images of violence as a standard form of behavior, they become desensitized and may view violence as an acceptable way to solve problems. They may imitate what they see on the screen.

The most important thing you can do as a parent is to supervise program selection. Limit the viewing of role models that you would not want your children to emulate. Be consistent in this monitoring, and do not hesitate to enforce the viewing rules you set down. Discuss characters and their actions to help your children make sense of what is happening on the screen.

Become familiar with the television rating system, which blends codes for age appropriateness and content type. Age and content codes are flashed on the screen at the beginning of every show and after each commercial break. They are also provided in the television guides and on the Internet.

The age codes include:

- TV-Y for programs designed for youngsters of all ages.
- TV-Y7 for shows geared for youngsters age 7 and over.
- TV- Y7 FV for programs appropriate for older children able to handle fantasy violence (such as cartoon characters fighting).
- TV-G for shows appropriate for general audiences of children and adults.
- TV-PG for content that may be unsuitable for some children and where parental guidance is advised.
- TV-14 for programs with material not suitable for children under age 14.
- TV-MA for programs specifically designed for adult viewers and not recommended for children under 17.

As children begin to accept the persistent images of violence as a standard form of behavior, they become desensitized and may view violence as an acceptable way to solve problems.

The rating system also uses several letter designations for program content. These are V for violence; S for sexual situations; L for coarse or crude, indecent language; D for sexually suggestive or provocative dialogue; and FV for fantasy violence.

The television rating system operates in conjunction with the V-chip technology, a filtering device installed in all new televisions to help parents manage their choices for appropriate family viewing. By using the remote control and the television's on-screen menus, you can easily block programs based on their ratings.

You should also be aware of the wide variety of violent material in movies and home video games and on the Internet. Some Internet providers offer a filter that can block out material that is unsuitable for children.

TEENAGERS WHO COMMIT CRIMES

Children under 18 may be responsible for offenses that society considers unacceptable. Some of them may be general violations of the law; others, called status violations, may be criminal only when committed by the young. For example, a college student may cut class and be guilty of no crime, but a middle-school student cutting class could be charged with truancy. The only difference is that the junior-high student is a few years younger. Besides truancy, other status violations include curfew violations, tobacco or alcohol violations, loitering, and being a runaway.

Many young people have committed at least one offense for which they could have been brought to juvenile court, including status violations, larceny, burglary, motor-vehicle theft, arson, and more—although few are. Only one in nine (one in six if you consider only males) is referred to juvenile court for non-traffic offenses prior to his or her 18th birthday.

So how can you protect your teenager from crime, either as victim or criminal?

Know where your children are, what they are doing, and with whom. Your child is just as likely to be bad company as to be in bad company, and if you are too quick to spring to your offspring's defense, you may be an unwitting accomplice. Admit that your child could run afoul of the law, and plan for this possibility with your teenager. Impress on teenagers the importance of respect for the law.

Encourage your teen to get a job or participate in sports or extracurricular activities at schools or clubs. These are excellent oppportunities for combating idleness and for building self-confidence.

Make sure you keep the lines of communication open between you and your children. Although it can sometimes be challenging to communicate with teenagers, you have nothing to lose and everything to gain by trying. Make your teenager feel like she is an important part of the family. Teenagers who don't feel a sense of belonging at home will surely look for places and groups where they can fit in.

CULTS

An unhappy teenager may be attracted to a cult. Typical "draftees" to a cult are middle-class children who receive good grades in school. Young people searching for meaning in life or spirituality are vulnerable, and many join cults because of frustration with established religion. Some are desperately searching for acceptance. The cultist group becomes their surrogate family; the cult leader becomes a father figure. Remember, a cult serves the specific needs of its followers. Recruits are not usually passive targets overpowered by mind controllers.

Also investigate to ensure that the institution your son or daughter is involved in is in fact a cult and not just a religious or social organization that differs from your child's background. Cults have unique characteristics that may include a charismatic and controlling leader who claims to have a direct line to a higher power; brainwashing techniques that instill fear, guilt, and shame and foster dependence on the leader; pressure to cut ties with family and friends; an intolerance of questioning of the cult's beliefs and practices; financial exploitation; criminal activities; and often an apocalyptic belief about the imminent end of the world. Evidence of cult involvement may include posters or other items depicting sacrifice of animals, violent illustrations involving humans, ceremony instructions, personal dress and tattoos that suggest a cult.

Once your teen has joined a cult, successful intervention is very difficult but not impossible. Prevention is the best, and perhaps only realistic, approach. What preventive action can you take?

- Never allow your home to be a meeting place for the cult's recruiters.
- Lobby to keep recruiters out of schools and off school grounds.
- Broaden the channels of communication with your teen. Be open-minded, tolerant, and willing to discuss sensitive subjects.
- Learn to be an active listener—be totally attentive and don't interrupt or impose your ideas before your teenager has finished speaking.
- Help your teen ask appropriate questions and think for himself. Young people vulnerable to cults often are unable to evaluate and choose among various options. They perceive cults as the only available alternative.
- Help your teen develop the art of critical thinking, make decisions and productive choices, and solve problems.
- Be a proper role model and instill confidence in your teen.

Identifying Signs and Colors

As a parent, you need to be aware of the various signs and colors of local gangs—they may be the key to identifying your own child's gang involvement. Pay attention to your child's clothing and accessories. Do they all tend to be the same color? Do his friends tend to wear that color? Is your child flashing hand signs to his friends? Is he drawing gang signs on his notebooks and backpack? Ask your local police department for information on gangs in your area, including their colors, signs, and symbols.

YOUTH GANGS

A delinquent gang consists of three or more youths who band together to commit crimes. Gang members share common symbols and defend exclusive territory, their "turf."

Gangs offer youngsters status, excitement, power, praise, profit, protection, mentoring, and opportunity for advancement—healthy goals fulfilled in unhealthy ways. Do everything in your power to prevent your child from joining and participating in a gang. Be on guard for early signs of gang involvement: drug and alcohol use, low grades, absence from school, a sudden change in friends, staying out late, and displaying lots of money and expensive merchandise that cannot be explained. Additionally, be alert for gang graffiti in your child's bedroom; gang uniforms or colors; special gang hand signals; photographs with gang names, insignia, and symbols; and talk of gang membership.

Prevention Is Best

While it is important that you are able to recognize the signs that your child has become involved in a gang, the best approach is preventative; try to steer your child away from joining a gang before it is too late. Here's what you can do:

- Speak to your child about the dangers of gang involvement.
- Keep the lines of communication between you and your child open.
- Get to know your child's friends and their parents.
- Recognize that not all sexual abusers are adults. Some older children,

who may or may not have been sexually abused themselves, may become sexual abusers. Be aware of older children who may come in contact with your child, including babysitters, cousins, and neighborhood kids.

- Ask school staff how they can be of assistance and what school programs are available to help your child.
- Get in touch with community organizations that may be able to provide help, guidance, and jobs.
- Seek aid from your religious leaders, who often are knowledgeable about neighborhood programs that strive to prevent gang membership.
- Form or join a Neighborhood Watch program, and if you observe gang activity, call 911 or inform your local police precinct. Ask to speak to a gang specialist trained in dealing with these matters.
- Establish a graffiti cleanup program. Organize neighbors and friends to report and remove graffiti in your neighborhood or from local school property.
- Offer alternatives to gang membership by establishing organized activities, including sports, outings, arts and crafts, picnics, and trips.

SEXUAL ABUSE

Sexual abuse can be particularly hard to catch, since the signs of abuse are often not readily apparent. The psychological and emotional effects of sexual abuse, in addition to the physical harm that can be caused, can be very serious and long lasting. Victims of childhood sexual abuse have been known to suffer from post-traumatic stress disorder (PTSD), depression, suicidal behavior, eating disorders, substance abuse, and anxiety, among other things. In addition, this type of abuse can have very serious effects on the child's ability to relate to other people and on his or her future attitudes toward sex.

You need to protect your children from this type of abuse and be aware of the warning signs that it might be happening. Unfortunately, older children are more likely than younger children to understand that they are being sexually abused but may be reluctant to tell someone about it due to fear of embarrassment. They might fear retaliation by their abuser. That's why it is vital that you maintain an open and honest relationship with your children. By having a close relationship with your child, you are more likely to spot changes in his behavior, such as becoming depressed, withdrawn, aggressive, or secretive. Take notice if your child suddenly refuses to go to school or participate on a sports team or is suddenly having behavioral problems.

A child sex offender is more likely to be someone your child knows than a stranger. Adults who come in frequent contact with your child, such as coaches and clergy, are in a position that allows them to get close to your children and to get them alone.

What can you do to prevent this abuse?

- Check the backgrounds of any adults who have the opportunity to spend time alone with your child. Make sure coaches have been through background checks, been fingerprinted, and had all references checked.
- Explain to your child the importance of not being left alone with any adults while they are at school or during religious education, and of not letting anyone touch them in inappropriate ways.
- Educate your children about sexual abuse and sexual harassment.

THE INTERNET

In addition to the people your child encounters daily in your community, there are countless potential predators who may try to gain access to them via the Internet. Social media networks (like Facebook and MySpace) offer opportunities to meet interesting new people with common interests, but they also provide an environment where your child may come into contact with sexual predators. The informal, conversational tones online lead people to quickly form friendships, even though you don't really know who exactly your new friend is. Pretending to be young teens, adult predators may try to find out if your child is home alone and where your home is, or try to lure him or her out of the house to meet up somewhere. (For more information on cybercrime, see chapter 19.)

Here are some steps you can take to keep your children safe online.

- Stay informed about parental control tools. Your Internet service provider offers some free control features, or you can buy blocking and filtering software, such as Cyber Patrol and CYBERsitter, from

Cyberbullying

Cyberbullying—when one person targets another using interactive technology, such as Facebook and other social networking sites, cell phones, and e-mail—is a huge problem among youth today. Children have committed suicide and even homicide after having been cyberbullied.

There are two kinds of cyberbullying: direct attacks, where a person targets and sends hostile messages to another directly, and attacks by proxy, in which the attacker uses the help of others to bully the victim.

Attacks consist of hateful or threatening words communicated via such avenues as instant messaging, text messaging, blogs, and Internet polls. Sometimes kids take pictures in a locker room or dressing room and send them through e-mail and cell phones. Within days the picture can reach millions.

So how can cyberbullying be stopped? Unfortunately, this is not an easy task. If schools get involved in disciplinary action for incidents that take place off campus and after school hours, they are often sued for exceeding authority and violating a child's right to freedom of speech. Parents tend to go too far, seeking revenge for the harm done to their child, which can often lead to worse consequences for the victim.

The best way to prevent cyberbullying is through education, beginning with the kids and teens themselves. Schools worldwide started to institute cyberbullying programs into their curriculum, teaching them about its harmful effects and sometimes fatal consequences, and the importance of respecting others. Schools and community groups have also set up anonymous tip hotlines so they can quickly respond and take action.

If your child has been victimized, contact law enforcement. Be supportive and talk to your child's pediatrician and guidance counselor to see if counseling may help.

your local retail store. These can monitor chat rooms or block them entirely, limit your child's ability to give out private information, and block private messages between your child and another user.

- Teach your children about the dangers of communicating with strangers via the Internet. Accompany your child in chat rooms until they understand the safety rules. Or block out chat rooms entirely.

- Tell them that they should never give out any personal information, such as their telephone number, address, school name, and birth date, and that they should never agree to meet an online acquaintance in person.
- Warn them to be suspicious of anyone who tries to turn them against their parents, teachers, or friends.
- Keep your home computer in a common area where you can keep an eye on what your child is doing.

SIGNS OF DRUG ABUSE

Drug use usually produces a variety of noticeable physical changes in a user: sleeplessness, diarrhea, bloodshot eyes, dilated pupils, vomiting, involuntary muscular movements (twitching), runny eyes or nose, inflamed nostrils, and loss of appetite. Other symptoms include lethargy or torpor not unlike intoxication, sudden weight loss, craving for sweets, excessive thirst, sweating, shakiness, and itching.

Drug use may also manifest itself in emotional or personality changes, such as inconsistency in behavior—for example, sitting for long periods in a trancelike state, then suddenly becoming hyperactive; volatility of temperament, ranging from extreme happiness to blackest depression; or uncharacteristic anger, radical changes in activity patterns or choice of friends, a sudden deterioration in physical appearance, sloppiness in dress, or inattention to personal hygiene. School grades may drop, and the drug user may lose interest in things that once held importance, such as school, athletics, and dating. The drug user may seem to be always tired, coming home only to fall asleep. A drug-troubled child may spend considerable time in the house, especially in a locked bathroom or bedroom. He may withdraw from family activities. A previously friendly and outgoing child may suddenly become secretive. A formerly easygoing child may become irritable and overly sensitive. The young abuser may be argumentative and have angry outbursts for no apparent reason.

There may be other evidence of drug use, too: yellow stains on fingers (caused by the high tar element in marijuana joints); needle tracks on the arms, legs, abdomen, and other parts of the body; the presence of drug paraphernalia, such as cigarette rolling papers, roach clips, plastic baggies, small pipes, a "work kit" with syringes, cotton, needles, and a

Where to Find Help

The best place for immediate help is a hospital with staff specifically trained to treat addicts. If your hospital does not have such a treatment facility, it should refer you to one that does.

The typical treatment program lasts 28 days and emphasizes individual and group therapy. Moreover, the patient's family is encouraged to participate in the rehabilitative process. Family members also receive individual and group therapy and attend educational lectures on substance abuse.

An aftercare program is essential because it recognizes the previous and special problems encountered when a recovering addict or alcoholic reenters the community. Therefore, the recovering addict or alcoholic is required, for at least several years, to attend regular "growth group" sessions and to participate in such self-help groups as Narcotics Anonymous and Alcoholics Anonymous. An effective aftercare program also provides counseling and support for family members.

Another possible source of help is a drug rehabilitation center, where the drug abuser can be treated as an outpatient or can live on the premises. These centers operate group sessions that teach people how to live drug-free lives.

Other users may benefit more from one-on-one sessions with a psychotherapist.

"cooker" (a metal bottle cap used for converting heroin into a liquid so it can be injected); burned ends of marijuana joints (often referred to as "roaches"); or small glassine envelopes tucked into a dresser drawer.

A number of stages may be observed in the behavior of those who abuse drugs. In the beginning stage, the abuser has the ability to take drugs or leave them alone. If the use of drugs becomes more frequent, with periodic or chronic states of insensibility or limited perception, that person is described as a chronic user. Beyond that point, a person who develops a compelling need, as opposed to a desire, to obtain drugs continually, at whatever cost in money or action, is addicted.

If you have a teenager with a drug problem, he or she needs help and so do you. Your family physician, even the child's pediatrician, can provide guidance.

Preventing Drug and Alcohol Abuse

It is far better to educate your children on the dangers associated with drugs and alcohol and try to prevent an addiction than to try to pick up the pieces after there is a problem. Here's what you can do:

- Curb your own substance use. Children are great imitators. If they see you using drugs or alcohol, they are likely to follow your example. Be a positive role model.

- Lock prescription medications safely away, rather than simply placing them in the medicine cabinet, so that your children cannot gain access to them. It is also important to communicate with the parents of your children's friends, to make sure that they take the same precautions. Be sure to talk to your child about the dangers of abusing prescription medications.

- Know your children's friends. Perhaps you can view them more objectively than your child can. Be sure to meet your children's dates for observation and dialogue.

- Encourage your children to say no to drugs. Teach them how to make responsible decisions and how to resist peer pressure.

- Help your teenager find positive activities. A child involved with school clubs, special projects, hobbies, and sports may not feel a need to use drugs out of frustration, boredom, or the need to fit in.

- Read up on drug abuse. Share current literature about drug abuse with your child, and include materials on related problems such as teen pregnancy, failure in school, crime, and family problems. Correct misconceptions about the incidence of drug use by peers.

- Know your child. This is the most important measure you can take. Make time to talk to your child about problems, worries, dreams, and goals. If your child knows you care about his or her problems, he or she may decide not to look to drugs for solutions.

- Participate in community prevention efforts. Join and support all community-wide drug prevention activities, including Neighborhood Watch programs and cooperative programs between law enforcement and the community. Also, encourage your school to develop a drug and alcohol curriculum and teacher training on how to manage students with a drug problem.

Frequently Abused Drugs

Alcohol is the most widely used of all drugs of abuse. A new study shows that 30 percent of Americans admit they have had alcohol problems.

Cannabis includes marijuana and hashish. It is usually smoked, although sometimes swallowed in solid form, often in brownies or cookies.

Depressants depress the central nervous system and are used medically to treat tension and some neuroses, to control pain and severe diarrhea, to minimize the effects of coughs and cold symptoms, and to treat insomnia. Included among the depressants are barbiturates, narcotics, heroin, morphine, codeine, hypnotics, and methaqualone.

Stimulants, such as amphetamines and cocaine, are deadly, addictive drugs. Amphetamines are usually taken in pill form, and cocaine is commonly inhaled as a powder.

Heroin, a derivative of morphine, is extremely powerful and widely abused. Heroin use increased dramatically throughout the 1990s due to lowered cost and the higher concentrations available. A recent national survey claims that 3.5 million Americans age 12 and older have tried heroin at least once.

Powder cocaine is used by roughly 34 million Americans age 12 and older at some point in their lives, representing nearly 14 percent of the population.

Crack is a highly concentrated, extremely addictive form of cocaine. Drug dealers sell tiny plastic vials of crack for $5 and $10. Crack is much more dangerous than cocaine because it results in an intense and instant high lasting around 20 minutes called a "rush."

Helping Teens Refuse Drugs

"Say no to drugs." Young people have heard this a thousand times, but in reality, resisting peer pressure to use drugs may require more than this one word. The National Crime Prevention Council has suggested additional ways to help them refuse drugs.

- Say that you have other things to do rather than take drugs—like go to the movies, play video games, jog, watch DVDs, and play sports—and then go do them.

- Explain that drugs damage your mental and physical health and you want to be at peak performance.

Methamphetamine, often known simply as meth, is a stimulant. When taken in its crystalline, smokeable form (which looks a lot like rock candy), it is known as crystal meth. Recreational crystal meth use has been on the rise among our nation's youth, becoming increasingly popular as a club drug. Each year nearly 1,000 deaths can be traced to meth abuse.

Hallucinogens alter one's perceptions of reality. These include PCP (angel dust), LSD, mescaline, and psilocybin.

Inhalants are abused by inhaling or sniffing. Among these are gasoline, airplane glue, paint thinner, dry-cleaning solution, nitrous oxide (laughing gas), and amyl nitrate.

Ecstasy is, perhaps, the heir apparent to the "in drug" mantle. According to researchers at the University of Michigan, about 4 percent of high school seniors recently surveyed had tried ecstasy at least once.

Rohypnol, commonly known as roofies, is 10 to 20 times more powerful than valium and has become notorious as the "date-rape drug" because it is tasteless and odorless and can be easily dissolved in a drink without the victim's knowledge.

Anabolic steroids are powerful drugs chemically related to the male sex hormone testosterone, used to rapidly strengthen muscles. For this reason, they are particularly attractive to athletes.

Prescription medications, such as OxyContin, Valium, Xanax, Ritalin, and Percocet, are now the second most commonly abused drugs today.

- Don't explain anything after you say no. If necessary, strengthen your protest by a stronger "No, not ever" or "Get out of here!"
- Never attend parties where drugs and alcohol will be available.
- Associate only with friends who reject alcohol and drugs.
- Learn as much as you can about the harm of drugs and alcohol, and make certain that lines of communication between you and your parents are open on this subject.

If you or a friend needs help and are afraid to go to your parents, call (800) COCAINE, (800) ALCOHOL, or the Center for Substance Abuse

Treatment at (800) 662-HELP. You can find numbers for local hotlines in your telephone directory, usually under alcohol abuse, drug abuse, crisis services, or under a special listing at the beginning or end of the directory. Websites such as www.addictioncareoptions.com can also help you find assistance.

TEEN SUICIDE

Adolescence is a tough time, and experts estimate that each year more than 500,000 youths attempt suicide.

Physicians treating suicidal teenagers report that the preliminary signs of suicide often are vague. Many of these symptoms also signal normal adolescent development. Frequent confusion, moodiness, and depression do not imply that an adolescent is contemplating suicide, although depression does significantly increase a child's risk of committing suicide. It is also important to remember that the availability of a handgun, often kept in the home for protection, substantially increases the likelihood of a successful suicide.

Warning Signs

Suicide warning signs include sudden changes in behavior, statements about dying—any reference your teenager makes to dying must be taken seriously—and situational factors beyond a youngster's control. Pay particular attention to:

- A decline in the quality of homework
- A general lack of consistency
- Preoccupation with death
- Uncharacteristic disregard for appearance
- Withdrawal from family and peers
- Marked differences in eating and/or sleeping habits
- Substantial changes in personality
- Noticeable boredom
- Unexplained crying
- A giving away of valued possessions
- Restlessness, defiance, recklessness, violent behavior, or rebellion

- Running away from home
- Abuse of drugs and alcohol
- Prior suicide attempts

Be especially attentive if the foregoing danger signals are accompanied by disappointing experiences, including the breakup of a close or intimate relationship, failure to achieve an important goal, serious physical illness, and above all, the suicide of a peer or loved one.

What to Do

If you observe suicide warning signs, you should start a frank conversation with your teenager. Don't be afraid to come out and say, "I feel like you've been depressed. Let's talk." Be prepared for your teen to say, "I am thinking of suicide." To assess the real risk, ask specific questions such as, What is your plan? Can you tell me about your plan? Who else have you talked to about this? The more thoroughly your child has thought about suicide, the more likely it is that he or she will attempt it.

If you sense a strong intention to commit suicide, or even if you suspect one, remain with your child until you can contact someone else to help you.

Be attentive and loving. Engage in "active listening," where you paraphrase what your child is saying. This technique assures your teen that you are paying attention and are concerned about the problem. It encourages a continuous stream of communication rather than suppressed feelings through parental domination. Here are some more simple rules.

- Don't use the word *why* very much; it encourages defensiveness.
- Try to keep an open mind.
- Don't make promises you cannot keep, since you can't make everything better.
- Be honest with yourself.
- Never interrupt or offer advice while your youngster is talking. He or she might simply shut down.

If you sense a strong intention to commit suicide, or even if you suspect one, remain with your child until you can contact someone else to help you, especially if your attempts at communication are failing. Whatever you do, never handle the situation alone. Call a suicide hotline; you don't have to be the one contemplating suicide to call and get help. Contact hospitals, suicide prevention centers, and school suicide intervention programs. Reach out to a psychologist, therapist, or psychiatrist who specializes in suicide prevention and treatment. Turn to close friends, relatives, or other adults whom your teen respects.

Copycat and Cluster Suicides

More and more cases are reported of young people imitating the suicide of others or of a group of people who make a pact to die together. If your teen's friend threatens suicide or actually carries out the threat, your teen may be in danger.

Young people similar to victims in age, sex, and social activities are at a higher risk than others of a copycat or cluster suicide. If your child is exposed to either, review the warning signs and suggestions mentioned above for preventing a lone suicide.

Help establish a suicide intervention program at your teen's school to prevent imitation suicides. This program should include group discussions that provide all peers with an opportunity to share openly their feelings, thoughts, fears, and concerns regarding the suicide. Self-esteem and personal confidence should also be addressed. School professionals should be available and accessible to the students, especially those reluctant to talk to a teacher or a group. And if your teen—or his or her friends—know someone who is suicidal, they must tell an adult.

CHAPTER 18

CYBERCRIME

Today more money resides in computers than in wallets. Computers also contain valuable information and intellectual capital that needs to be preserved from disclosure, misuse, or destruction. With new viruses and tools to steal personal information being developed every day, it's imperative to stay on top of hackers and what has come to be known as crimeware.

HACKING, VIRUSES, DATA BREACHES, AND IDENTITY THEFT

The traditional mainframe computer has been replaced with a network of desktop, laptop, and microcomputers, often interconnected through the Internet, wide-area networks, or wireless connections. Add to this the explosion in Personal Digital Assistants (PDAs), mobile phones with wireless e-mail capabilities, smartphones, remote computing for traveling employees, employees working from home, and individual personal computers connected to the Internet, and the result is an ever-increasing opportunity for computer hackers and criminals to exploit weaknesses in poorly implemented computer security and to commit crimes via online scams or fraud.

It's All Too Easy

Computer crime is surprisingly easy to carry out. Instructions for creating damaging computer viruses and malicious code are readily available on the Internet. The only resources required are a personal computer and an Internet connection.

If you receive an e-mail claiming to be from your bank or credit card company, don't click on the link in the e-mail, no matter how authentic the message appears.

The Internet can also be used by pedophiles to prey on children. If fact, there are numerous chat rooms and discussion groups on the Internet where pedophiles share information. The pornography industry uses the Internet to distribute images and streaming video of a graphic and sexual nature. And as the Internet is increasingly used to buy and sell goods and services, criminals continue to find new and inventive ways to commit on-line fraud.

Computer Abuse Techniques

Hackers and computer criminals are continually developing new and more sophisticated computer menaces. Here are some of the more prominent ones:

- **Trojan Horse Programs.** A Trojan Horse is a malicious software program ("malware") that appears to be useful but in fact is designed to cause harm to the infected computer. Authors of these programs might e-mail them to recipients under the guise of a free utility program, such as a screensaver. However, when the program is downloaded, it unloads a hidden program, often allowing the author unauthorized access to the user's computer without his knowledge. Trojan Horses can be used to log keystrokes to steal information such as passwords and credit card numbers, corrupt files in a subtle way, install a virus, and even harvest e-mail addresses and use them for spam.
- **Backdoor and Remote Administration.** These are programs specifically designed to give intruders remote access to a computer without the

Are Cyberattacks an Imminent Threat?

More than 300 computing and computer-security executives in 14 different countries believe their companies have already been victimized by sophisticated government intruders, according to a recent report issued by the Center for Strategic and International Studies and the software-protection company McAfee. And even more believe that a major cyber incident—one that causes loss of life or an outage or company failure—is expected to happen within a year. This study, based on responses from 600 executives, indicates that the threat of cyberattacks is on the rise and has become a very real and serious issue.

Even more alarming is the fact that more than half of these executives believe their own nation's laws are inadequate for warding off these attacks and that the United States is the most vulnerable, followed by China and Russia.

The report focused specifically on critical infrastructure—networks such as the financial system, transmission lines for gas and electricity, water supply, and voice- and data communication.

The solution, according to McAfee? To better protect industrial systems or to move to more private networks and not use the open Internet.

user's knowledge. They are often attached to a Trojan Horse. They can give the hacker "backdoor" access to your computer as a Denial of Service (DoS) agent to attack other computers or send information from your computer to the hacker's computer.

- **Denial of Service (DoS).** Denial of Service attacks are designed to force a computer to become so busy processing data that it becomes unusable. DoS attacks are often launched on domain servers in order to force a website to crash or become unresponsive. A disgruntled employee may be motivated to launch this type of attack, or an activist group targeting a firm's stance on a controversial topic. Likewise, there are more and more certain reports of government officials utilizing this type of attack—as a form of Cyber Warfare—to disrupt an enemy's information infrastructure prior to an invasion.

Identity Theft

Always remember that if someone steals your personal information online, they can electronically clone you and steal indiscriminately through transfers, bank withdrawals, and credit card purchases. Computer users often provide detailed personal identification information through careless Web surfing, through social media like Facebook, or by using a computer infected with spyware. Others fall victim to phishing attacks, where hackers trick e-mail recipients into visiting bogus websites to divulge bank-account details or credit card information. Follow these tips to protect yourself from online identity theft:

- If you receive an e-mail claiming to be from your bank or credit card company, don't click on the link in the e-mail, no matter how authentic the message appears. Banks or credit card companies will never send you an unsolicited e-mail asking you to divulge bank account details or credit card information.
- Remember to monitor your credit by obtaining a free credit report annually from one of the three major credit-reporting agencies. Likewise, consider subscribing to a credit monitoring service, which can alert you immediately to any suspicious transactions that would affect your credit.

- **Botnets.** Botnets are networks of computers controlled remotely without the knowledge of the owner and are often created through the distribution of a Trojan Horse. The computers that form the botnet can be programmed to redirect transmissions of data to a specific computer.
- **E-mail Viruses.** Tens of thousands of known viruses can, if they find their way onto your computer, affect your computer system, from displaying annoying messages to deleting important data. These viruses are often distributed in the form of an attachment to an e-mail message. In some cases, hackers will disguise the origination of the e-mail and make it appear as if it were sent from a familiar address so you'll be more likely to open it.

- **E-mail Spoofing.** E-mail spoofing is when an e-mail appears to have been sent from one source but in reality was sent from another. Hackers use this to trick the recipient into releasing personal information or a password. One common scheme involves an e-mail that appears to originate from a bank advising the recipient to provide bank account details and PIN numbers in order to verify her account. The hacker then uses this information to access the victim's bank account.
- **Chat Clients.** Instant messaging or chat clients allow users to exchange dialogue, Web URL's, and even files between computers on the Internet. Because the hacker can download executable code through these exchanges, hackers can use chat clients to remotely inject their malicious codes onto a victim's computer.
- **Packet Sniffing.** A packet sniffer is a program that allows the user to capture data packets over the Internet. These data packets may contain sensitive personal information or proprietary information if they are sent unencrypted. With the use of a packet sniffer, a hacker could glean hundreds or thousands of usernames and passwords and launch widespread attacks—or steal personal data for identity theft.
- **Manipulation of Data.** Thieves can use computers to manipulate data for embezzlement or to commit fraud, including creating false invoices for equipment or writing checks in favor of the computer operator.
- **Telecommunications Phreaking.** Hackerslang for attacks on phone, PBX, or voice-mail systems, "phreaking" may result in toll fraud, misuse of systems, or the interception or destruction of valuable data.
- **Hardware thefts, software piracy, and proprietary information theft.** This includes the theft of computers, printers, programs microprocessor chips, or trade secrets.

Portable Media Safety

External hard drives, flash memory, and USB thumb drives are commonly used to share files with colleagues. Exercise care to keep these devices from falling into the wrong hands. Use passwords and enable encryption on your portable media devices. Do not plug a USB device into your computer unless you know where it came from, as it may contain malicious codes that can infect your computer.

INTERNET SCAMS

Given the amount of money flowing through cyberspace, it's not surprising that Internet-related scams have mushroomed. Some common Internet scams include:

- **Nigerian Fraud.** An unsolicited e-mail—ostensibly from a government official from a country like Nigeria—that tells the victim he can share in a large amount of money if he uses his bank account to transfer these funds to an offshore account. The scammer takes the bank account information and disappears.

- **Phishing Schemes.** A phony e-mail that appears to be from a credit card company or bank to a recipient, with a request for account-update details. The e-mail may contain a link to a website that appears to be legitimate, but the sole purpose is for the scammers to obtain personal identification information and bank or credit card details used in identity theft. The perpetrator uses the information to create bogus credit accounts, which are charged to the victim, or to sell the information to other criminals for fraudulent purposes.

- **Fake Work-at-Home Offers.** These often take the form of employment listings on job-opportunity websites, where scammers offer applicants the opportunity to work at home—if they provide bank information to get set up in business. The jobs and the scammers vanish once the victim provides the information.

Log on to your e-mail only when you are at your own desk, so that no one else can receive your messages or send one in your name.

- **eBay scams.** These scams involve fraud and misrepresentation by sellers of items listed on Internet auction sites like eBay. Victims give up passwords and other account information—even wire funds abroad—at scammers' request.

- **Sabotage.** Other criminal specialties that have surfaced over the last few years include "crashers," who purposely damage computer systems, and "cyberpunks," who threaten to use computers to paralyze the econ-

Laptop Computers and Wi-Fi

Always keep in mind that laptop computers are an attractive target for thieves and that the data on them may be far more valuable than the computer itself. Laptops should always be in your possession—never left in checked baggage or in an unattended vehicle when traveling. Avoid flashy or expensive-looking computer cases; they will certainly attract a thief's attention.

Use caution when utilizing wireless network services (Wi-Fi). With unencrypted Wi-Fi every password, e-mail message, and Web page can be read by any other user on that network. That means you should only use secure (encrypted) e-mail and never enter a password or confidential information on a Web page over Wi-Fi unless it is a secure connection. Also, enable a password in order to log onto your computer when powering up. Never make it easy for a thief to get your laptop or the information contained on it.

omy or destroy worldwide communications systems. Some use viruses to damage computer systems or networks. To lower the risk of getting a virus, never copy or download software unless you know and trust its source, and be sure to use an anti-virus program that can detect and eradicate viruses. Since new viruses turn up at the rate of 20 or more each month, be sure to keep current on the updated virus profiles provided regularly by the manufacturers of your anti-virus package.

- **Theft.** Whether an employee uses the computer at work to mail out bills for a private business on the side, place orders for merchandise and have it sent to an unauthorized location, transfer negligible amounts from each transaction to his or her own account (a technique called "salami slicing"), or steal data in the form of computer programs or output, theft of computer services is extremely common. Computers can also be used for much more sophisticated theft, such as complex financial swindles. False companies can be established, or misleading information can be provided to investors.

E-mail Traps

E-mail is susceptible to many pitfalls, dangers, and breaches of security. Electronic messages can be accessed, intercepted, read, and altered

Power Problems

Computers are sensitive to power glitches and interruptions, potentially damaging internal components and making the computer inoperable. Install a surge protector on your computer to protect it against power surges.

unless proper precautions are taken. For example, e-mail stored on backup media for safety can be easily loaded onto another computer for illicit access.

Consider this scenario: An e-mail message from the company's CEO stated that the company was undergoing a major reorganization, and substantial layoffs should be expected—but the message was a fraud. A prankster engaging in the practice known as "spoofing" decided to create havoc among company employees.

How can you—and your company—protect against this type of fraud? Employ a cryptographic technique known as a "digital signature," as well as passwords and encryption systems (which allow coding and decoding).

Here are some other ways to get around e-mail scams:

- Log on to your e-mail only when you are at your own desk, so that no one else can receive your messages or send one in your name.
- Log off your computer when you leave to deny access to anyone interested in snooping.
- Be sure to change all passwords often.
- Before opening e-mail attachments, be certain that you know the source of the e-mail and the attachment. Computer viruses spread quickly because they can use e-mail addresses from a victim's computer to resend the virus to each of those addresses.
- Never open unsolicited e-mail, or spam. Simply delete it without reading it. Besides being a nuisance, spam is a major source of virus distribution.

HOW TO PROTECT YOUR COMPUTER

While the Internet has many virtues, you need to implement security precautions to protect your computer from many of its unpleasant aspects, such as viruses, spam, and hacker attempts.

Be sure to use a firewall to protect your computer from network attacks and malicious users. The firewall may be a part of your DSL or cable modem, or it can be software that is installed on your computer. Firewalls act by screening the network traffic and filtering out unwanted traffic.

Install antivirus software on your computer and download and install updates frequently. Some of the antivirus products on the market automatically check for updates.

Perhaps you've installed a wireless home network or Wi-Fi, allowing you to operate your computer from anywhere in the house without the need to run a network cable directly to the computer. However, without proper security precautions, anyone in close proximity to the wireless network could easily intercept your e-mail or use your Internet service without your knowledge. Always enable the encryption option that comes with the wireless LAN (Local Area Network) device.

Turn off your computer or disconnect it from the Internet when it is not in use. There is no way for a hacker to gain access to your computer if it is off or disconnected from the Internet.

PART FOUR

COMMUNITY SECURITY

CHAPTER 19

NEIGHBORHOOD CRIME PREVENTION

The best way to avoid becoming a victim of crime is to prevent it in the first place. And one of the best ways to prevent it is for neighbors to join together to keep crime out of the neighborhood.

FORMING PROGRAMS WITH YOUR NEIGHBORS

Approximately 50 million Americans participate in some sort of crime-stopping organization such as a Neighborhood Watch or Block Club. These programs are not difficult to develop, and they have been found to reduce the chances of victimization. At the very least, the programs increase the cohesiveness, unity, and solidarity of your neighborhood. These characteristics alone will have an impact on crime.

Block Clubs

Block clubs generally consist of the residents of one block. People in a block club organize efforts to educate neighbors and make them aware of crime and public safety. Many block clubs also conduct street surveillance. Block-club participants, including children, are encouraged to report crimes and suspicious-looking people to the police.

Don't Fail Your Neighborhood Watch

If you start or get involved with a Neighborhood Watch program, make sure you stick with it. The biggest problem with these programs is that members have a tendency after an initial rush of activity to let the organization stagnate or to stop participating. A non-operating program will assist only those whose activities it was designed to curtail.

Neighborhood Watch

Neighborhood Watch programs are similar to block clubs but cover a broader area. Participants are trained by police crime-prevention units to report crime to law enforcement and suspicious events or people in the neighborhood. Neighborhood Watch programs may also offer short- and long-term victim assistance, including emotional support after the crime and direction on how to get through the complexities of the criminal justice system (see chapter 30).

Interviews with criminals reveal that the Neighborhood Watch program is a very effective deterrent against robbery. Most burglars claim that they would leave a neighborhood if they were observed or challenged by a resident. Contact your police or sheriff's department for information on the national Neighborhood Watch program.

Citizen Patrols

The fear of crime has motivated neighbors to organize crime patrols. In some areas residents carry out the patrol activities, and in others they hire professionally trained security officers. Some patrols concentrate on specific buildings or housing areas, while others cover entire neighborhoods. The patrols are usually equipped with citizens band radios.

Many neighborhood patrols have followed the lead of the police and have taken up bicycle patrols, which offer more visibility and mobility than foot patrols, and which offer more interaction with neighbors than motor vehicle patrols. Bicycles can also get into areas automobiles can't, such as alleyways and parks.

Unlike building patrols, which may prevent unwanted visitors from entering buildings, neighborhood patrols cannot deny people access to their streets. Instead, they concentrate on uncovering suspicious and criminal behavior, which they report to the police. Some patrols also perform social service functions, such as escorting senior citizens on shopping trips. Others monitor police activities and may be organized when police-community relations need improvement.

Most burglars claim that they would leave a neighborhood if they were observed or challenged by a resident.

Crime-Reporting Programs

If you're interested in crime-reporting programs for your community, you may want to consider some of the following options:

- **The Whistle-Stop program.** Whistle-carrying citizens sound off when they are victimized or when they see a crime in progress. The whistles serve as a community signal system. Neighbors who hear the sound also blow their whistles to disrupt crime and alert the police.
- **Radio watch projects.** Radio-equipped cars patrol neighborhood streets, looking for criminal activity or suspicious people. When the drivers spot something amiss, they report it, either to a dispatcher who then notifies the police or directly to the police on special emergency frequencies.
- **Dedicated telephone lines.** These projects provide special telephone lines that allow people to report suspicious behavior or criminal activity without revealing their identity. Law-enforcement or civilian agencies then offer rewards to callers for their assistance. Crime Stoppers is a successful example of this type of program.
- **Drug watch.** This recent but excellent program involves the community in combating drug dealing. One such program in New York City provides its members with drug-watch training sessions. They see slides of drug arrests, drug-selling locations, and visible signs of drug transactions. A retired police lieutenant with experience in narcotics enforcement teaches participants how to accurately report drug dealing to the police.

Other Community Programs

The following community programs may give you further ideas for ways to stop crime.

- **Anticrime campaigns.** These organized neighborhood citizen groups combat crime by observing and reporting.

- **Police-community relations programs.** Their objectives are to improve formal and informal communication between local police and neighborhood residents to prevent crime and to combat juvenile delinquency.

- **Community policing.** In this situation, residents work with police officers to develop creative ways to combat "quality-of-life offenses," including public drunkenness, prostitution, and low-level drug dealing, and neighborhood deterioration problems such as uncollected trash, run-down housing, and absence of drug-treatment facilities, all of which set the stage for social decay and criminal behavior. Residents are also empowered to take a proactive role in solving neighborhood crime problems, helping staff local police stations, offering information on local crimes, helping identify neighborhood delinquents, or supervising sports activities for community youth. For more information on community policing, go to www.policing.com.

- **Auxiliary or reserve police.** Many police departments have helped organize auxiliary-police organizations, where civilian volunteers are trained in police methods and procedures. They wear uniforms similar to those of police officers, and they often patrol on foot and in vehicles supplied by the police department. Their main function is crime prevention and deterrence. They report crimes to the police but will come to a person's aid if necessary. Auxiliary police officers are usually discouraged from making arrests. Instead, they are urged to summon police officers to do this. Auxiliary police officers often assist regular police officers in crowd and traffic control, at demonstrations, or at an accident scene.

Vigilantism

Although it is always a good idea for community members to come together to try to prevent crime in the neighborhood, make sure that a vigilante mentality does not develop. You must let law-enforcement officials enforce and uphold the law. You should never try to take the law into your own hands. Never go after criminals yourself or try to punish them in some way that you see fit. You must have faith that our criminal justice system will be effective in bringing offenders to justice and respect the right of every American citizen to due process.

Although it is always a good idea for community members to come together to try to prevent crime in the neighborhood, make sure that a vigilante mentality does not develop.

Booby Traps

While "booby traps" usually calls to mind exploding devices, there are some non-lethal booby traps that can be used to defend your home and your community against unwanted trespassers. For example, you can protect your property by setting up booby traps that transmit a strong electric shock to anyone who trespasses. You can also use noisemakers and pepper sprays—just about anything can be turned into a booby trap.

Keep in mind, however, that depending on where you live, booby traps may be illegal. This is especially true if the trap results in a fatality; you will not be able to hide behind a self-defense argument. As a result, you should probably stick to more traditional means of security such as alarm systems, Neighborhood Watches, and guard dogs.

PRIVATE-SECTOR SECURITY

Lacking most of the police powers of their public-sector counterparts, the private-security industry has long emphasized the prevention of crime. Private security is not concerned with arrests, only with preventing incidents.

Businesses are using private-sector security more than ever, often in capacities once performed by the police, such as employee or customer protection or in escort service to parking areas. In this way, private security supplements the public police.

Private security in various parts of the country is also expanding its role in public-building protection, residential-neighborhood patrol, traffic control, parking enforcement, crowd control, and court security.

The problem with private-security forces is that an ill-trained force can be more dangerous than none at all. An officer's abusive or unwarranted behavior can lead to lawsuits or violent confrontation. Should you decide to employ private security, be sure to hire security officers from a reputable company that ensures stringent standards of recruitment, screening, and training. On the whole, private-sector security is a good idea because it can complement traditional venues of security. But remember: It is unwise to believe that writing a check is going to make someone safe. Personal safety starts with personal responsibility.

The problem with private-security forces is that an ill-trained force can be more dangerous than none at all.

INDIVIDUAL CRIME PREVENTION

The programs and strategies listed below, which rely on individual crime-prevention efforts, may be useful in your neighborhood:

- **Residential risk assessments.** A residential security inspection often conducted by a law-enforcement crime-prevention bureau officer offers a practical and simple solution to security evaluation. It usually consists of a thorough examination of your residence to identify its security deficiencies. The survey determines the protection required and shows how to minimize opportunities for criminals. Studies have shown that such surveys reduce your chances of victimization.
- **Property-marking programs.** Residents borrow marking equipment, often from the police department or a civic organization, and engrave identification numbers on portable property. The numbers are then recorded with the police. Program participants post decals on their doors or windows indicating that their property has been marked. Marked property is less appealing to a thief, and in the event of a theft, your personal property may be identified and returned to you.

This crime-prevention effort became popular over the last few years and has been shown to reduce burglary rates.

- **Assisting elderly neighbors.** Individual crime-prevention efforts may be as simple as replacing a burned-out lightbulb for an elderly neighbor, thus increasing his or her nighttime security. You can also take your elderly neighbor to the bank to deposit a Social Security check, and, while you are there, point out the advantage of electronic mail deposits to eliminate the possibility of mailed checks being diverted to criminals.

- **Block parents.** These neighborhood volunteers offer guidance or shelter for neighborhood children who may need assistance. On a more formal basis, McGruff Houses perform these and other services and have the additional advantage of being part of a nationally advertised endeavor to provide for neighborhood children.

A nosy neighbor can be a neighborhood treasure who will tell you when your floodlight is out, that you have allowed the vegetation to grow too high around your trashcan area, or that you failed to close your garage. When you reciprocate and advise your neighbors of security shortcomings at *their* homes, you have the beginnings of a crime-fighting neighborhood organization.

CRIME PREVENTION THROUGH ENVIRONMENTAL DESIGN

Along with enhancing lighting around your home and eliminating overgrown hedges and other places criminals can hide (see chapters 1 and 2), you can take additional steps to prevent crime in your neighborhood, primarily through environmental design, such as incorporating benches, hedges, or fences into a security plan. Here's how:

Divide common lawn areas into private yards or patios using small picket fences, well-trimmed shrubbery, or concrete curbing. These simple steps can make it easier to distinguish between people who belong in an area and those who don't. They will also extend the social control of residents from their houses and apartments into nearby common areas. Enhance this approach by limiting the number of public-access points to your apartment building or condominium complex and by providing the remaining entrances with adequate lighting, visibility, and security.

Get traffic rerouted so that the residential character of your neighborhood is preserved. Modifying the environmental design of streets reduces crime. You may also want certain avenues narrowed and selected streets turned into cul-de-sacs to avoid through traffic.

Improve the appearance and attractiveness of your house, property, and areas shared with your neighbors to promote a sense of responsibility among all of you. Decorative painting, lighting, installation of benches at strategic spots, and careful landscaping will motivate neighbors to care for each other's welfare and safety. (See "What Is the Criminal Thinking?" page 5.) These steps also will increase the use of streets, parks, and surrounding land. Criminals are less likely to commit crimes in attractive, well-populated neighborhoods than in run-down, deserted areas.

CHAPTER 20

SCHOOL AND CAMPUS SECURITY

School shootings like Columbine and Virginia Tech made national news and thus educated Americans on the need for heightened security on school campuses. But there are many other incidents of school violence that happen each day that haven't made headlines. You need to know how to protect your children from these acts— and teach them how to protect themselves.

PERSONAL SAFETY FOR STUDENTS

By the time your children are old enough to attend school, they should know the basics of personal safety. Still, until you are sure they can travel alone—they know their way or can take the school bus—drive or walk with them to and from school.

If they travel on their own, do not let them take dangerous shortcuts. They should not walk past construction sites, empty stores, or deserted buildings, and they should avoid walking near or through parks. Check immediately by cell phone to the child or to a school official. Forbid them to hitchhike or accept rides from anyone other than those you have designated beforehand. They must learn to tell you and their teachers about any strangers who approach them.

Martial Arts

Older children may benefit from learning jujitsu, karate, or another form of self-defense. Martial arts encourage self-confidence and discipline and may assist your child if he or she is confronted by a threatening person at school— or anywhere else.

Remind them not to take large sums of money to school and to keep as few valuables with them as possible. This is especially true for older children. Encourage them to place all personal possessions in locked school lockers and never to give out the lock's combination. They should report crimes or situations involving drugs or alcohol in or around the school to the school's main office, or at least to you. Then it is up to you to alert the school.

Promote the idea that it is *their* school, and encourage them to work with teachers and school personnel to improve awareness, protection, and prevention.

Warn your children about the danger of walking alone in deserted hallways, corridors, and stairwells—no matter what their ages. "Safety in numbers" rings true at school as well as on the street.

Know your children's playmates, friends, teachers, and school officials, and communicate with them. Demand proper security measures in the schools, especially in high-crime areas. If weapons and violence are threats to your children's safety, insist that the school install metal detectors, X-ray bag scanners, and ID card–controlled access systems. Also, insist that your school have an adequate staff of well-trained school safety officers. Suggest self-defense instruction. Become involved in the school board or parent organization, such as the PTA, even if only by voicing your dissatisfaction and insisting upon safe conditions in the schools.

Teach your children to keep an eye out for violence and vandalism against the school. Some schools promote a Neighborhood Watch that enlists neighbors near the school to watch the school and report suspicious incidents to authorities, while other programs focus on student involvement in deterring vandalism and repairing its consequences. Stress the undesirable effects of destructive behavior and encourage your children to report vandals to school authorities or to you. Promote the idea that it is *their* school, and encourage them to work with teachers and school personnel to improve awareness, protection, and prevention.

BULLYING

One of the biggest security threats to your child while he is at school can come from other students. Bullying—when a child is repeatedly subjected to negative treatment by other students—is a widespread problem. The actions of a bully can range from taunting and gestures to physical violence. Cyberbullying is an increasing problem.

Here are some things to watch out for:

- signs of physical violence, such as bruises and scrapes
- refusal to go to school
- unusual anxiety
- nightmares
- sudden poor grades
- noticeable isolation from others

And what you can do to help:

- Encourage your child to speak openly to you about what is happening.
- Keep a log of when the bullying occurs.
- Be a good listener and don't overreact.
- Encourage your child to ignore the bully's taunts and to just walk away.
- Help children try to avoid being in the wrong place at the wrong time.
- Talk to your child's teachers and principal about your concerns.
- Make sure the school has adequate adult supervision in the hallways, bathrooms, and schoolyard.
- If your child does not want you to get the school involved, try setting a time limit. For example, if the bullying doesn't stop in two weeks, then seek assistance from the school. If your child is insistent that you not tell anyone, then unless the situation is dangerous, try to respect that wish. But continue communication with the child about the situation.

Special Considerations for Teachers

Communication is necessary for effective teacher-pupil relationships, but in some cases it may not be enough to prevent increasing violence and abuse. What can you do to protect yourself and at the same time fulfill your professional obligations?

- Establish good communication with your students, and involve them in setting up classroom rules, but be sure they understand that you are in control. When trying to control students, never use sarcasm, shouting, or embarrassment, and do not threaten punishments unless you are willing to carry them out. Know the problem students, and consult with other school personnel to determine how to handle them.
- Immediately report to administrators and the police any threats by students. Never walk in secluded areas alone or stay late at school without others present.
- Help build or maintain self-esteem by supporting your students' successes. Most students still look up to their teachers; your advice may be just what they need.

The Rise of Anti-Violence Curricula

Many schools are now building anti-violence programs directly into their curricula. Some of these programs teach elementary students social skills, anger management, impulse control, and empathy. Studies have found that the effects of these lessons are immediate and long-lasting, resulting in substantial declines in aggressive behavior. High schools throughout the nation also use anti-violence curricula to teach their students about problem-solving techniques, as well as about how violent interactions may begin and escalate and how to manage conflicts with peers.

CRIME ON COLLEGE AND UNIVERSITY CAMPUSES

Although many young people between 18 and 22 feel that they are immune to crime, statistics prove otherwise. Crime on campus includes aggravated assault, sex offenses, robberies—even homicide. And campus crime can be committed by outsiders or students themselves. College students need to know how to protect themselves from all types of crime.

Choosing a College

Most parents and teenagers select a college based on its tuition, size, location, and type of student body, as well as its reputation for teaching, research, and social activities. However, the incidence of crime on campus is also becoming an increasingly important consideration.

When considering a college, always ask about its safety record and security features. Consult the FBI's *Crime in the United States: Uniform Crime Reports*, available online at www.fbi.gov, which includes information about crime on the nation's campuses. Colleges and universities are required to report campus crimes to the United States Department of Education as mandated by the "Disclosure of Campus Security Policy and Campus Crime Statistics Act," also known as the Clery Act. This information is available online at the U.S. Department of Education's website. Also ask about crime-prevention orientation, a mechanism for immediately informing students about serious crimes, a student newspaper that provides information on campus crime, and

Campus Security Basics

Although safety experts debate certain aspects of campus security, many agree on these precautions:

- All buildings should be secured on nights and weekends so that only students and employees with proper identification can enter.
- An emergency notification system must be in place so that all students, faculty, and employees can be alerted in the case of an emergency.
- Possession, consumption, and sale of drugs and alcohol cannot be permitted on campus.
- All weapons of any type must be prohibited on the campus.
- Security personnel should be on campus and accessible 24 hours a day, including safety escorts.
- All emergency exits from buildings should be clearly marked.
- A daily crime log should be kept and made accessible to the public.
- Campus dorm or resident advisers should be trained in the recognition and awareness of emotionally troubled students and behaviors associated with physical abuse, substance abuse, and potential suicide.

policies on drug abuse, alcohol consumption, sexual harassment, and sexual assault.

Compare the amount that the college or university spends per capita on their law enforcement or security program with other schools. It is also a good idea to research the number of incidents that occurred in the preceding three years.

Be certain that your college or university has enough campus law-enforcement officers. *Crime in the United States* provides data on the number of officers and civilian law-enforcement employees who work at selected campuses. You can also request this information from your college representative, admissions officer, or counselor.

Security in Dorms and on Campus

Student dorms are, in fact, apartment buildings, and the security measures in a dorm must be no less serious than those for an apartment. There are also special considerations for dorm students, who are in much closer contact with others (their dorm mates). Many more people are likely to be in and out of a dorm room than a typical apartment.

As a college student, you can protect your residence by following a few simple security rules.

- Note the conditions of door and window locks, and the lighting both outside and inside your room. Demand improvements if necessary.
- Always lock your doors and windows, even if you plan to be gone only a short time.
- Become familiar with your roommates and neighbors, and encourage their efforts at crime prevention.
- Prepare for dangerous encounters by discussing what you would do if you were threatened or attacked.
- Look out for each other's safety, and report any crime to the campus police.
- Don't keep valuables or large sums of money in your dorm room.
- Keep a complete and up-to-date inventory of your valuables.
- Determine if the campus security office has an organized tagging or labeling system for stereos, TVs, computers, and so on. Use the system if it's offered.
- Always lock your bike or vehicle securely, and be cautious in parking areas. Park only in well-lighted areas that are well traveled.
- Maintain a record of anyone with a key to your room, and be sure to request a change of lock if a key falls into the wrong hands or if it is lost.
- Do not leave visitors alone in your room when you are away. Never let a stranger into the room, especially if you are alone.

In addition to dorm security, follow these rules for campus security:

- Exercise caution when giving out your phone number.
- Keep a list of emergency numbers handy, including campus security.
- Provide an updated list of emergency and next-of-kin information to the college's registration office.
- Do not give your student ID number or Social Security number to anyone other than college faculty, administration, or staff. Never leave any papers lying around that have your ID number on them, especially in registration areas.

- Secure your personal belongings in class, the restroom, library, cafeteria, and computer facilities.
- Never let your handbag, books, or backpack out of your sight.
- Avoid deserted and isolated areas such as empty classrooms, stairwells, elevators, library stacks, laboratories, and department offices.
- Follow safety rules when walking alone off campus. Be especially alert if the surrounding area is a high-crime neighborhood. Ask the security office for an escort or shuttle service across campus at night, or form your own.
- Avoid exercising or jogging outside at night or early in the morning, unless with a group.
- Ask your security office for further crime-prevention tips, and be aware of security problems on campus.
- Identify two separate exits from each campus building that you frequent.

Fraternity and Sorority Hazing

Fraternities and sororities are known for their hazing rituals, in which prospective members, or pledges, are required to carry out dangerous or humiliating tasks before they are granted membership to the group.

While hazing is illegal in most states and is prohibited by most colleges and universities, these rituals continue at colleges and universities across the country and the dangers are very real. Make sure you speak to your college-bound sons and daughters about the dangers of these hazing rituals, and encourage them to avoid any fraternity or sorority that uses them.

CHAPTER 21

SECURITY IN HOSPITALS AND NURSING HOMES

As hospitals and nursing homes become more crowded, the need for security and safety is increasing. Patients, staff, family, and other visitors need to exercise special care to protect themselves and their loved ones. This is particularly true in the current healthcare environment, where reduction in staffing is a common occurrence.

STAYING SAFE IN THE HOSPITAL

Hospitals present unique security problems because they operate 24 hours a day and often have open campuses. Another unique feature of hospitals is that they never close. Nights, weekends, and holidays large numbers of staff members—including physicians, nurses, health aides, pharmacists, cashiers, clerks, housekeepers, and repair and maintenance people— enter and leave through the many often-unlocked entrances and doors. The patients, on the other hand, are unable to provide minimum defense against crime, because they are often too ill to walk, move, or talk.

In such circumstances staff, patients, family, and visitors must take special precautions, but unfortunately, these groups are often distracted with medical concerns. Research conducted by the International Association for Hospital Security and Safety (IAHSS) found that theft was the most common crime occurring at hospitals.

For a scheduled admission, leave all unnecessary items at home. Bring only your insurance information and other pertinent medical records. For an unscheduled admission, turn over all valuables to a family member. If no family members are present, contact the nursing staff and request them to secure the items. Some hospitals require waivers absolving them of responsibility for valuables not secured in their vaults. Patients who are too ill at the time of admission to secure their personal belongings can request that a nurse provide a safe-deposit envelope to store valuables. The envelope should be sealed in the patient's presence and signed on the outside by the patient and the hospital representative. The inventory list should be placed in the patient's medical care record file until release and redemption of the envelope.

Other rules for protection against hospital crime are obvious.

- Do not wear expensive jewelry.
- Keep only small change and a few small bills in a drawer next to your bed, and don't leave clothing or drugs lying around.
- Lock away your wallet, credit cards, keys, rings, watches, and other valuables. (A thief can steal a purse with house keys and an address, then ransack the patient's empty home.)
- Do not place dentures, hearing aids, eyeglasses, radios, or similar objects in the safety deposit box, because they are likely to be damaged during handling and storage. (Many hospitals require patients to remove their dentures, because precious metal in them attracts thieves.)
- Immediately alert the staff if you observe any suspicious behavior or individuals.

Many hospital and healthcare facilities provide security brochures. When you are admitted, ask for a copy of the facility's security rules or brochure. Make use of the security suggestions and services that are offered. And remember, if there is a theft, notify hospital security at once.

Emergency Room

Because of its very nature, the emergency room is a potentially risky area. Intoxicated individuals, people high on drugs, criminals, and disoriented people arrive regularly at emergency rooms. Many of them are brought there against their will by friends or family members, and some may even be carrying concealed weapons.

The long waiting periods before treatment often make emergency-room patients anxious. Beware of overwrought individuals, but never attempt to calm them down or provide assistance to resolve a dispute. It is the job of hospital personnel, especially the security department, to handle these highly volatile situations. If someone nearby is disruptive or abusive, change seats immediately, moving as far as possible from the area of disturbance, and if safe to do so, alert the hospital staff. The new seat should be near the nursing station or at least within sight of the emergency-room security officer or other hospital personnel.

Be particularly careful if no security officer is on duty. Do not wander around hospital corridors while waiting for treatment, especially at night, when many areas are deserted. Finally, keep track of your valuables.

Labor and Delivery Unit

The safest place in a hospital ought to be the maternity ward, where mothers can peacefully recover from childbirth and rest knowing that their newborns are safe. However, all hospitals are concerned about infant abductions and need to take appropriate precautions. Dressed as hospital personnel, nurses, and physicians, kidnappers may gain entry to the newborn section, nursery, or mothers' rooms and abduct infants.

Well before you are due to give birth, ask about your obstetrician's hospital affiliations and research those hospitals. Check the security procedures for the maternity ward and newborn nursery at each hospital. Make certain that the entire maternity ward is a restricted area. At the very minimum, the newborn section should be locked at all times, with carefully monitored visiting privileges. You should inquire how patients and staff are educated regarding special precautions.

What else do hospitals do to enhance security in the maternity ward? Some monitor patient rooms and nurseries, while others place special identity bracelets or anklets on newborns; these cannot be easily removed and will sound an alarm if the child passes out of the maternity ward area. Ideally, the parent should wear an ID band that matches that of the infant. This not only provides help with administrative problems but may also prove useful in kidnappings. Another system utilizes sensors on both the infant and the mother. When the two sensors are placed next to one another, a tone sounds. If the wrong infant and mother are paired, a different tone sounds. In summary, you should never give your newborn to anyone you are not 100 percent certain is a staff member on the unit!

Visit the hospital. Are you challenged when you walk past the entry point into the maternity ward? Do all hospital personnel who care for the babies wear uniforms of the same type and color, bearing special employee identification badges? If not, anyone could don hospital garb, mix with the staff, and walk off with your newborn.

Stroll the corridors to get a sense of the security. If dissatisfied, there probably is something wrong. Discuss your impressions with a hospital representative. If unhappy with the response, choose another hospital.

Parking Areas

Parking lots and garages at hospitals may be even more isolated and deserted than those at shopping centers or malls and are accessible 24 hours a day. The last thing you want after visiting a sick loved one is to find your car vandalized or stolen. Even worse, on the way to your car, you may be robbed or sexually assaulted. Most hospital security departments provide you with an escort to your car. If you feel uncomfortable going to your vehicle alone, do not hesitate to take advantage of this service. Many of the security procedures discussed for parking while shopping should be followed for hospital parking as well (see chapter 12).

Precautions for Hospital Staff

Because hospital employees come and go at all hours, you need to be especially careful in the parking lot. If your hospital separates employee from visitor parking, take advantage of this safeguard. Allow security to protect you by spotting loiterers who can easily be identified between shift changes.

Be alert and cautious when police officers bring a prisoner in to be treated. And be particularly careful as you walk around the maze of deserted hallways.

Some hospitals provide training in security procedures for all employees. Topics covered include managing intruders, recognizing the beginning stages of altercation, and intervening without escalating the altercation.

CRIMINAL MISCONDUCT IN NURSING HOMES

Nursing homes differ according to cost, level of medical care, convenience of location, visiting rights, accreditation or licensing, quality of food, privacy, adequate lighting, proper staffing, numbers of personnel and atmosphere—and security and safety. Highly publicized scandals and investigations into criminal misconduct by nursing home owners over the last several years have highlighted the terrible dangers and conditions found in some nursing homes. Patients and their families should practice the same precautions regarding their valuables as previously described, on page 256.

When searching for a source of elder care, check with your local agency on aging. Also consult The American Association of Retired Persons' *Guide to Long-Term Care*, which is available online. Investigate alternatives to residential nursing homes, such as assisted-living facilities. Part-time domestic help, a nurse, or aide may be a better option. This allows an elderly person to remain at home with a higher level of independence and in familiar surroundings—with less chance of suffering abuse.

Staff Abuse

Although any member of a nursing home's staff can abuse residents, research by the U.S. Department of Health and Human Services' Office of the Inspector General indicates that the primary abusers of elderly people in nursing homes are aides and orderlies, those most responsible for daily care. The research also found that a major cause of the abuse is that staff is inadequately trained to handle stressful situations. In addition, according to Adult Protective Services Administrators, inadequate staff supervision, poor communication among staff regarding changes to residents' needs, and unclear expectations for staff are also factors leading to elder abuse and neglect. If you suspect that a family member has been abused, immediately notify the senior administrator at the facility.

Consider the Staff

The positive staff working conditions below could decrease incidences of abuse.

- High staff-to-resident ratios
- Highly skilled and trained staff
- Low staff turnover rates
- Sufficient staff supervision
- Well-paid staff
- Low-stress working conditions
- Minimal number of critically ill patients
- Staff empathy and understanding of the elderly and their needs

Choosing a Facility

Because abuse by nursing-home staff is not uncommon, you must exercise extreme caution in your selection. Ask your doctor, local health department, or area agency on aging for references to several nursing homes. Be sure the nursing homes you are considering are certified and that the staff is thoroughly screened. Ask to see the home's latest state survey results that report any problems the facility has had, and compare these with past reports. Do not admit yourself or a loved one to a home that does not allow you to see this report. The administrators may be hiding the report for good reason. Avoid nursing homes that have had a record of abuse.

Observe how attentive (or inattentive) staff members are to residents' needs. For example, see how quickly they respond to call bells.

Visit nursing homes with members of your family before selecting one. Spend several hours at each, preferably during an event or activity. During your visit, observe the staff and residents. Find out if the staff is caring, compassionate, understanding, and energetic. Observe how attentive (or inattentive) staff members are to residents' needs. For example, see how quickly they respond to call bells. Make sure the staff respects and adheres to basic patient rights, such as confidentiality and privacy and safety from exploitation. Determine what residents think about the nursing home. Make sure they look clean and healthy, and that if any are restrained, it is for safety purposes only. Look for resident awareness. Avoid a nursing home in which a lot of residents appear "drugged."

Nothing undermines the morale of a resident more than an unsafe nursing home. Crimes include physical and sexual assaults, robberies, and even homicides. Be sure that the nursing home administration is truly concerned about the security of your family member, and that its plan of action ensures a safe environment. (Review the guidelines offered above for safety in hospitals, which apply equally to nursing homes, and the procedures for preventing elder abuse in chapter 15.) Be aware that local police and fire departments can provide detailed information regarding incidents that have occurred at the facility.

Ask if your nursing home has a property identification program ("Operation ID") to engrave valuable personal property with a unique identification number, and use it.

Since theft is the most common crime in nursing homes, sit down with administrators and determine which valuables (if any) should be brought along. Put them in a safe-deposit box maintained by the nursing home or in a locked property-storage container mounted on a wall, cabinet, door, or similar convenient location. A safer (but less convenient) alternative is to store valuables at a local bank or send them home with a family member.

Ask if your nursing home has a property identification program ("Operation ID") to engrave valuable personal property with a unique identification number, and use it. Then display a decal indicating that your belongings have serial numbers and that a thief will have difficulty fencing them. Make an inventory of personal property. Update it frequently and keep in a safe place; it will be useful in recovering lost or stolen items.

Hallway Watch

At some nursing homes, residents on the same floor get together to organize a hallway or floor watch. They meet periodically to discuss security and arrange to watch out for each others' safety the same way groups of neighbors do in the Neighborhood Watch program (see "Don't Fail Your Neighborhood Watch," page 240). Try to organize a watch at your nursing home to prevent crime by both outsiders and employees. Members of the hallway watch should always be alert for strangers, suspicious persons, and people having no legitimate business in the nursing home. If someone suspicious is spotted, report this to the staff as soon as it is safe to do so. Missing property should also be reported to the nursing staff as soon as possible.

For more information on how to select a safe and secure nursing home, check your local agency on aging. You can also consult the American Association of Retired Persons' *Guide to Long-Term Care*, available online at www.aarp.org/families/caregiving/guide_to_longterm_care, for similar information.

CHAPTER 22

KEEPING SENIORS SAFE

Although senior citizens have a lower crime victimization rate of any age group, they are particularly vulnerable physically, psychologically, and financially. They may be targeted because they are less able to flee from danger than younger victims, and therefore less likely to protect themselves.

COMMON CRIMES AGAINST SENIORS

The senior's worst enemy, as far as crime is concerned, is themselves. Three quarters of the burglaries victimizing older people involve unlocked doors or windows. The risk of burglary and other crimes increases when an individual lives alone, because of lack of activity around the residence. The burglar is not the senior citizen's only threat, though. Purse snatching and petty crime are frequent crimes against the aged. A thief typically grabs a purse with one hand, shoves the victim with the other, and runs away. The victim may end up with broken bones—which is often more serious than losing a purse.

Instead of a purse, use pockets in slacks, jackets, or coats. If necessary, sew pockets in your clothing. You may still be stopped on the street and robbed at gunpoint, but without a purse you're less likely to become injured as a result of being knocked to the ground.

Three quarters of the burglaries victimizing older people involve unlocked doors or windows.

What Senior Citizens Should Do

If you're a senior citizen, establish daily telephone contact with your adult children and/or friends, encourage frequent visits, and check with neighbors on a regular basis. If no one is available for daily contact, join a neighborhood program that provides this service. The U.S. Postal Service, for example, has mail carriers report when older residents have not picked up the previous day's mail. Many utility companies sponsor similar programs. You should also join others for mutual self-protection, whether in a citizen crime prevention group, a property identification program, or similar activity.

When returning home, have your key ready, and don't linger at the door. Whenever possible, have someone walk you home, especially at night. If you observe suspicious-looking people around your entrance, don't go in. Go to a nearby store or to the house of a neighbor, friend, or relative, and call the police. If you live in a building and someone is standing near your apartment door, ring a neighbor's bell and pretend to be a visitor. Keep in mind that a crime prevention specialist from your local police precinct can give your residence a home security survey, which will help you determine which security features you need to improve.

When you need to go shopping or on other excursions that take you out of your home, follow the guidelines described in chapters 11–13. Seek out a friend or relative to accompany you when shopping or running errands. There is safety in numbers. Keep your shopping money separate from your lunch or transportation funds.

Criminals are on the lookout for predictable schedules, so vary your routes and routines. This is particularly important when making a trip to the bank, especially at the beginning and end of the month when you receive checks. Arrange for direct deposit of your checks if possible, so that you don't have to carry them to the bank. Many communities have at least one bank that provides free checking accounts to seniors. (If your Social Security check is more than three mailing days late, report it to the Social Security Administration at (800) 772-1213 and request a replacement check.)

If driving, park as close as possible to your destination. If you have a health problem or disability, ask your doctor about your eligibility for a "handicapped" sticker, hang tag, or license plate for your car. It will allow you to park near building entrances.

What Senior Citizens Should Avoid

Avoiding certain behaviors can be as important as taking steps to prevent crime. Here's what you shouldn't do:

- Don't let strangers stop you for conversation.
- Avoid parked cars with running motors.
- Don't be conspicuous wherever you may be; dress simply and avoid displays of cash or valuable jewelry.
- Avoid large groups of adolescents.
- Avoid isolated, sparsely traveled streets or roads.
- Don't carry a purse if at all possible, but if you must, never let it out of your sight.
- Never keep your keys in your purse or in the same pocket as your wallet. If your purse or wallet is stolen, the criminal will also have your address (from identifying cards). If your keys are stolen also, change your locks immediately.
- Don't be a hero—surrender valuables if you're robbed.

TELEPHONE SCAMS AND OTHER TYPES OF FRAUD

The social isolation and cognitive dementia of the elderly make them easy targets for scams. Typical scams used against seniors include fraudulent prizes and sweepstakes, investments, charity contributions, insurance, health remedies, home repairs, and travel. View anyone offering these types of deals with suspicion, and don't agree to anything over the phone or in person without first discussing it with your lawyer or family member. (See page 269 for more information on telephone scams.)

In addition, follow these cautions to the letter:

- Don't give "good-faith money" for any investment that hasn't been thoroughly checked by someone you have known and trusted for many years.
- Never disclose personal information, bank account numbers, or credit card numbers to a telephone caller, even if the caller claims that he is a bank official or that you have won a prize. Also be wary of mailings that offer prizes, especially when they request money.
- Do not withdraw any of your bank funds as a part of an alleged investigation of bank procedures.
- Don't pay in advance for any significant purchase, unless you are buying from a reputable merchant who you've dealt with for years. Always get a receipt. Use credit cards (or checks) for payment—never cash.
- Don't sign any contracts without first checking with your children, a trusted friend, your attorney, or the Better Business Bureau. You can also call the police department's fraud division, your local consumer affairs office, the district attorney's office, and your attorney general to check out a particular business.

Even if you don't fall for a scam, report it. You could prevent someone else from falling into a trap.

WHERE TO FIND HELP

Know emergency phone numbers: In most communities help is available by dialing 911 or the operator (0). Keep a list of emergency telephone numbers next to your telephone, including those of friends or relatives nearby who can help when needed. Often, important numbers can be programmed into the phone so the person can speed-dial. Keep a list of codes on or near the phone. Help is always available at a police station, a fire station and sometimes even at a business that you patronize. Tape your phone number and address to the back of your phone. If you need help, ask for it directly and clearly. If you are the victim of a crime, do not hesitate to report it!

CHAPTER 23

CONSUMER FRAUD, CON ARTISTS, AND CON GAMES

Con artists, con games, and scams may seem antiquated, and we all like to think we're too smart to fall for the bait. However, all too often we fail to realize that we're being baited in the first place. According to one study, millions of people are victimized by fraudulent activity each year in the United States, resulting in losses of more than $100 billion.

DISHONEST BUSINESS PRACTICES

Most businesses are honest. However, there are always those that will try to cheat you if they think they can get away with it. Try to do business with a firm that has been recommended by your relatives or trusted friends. Before contracting for a service or making a major purchase, check the reputation of the company by calling a consumer service bureau, such as the Better Business Bureau.

Unscrupulous Contractors

Remember that even though a business may be licensed, there is no guarantee that its personnel are honest or that it provides quality work. Before you authorize any work from a contractor, get a written estimate.

Ask the contractor to itemize each item of cost before you approve the estimate. If you need clarification, do not be ashamed to ask questions and always get at least three estimates.

Advertising Swindles

Every advertisement you encounter should be taken with a grain of salt; however, fraud and inaccuracy are most often associated with ads involving medical aids, wonder cures, sure-fire investments, work-at-home opportunities, travel opportunities, credit repair, and weight loss or fitness programs.

Offers that appear to be too good to be true—such as "overnight weight loss" or "earn thousands a week" or "bad credit history erased"— are almost always worthless and expensive scams. Any ad that directs you to call a 1-900 number for information (which can result in charges to your phone bill of anywhere from $3 to $50 a call) is most certainly not legitimate; unfortunately, even some 1-800 numbers now charge for the call. A business that offers an honest product or service will not charge you for more information about it.

Remember, if an ad has fine print or lists several conditions, you must carefully read all the information before making a decision to buy the product. Never buy on impulse because of the selling power of an ad. Something that's truly good today will still be good tomorrow, after you've had time to think about it.

Retail Swindles

Beware of consumer rip-offs when shopping in retail establishments. Here's what you need to know.

- Watch out for signs such as "Lost Our Lease" or "Everything Must Go"—they may be used to lure you into the store.
- When paying by check, make it payable only to the company, not to an individual employee of the store.
- Always have a secondhand car checked by a mechanic before you buy it. Used-car dealers are skillful at hiding the defects of their wares.
- Watch the scanner as the supermarket checkout clerk rings up each item. Price mistakes are often made unintentionally—and also deliberately.

- Compare warranties when making a major purchase, such as an appliance. Some warranties offer full service, while others provide only minimal coverage on certain parts of the product. Ascertain who guarantees performance under the warranty and the ability and resources of the guarantor to meet the contractual obligations. Save all receipts, and note the installation date. This information will be essential if you wish to file a complaint against a company. Before buying any extended warranty, check with your local or state consumer advocacy agency as to the applicability of the terms.

Mail and Telephone Fraud

Fraudulent activity involving mail or phone lines includes insurance offers (especially health insurance); debt consolidation; magazine subscriptions; land, property, and condominium offers; securities and oil leases; franchise deals; work-at-home plans; publish-your-own-book arrangements; home improvements; medicine and miracle cures; weight-loss or fitness programs; sweepstakes opportunities; travel opportunities; and discount purchasing clubs.

Telemarketing calls must legally be made between 8:00 A.M. and 9:00 P.M., so if you receive a call outside of those hours, it is sure to be a scam.

What you should know about phone and mail scams:
- Be wary of work-at-home schemes that require cash deposits or payments or that require you to call a 1-900 number to receive more information.
- One of the fastest-growing frauds is a telephone call or a postcard that promises an exotic vacation, an exorbitant gift, or cash in exchange for a processing fee, or for your purchase of an item the caller or postcard is selling. Ignore them.
- Telemarketing calls must legally be made between 8:00 A.M. and 9:00 P.M., so if you receive a call outside of those hours, it is sure to be a scam.

- Remember, it is the *law* that no purchase is required where a sweepstakes is concerned.
- Wondering about the legitimacy of a "prize" offer? Check the postage on the letter; if it's bulk rate, you haven't won anything of value—in fact, thousands of other people have received the same notice.
- Don't forget that you have no obligation to stay on the phone line; it is your right to hang up at any time.
- All legitimate mail- and phone-order operations have clearly detailed return and warranty policies and will gladly answer any questions you have; they seek your *repeat* business. If they are unclear or evasive about their policies, or use high-pressure tactics to get you to commit, go elsewhere with your business.

Check the postage on the letter; if it's bulk rate, you haven't won anything of value—in fact, thousands of other people have received the same notice.

- Never give out any personal information without fully understanding to whom and why you are giving this information. The only information you need to give is your credit card number, and that should only be on a call you initiated with a business of confirmed legitimacy. (Never send cash in the mail.)
- Be on the lookout for a phony IRS agent calling to say that he needs an immediate cash payment to settle a problem, or your Social Security or credit card number so that he can set up an "audit." Ask what office the agent is assigned to and call back only after obtaining the office number from the telephone operator. Call the U.S. Treasury Inspector General's Hotline at (800) 366-4484 for verification or to report an IRS imposter.
- Beware of organizations offering to find you a low-interest credit card or to repair your credit history. If you need this service, call the Consumer Credit Counseling Service at (877) ASK-CCCS.

Counterfeit Drugs and Cigarettes

One of the most dangerous types of consumer fraud is the counterfeit drug, the consequences of which can be fatal. Common forms of counterfeit medications include drugs that have already expired and those in which the active ingredient has been diluted, adulterated, or substituted with some other substance.

Look for signs that your medication might be counterfeit. For example, has the appearance of your medication—its size, shape, and color—been altered? Make sure your medicine fits the description on the bottle. Pay attention to the packaging: Never use medication from an unsealed container or a container whose label has been altered. Make sure you buy your medications only from a safe and reputable source. Many counterfeit drugs are sold on the Internet, so if you buy your medications online, make sure you do so from a licensed seller.

You may run into counterfeit cigarettes. These, too, can be very harmful—even *more* harmful than real cigarettes. Counterfeit cigarettes often contain higher concentrations of carcinogenic heavy metals, such as arsenic and cadmium. To protect yourself, buy your cigarettes only from safe and reputable sources. Never buy or smoke cigarettes from unsealed packages, and always stick to brand names you know.

CON ARTISTS AND THEIR GAMES

Though con artists are glorified in movies, they are actually criminals who prey on the uninformed and elderly, often taking their life savings and leaving them to lives of privation and despair.

A Stranger at Your Door

One of the simplest cons is initiated by a person masquerading as a repairman, often for a utility, electric, or cable TV company, who knocks on your door and asks for a glass of water. Their aim is to keep you occupied in the kitchen while an accomplice sneaks in and steals money, jewelry, credit cards, or other valuables. Never let anyone into your home unless you know who they are (see chapter 1).

These people would never show up at your door without prior notification. In any case, always demand to see proper ID and documentation and contact the worker's employer to verify his legitimacy before you open the door.

Another con involves the "funeral chaser," who reads an obituary and shows up at the home of the deceased with highly overpriced merchandise that the deceased ostensibly ordered—which you then must buy. Of course, it isn't true, but the salesperson may threaten to tie up life insurance proceeds until you pay. If you are not previously aware of the purchase, immediately notify law enforcement.

Street Swindles and Other Common Con Games

Watch out for con games that take place on the street.

- Beware of a person who approaches you on the street and says you can buy a case of expensive liquor at a low price. He takes you to a store, asks you to pay for the liquor, and tells you to wait until he returns with it. Your "friend" *leaves* the store, never to return with either your money or the goods.

- Avoid street hawkers who appear to be selling expensive goods such as watches, necklaces, rings, bracelets, sweaters, shirts, and so on at discount prices. The peddler's aim is to convince you that you are purchasing expensive merchandise at a bargain-basement price when in fact you are overpaying for a nearly worthless item. Also, beware of national brand or designer clothes peddled by street vendors. Most likely you will be overpaying for "knockoffs," or counterfeits, of the original.

- Watch out for cons that use honest citizens as unsuspecting accomplices. For example, the swindler buys a few regularly priced television sets and then sells them to prominent citizens at a discount, saying he got the sets from an electronics store that was going out of business. He then uses telephone solicitation to sell hundreds more to people in the community, who are told—when referred to the original buyers— that the deal is a legitimate bargain. Of course, he has no more televisions to sell, and the community loses thousands of dollars.

- Beware of the "pigeon drop," which generally targets senior citizens. A person makes a deposit into a savings account and leaves the bank. A stranger flashes a wad of money, indicating that he just found it, and asks the victim what should be done. A "passerby"

Don't Get Ripped Off by a Mechanic

How can you prevent getting ripped off by a mechanic? Know how to do minor repairs and maintenance on your own. Know how to change a tire and how to check tire pressure with a gauge. Learn how to check the fluids (oil, antifreeze, transmission, windshield washer, and so on) in your car and how to refill them. Know how to put water in the radiator in a pinch if your car overheats. You should also keep jumper cables, a flashlight, flares, a can of flat-tire fix, a tool kit (including a lug wrench to change a tire), and a first-aid kit in your car.

(actually another con man) states that a friend at a nearby bank would know what to do and agrees to telephone the banker. He tells the group that the money should be split among them, providing that it isn't claimed by the real owner by the end of the day. The problem, however, is that a $2,000 fidelity bond is required "to protect the bank." The victim (or pigeon) is prevailed upon to provide the bond (with the promise of half the windfall). The con man with the banker friend takes the money and heads for the bank. The victim awaits the return of the con man. Of course, no one returns at the end of the day.

- Avoid charity fraud. People may masquerade as representatives of a charity, soliciting donations for "needy children" or "cancer research"—and using the money for themselves. Giving to charity is a selfless thing to do; however, it is best to stick to giving donations to well-established and well-known charities.
- Never play three-card monte. It is ostensibly a game of skill, but you will never come out ahead, even if you win the first game or two. The dealer may be very skilled at the game—or the dealer may have rigged the game. But that isn't all. Pickpockets frequently mingle among the players and spectators surrounding the dealer and players.

One final note: When trying to find police assistance after being victimized by a scam, make sure the person you contact is a real officer. Con men often have accomplices who pretend to be law-enforcement agents; their job is to keep the real law out of any dispute and, if possible, to swindle even more money from you. Remember, all police officers must have proper ID at all times and will never ask for money or valuables.

When trying to find police assistance after being victimized by a scam, make sure the person you contact is a real officer.

Real Estate Con Games

Real estate cons offer a large potential haul for a thief. A common real estate scam is the time-share or campsite swindle. An "agent" informs you that she is in contact with a party interested in buying your property. But first you must pay a finder's fee to the agent for the service. Of course, it's a scam; there is no buyer, and your "agent" disappears with the finder's fee.

The multiple rental scam is common in large cities. The con artist leases an apartment, using an assumed name. He sublets it to as many as 50 other people, receiving a month's rent and a security deposit from each of them.

Repair or Rip-off?

Other common rip-off schemes include "repairmen" or engineers who offer you repair work at unbelievably low prices. A phony engineer might inspect your home and determine that the heating, plumbing, or chimney needs repair. He might ask you to sign a contract for the repairs and give him a down payment, but you'll never see the "repairman" again. A fraudulent repairman might say that he has enough material to blacktop your driveway or repair leaks in your roof. The work is done with black oil that never dries, but you have already paid cash, as requested. A "gardener" offers to cover your property with topsoil. Later you learn it is sawdust mixed with motor oil. To avoid these types of swindles, use only those businesses that have been around for years or have been referred to you by a trusted source.

Customers are particularly vulnerable at car-repair shops. Make sure the repair shops you deal with are registered with your state. They should

Getting Help

If you've been the victim of fraud, there are places you can turn for help and information. You can contact state and local consumer protection agencies, the local Better Business Bureau and the state attorney general. You can also contact the National Fraud Information Center by calling (800) 876-7060 or going to www.fraud.org. If you have a problem involving mail fraud, contact the U.S. Postal Inspection Service. If you have a problem with telephone scams, contact your phone service company and report your concerns to the security department. If you're the victim of street fraud, contact the police.

have a current Department of Motor Vehicles registration certificate. Ask friends and relatives to refer you to a reputable business.

Give the mechanic a written list detailing what's wrong with your car, and ask for a written estimate for all repairs. Write down the date, time, price, and with whom you've spoken when authorizing repairs, especially by telephone. The repairman should answer all questions you have. If he fails to, look for a new repair shop. If you aren't very knowledgeable about your vehicle and its parts, try to bring along someone who is.

Keep a written record of all repairs. You will need to supply these materials if you file a complaint.

After the work is completed, make sure you are given a written, detailed invoice, and inspect your car before paying. Ask for the old parts back after they are replaced. If you are not satisfied, speak to the manager or owner. If this proves unfruitful, file a complaint with your state Department of Motor Vehicles. The department will try to settle the dispute by telephone; if it's unsuccessful, it will refer the case to a state investigator. You can also contact the state attorney general, the Better Business Bureau, and the Department of Consumer Affairs for help.

Never accept offers for repairs from people on the street. One very common con involves people in cars who look for autos needing bodywork. They offer these repairs at a low price—using materials that disintegrate after a short time.

DATING SERVICE DANGERS

A dating service may seem like the ideal venue through which to meet people. Be aware, however, of the very serious perils involved in the use of these agencies.

Before disclosing personal information to a dating service, investigate the business fully. Some services may be fly-by-night organizations that disappear shortly after collecting your money. Others may collect personal information about you to find out if your home is worth burglarizing.

The best way to find a legitimate service is through recommendations from people you trust. Before committing yourself, check with the local Better Business Bureau, Chamber of Commerce, and Small Claims Court for complaints against the agency. Ask the agency how long it has been in business—obviously, the longer the better. A legitimate business should be able to provide you with references from clients. Be wary about signing any contract, and find out about all fees before making a commitment. Make certain your personal information will be kept confidential and that the service conducts thorough background checks of all its members.

Avoid personal ads altogether. Criminals often use them to meet victims.

Charlatan Lovers

The ultimate con involves a person who pretends to love you but whose heart is focused on your money. It usually begins when your "lover" asks to borrow a little money and ends when your credit cards, jewelry, home, business, and life savings are taken. All of a sudden your lover has disappeared, whereabouts unknown.

How can you identify a charlatan Romeo or Juliet? Watch for these warning signs.

- The person appears slick, too perfect. He is extremely attractive and a perfect dresser.

- Your partner rarely if ever talks about herself, displaying excessive interest in everything about you. This tactic may be flattering, but it is also unrealistic.
- The relationship proceeds rapidly emotionally, intellectually, and physically.
- You can't pin your partner down on a home or business address.
- You learn that your partner has a history of avoiding commitments.
- Your partner has no visible means of support and is vague about job and personal resources.

Your best defense against such a person is a strong offense. Always take care of your personal property yourself; do not be lax or careless with your money or jewelry. Never lend money to a partner you have known for only a short period of time and whose history and background have not been revealed. If you decide to invest in your partner's business, work through your lawyer or a business adviser.

Should you be conned, report the crime to the police or the office of the district attorney. Also, immediately report to law enforcement and the issuer of the credit cards that have been stolen. Stolen checks, jewelry or other assets should be immediately reported to law enforcement. Above all, do not shy away from pursuing the case; if you don't, your former "lover" will be someone else's problem tomorrow.

CHAPTER 24

INVESTMENT FRAUD

New-venture underwritings for nonexistent products, diversion of trust funds by attorneys for their personal use, and insider trading are common instances of fraud. To avoid swindles, large and small, you must be very careful when you decide to invest your hard-earned cash.

COMMON FINANCIAL FRAUDS

Whether over the phone or on the Internet, financial frauds abound. You'll be able to better protect yourself from these schemes if you know what pitches may come your way.

Blue-Sky New Ventures

One of these days your phone may ring, followed by a pitch for shares in a hot new stock offered only to savvy investors.

Telephone pitches for these sensational underwritings come from fast-talking, smooth telephone solicitors in an office crammed with phones—a so-called "boiler room." The first contact that you receive is typically made by a low-paid individual called an "opener." Once you express interest in the pitch by committing some money or requesting more information, you are turned over to a much more accomplished high-pressure sales artist called a "loader." He will add some exciting, confidential embellishments to the preliminary pitch that will make the offer seem very plausible and irresistible, and will try to convince you to extend your commitment even further.

You discover too late, after your money is committed, that the entire undertaking was a fraud and that there is little hope of ever recovering your investment. Report such attempts through the consumer crime department of your state attorney general office or the U.S. Securities and Exchange Commission.

Shell Games

A close relative of the new venture fraud is an existing corporation without any substantial assets—frequently a relatively new business gone sour. The essentially dormant company, not yet having taken the formal steps for dissolution, thus becomes a marketable asset in itself, appropriately referred to as a "shell."

Stock fraud con artists acquire the company, apply for a name change, and then install management figureheads. The next step after the takeover is to reduce the equity of the shareholders of the original corporation through a reverse stock split—for example, issuing one new share for each 100 original shares.

If the SEC detects the scam, it promptly halts trading in the shell's stock, but the action usually comes too late for victimized investors.

Using telephone pitches, brokers foist the fundamentally worthless stock on unwary investors. The fraud is completed when the shares held by the criminal backers are completely liquidated. At this point, the price quickly plummets, leaving the investors holding the worthless stock. Alternatively, the con artists may pass off the valueless stock in exchange for valuable assets or as collateral for a loan.

The SEC and You

Does the Securities and Exchange Commission (SEC) really protect you from investment fraud? Under current SEC regulations, individuals can solicit investments by phone without disclosing all the facts in the written offering prospectus. That document need only accompany the first written communication, usually with the order confirmation. Understand that federal law and SEC requirements provide only limited protection, and there is no substitute for individual research and due diligence in evaluating investment solicitations.

The SEC and other regulatory agencies primarily serve to make sure that full and accurate disclosure of all the relevant investment information is publicly available. They cannot protect you from devious financial schemes; they cannot tell you what is likely to be a sound or unsound investment; and even when you've been victimized, they can only help after the fact and generally in a way that attempts to enhance the future fairness of the investment markets.

If the SEC detects the scam, it promptly halts trading in the shell's stock, but the action usually comes too late for victimized investors. Most often, the "financial advisers" abscond with the fortune, spend all the money, or end up in prison. Report your suspicion to the Securities and Exchange Commission.

The Financial Fortune-Teller

You receive a phone call from a "Mr. Wingate" who wants to give you a taste of his "forecasting abilities" by telling you about a commodity whose value is about to increase dramatically. Sure enough, it increases as promised.

"Mr. Wingate" calls back; he wants you to consider his firm the kind of firm you can trust your money with. He gives you a tip that a certain commodity is about to experience a sharp decline. Sure enough, within a short period of time, the commodity's value has decreased.

Who can argue with these results? Certainly not you, so you promise with the third phone call to give "Mr. Wingate" and his "firm" quite a bit of money to invest on your behalf.

What you don't know, as you're helping to make "Mr. Wingate" a very rich man, is that he originally called 300 people, telling half that the price of that commodity would go up, the other half that the price would go down. When the commodity increased in value, he called the 150 people for whom he'd made the "correct forecast," telling 75 of them that the next commodity's value would decrease, and the other 75 that it would increase.

This means that he had 75 people impressed with his unerring accuracy ready to invest. It also means that he had 75 people willing to give him money that they'll never see again.

Fast-Buck Commodities Futures

Increasing numbers of amateurs are being lured into commodity futures trading. The attraction of these contracts for the future delivery of commodities like gold, silver, platinum, and the like is that they are highly leveraged. Relatively few investment dollars can control sizable sums. The problem is that the likelihood of turning a profit is well below 10 percent.

As in the earlier examples of securities fraud, commodities fraud is frequently perpetuated by professional-sounding operators in boiler rooms temporarily located at prestigious Wall Street addresses or other financial centers. Therein lies part of the danger to the investor: Legitimate commodity futures brokers also operate by phone and have similar addresses. Con artists rely on the inexperienced investor's limited understanding of commodities and the complex array of factors that dictate the future price of the commodity. Thus, the con man can play on the investor's ignorance by identifying a couple of well-known recent events that suggest the future price of the commodity is worth gambling on.

Of course, the words *gamble* and *risk* never arise in the salesperson's pitch; instead, he practically guarantees immense profits. As in the earlier scams, things move very quickly. Lest the hot opportunity be lost, the con artist urges the investor to wire bank funds to the fly-by-night brokerage firm, with the usual promise that informational literature will be immediately forthcoming. The scam centers on the fact that the investor will not get a genuine futures contract. Instead, the investor will receive—if anything at all—an *option* on the touted commodity (a so-called deferred-delivery contract). Unfortunately for the investor, these contracts were banned in 1978 and no longer exist in U.S. futures markets.

Con artists rely on the inexperienced investor's limited understanding of commodities and the complex array of factors that dictate the future price of the commodity.

Internet Investment Fraud

The Internet offers a new venue for old tricks of investment fraud. As careful as you should always be when you decide to invest your money, you should be *doubly* cautious when you invest in anything you learn about online. Many online investment newsletters are fake or make false claims. Fraudsters often use online bulletin boards to post phony "inside" information or to talk up their company. There is also the "pump and dump," in which the fraudster tries to boost the price of certain stock to entice you to buy by giving you false or misleading trading advice and tips via the Internet. When the demand for that stock reaches a peak level, the schemer sells the stocks and you lose your money.

As with any online interaction, you can never be sure of who you're dealing with, so if you're going to be investing a lot of money in any online venture, you'd better take every step to ensure that you know exactly where your money is going and that the venture is legitimate. Get financial statements from any company you're considering investing in. Verify any claims made in online newsletters or bulletin boards. If an investment sounds too good to be true, it probably is.

Pyramid Schemes

In a pyramid scheme, investors are tricked by quick profits on initial trades into committing further capital (and spreading the word of their success to friends, who then invest). The con artists who set up these frauds, sometimes called Ponzi frauds, use the funds of later investors to pay off original investors—until the pyramid collapses, leaving later investors without their money. (See "20 Ways to Avoid an Investment Scam," pages 284–285.)

Dishonest Brokers

Some fully licensed but dishonest brokers institute buy orders for commodities that are intentionally not executed. If the commodity price falls, the faked loss is posted to the investor's account, and the broker pockets the money. If the price rises, the broker declares that a clerical error resulted in the order not being processed and pockets the difference. Report such suspicious transactions to the Securities and Exchange Commission and be certain you fully understand commodity trading before investing.

Keep in mind that the account agreement that you long ago signed but barely read—the one with the fine print indicating that you would not sue your broker but instead subject all claims to an arbitration board dominated by the investment community—may have left you with little effective recourse.

Land Frauds

Frauds come in many varieties, but perhaps the most enduring of all are land frauds.

One typical fraudulent operation offered coal-mining rights on land in a southern state. In reality, there was no coal in the field. Part of the success of the operation was due to the efforts of a shill, who was introduced to potential investors as a customer pleased with his investment and impressed with the reputable management of the operation. Mining rights were sold throughout the United States and overseas—and every investor lost money.

SPOTTING A BAD DEAL

To avoid falling prey to investment fraud or deception, you need guidelines on investment security that will help you to be prudent and cautious. Do not, on the other hand, be so restrained that you become paranoid and miss important, legitimate opportunities to enhance your future net worth through astute, carefully considered investments.

There is risk in any investment. But a strategy that diversifies by institution, investment type, issuer within these financial alternatives, and

(continued on page 284)

20 Ways to Avoid an Investment Scam

Broker and investment-house fraud is another avenue to tempt you to become involved in illegal stock transactions. Keep these 20 things in mind if you're looking to stay in the investment game but want to avoid a scam.

 Be alert to transactions that involve secretive foreign aspects such as off-shore financial institutions.

2 Watch out for unusual delays by brokers in making delivery of your securities or your investment proceeds; you may be caught in a fraudulent operation or in the misappropriation of your assets.

3 Be suspicious if transaction confirmations do not arrive promptly.

4 Keep an eye out for evidence of excessive buying and selling by your broker; periodically check through your trades of the past couple of years.

5 Buying and selling should be based on sound reasoning, not the whim of the broker.

6 Always check the financial soundness of the issuer of fixed-yield investments in Standard & Poor's, Moody's, or similar agencies, whether the issuer or instrument is a bank or savings and loan (S&L), CD, municipal or corporate bond, or other investment.

7 When buying stocks, determine whether your account representative is a broker or broker-dealer; the latter buy and sell for their own accounts and therefore have a vested interest that may seriously bias the advice you are getting.

8 When first opening an account, obtain the firm's recent financial statements, and be cautious of doing business with those having net capitalization of under $1 million.

9 In regard to new accounts at unknown firms, always request evidence that both the firm and the broker are licensed. Inquire about the number of years in business, as well as the experience of the broker and/or lesser-known firms. Get bank references, and check with regulatory agencies.

10 If the brokerage also has an investment banking division, find out the firm's policy about recommending stocks when there is potential for conflicts of interest. Inquire not only about the institution's underwritings but also about senior partners who may serve on the boards of various companies having publicly traded stock.

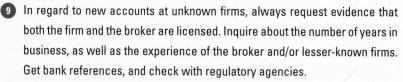

11 Although deposits in banks and S&Ls are insured by the FDIC and FSLIC, it is wise to obtain a copy of the institution's recent balance sheets, since the government auditor's roster of "problem banks" is not readily available. Certainly, split any joint accounts over $250,000 into separate ones if at the same bank.

12 In regard to "penny stocks" of new ventures, insist on seeing the written prospectus, no matter how sweet the deal seems or the sense of urgency that you are given.

13 Always ask the broker how many shares of penny stocks are outstanding, how many employees the company has, and the company's record of profitability, if any.

14 When you receive the prospectus, look to see if a substantial portion of the underwriting will be siphoned off to pay expenses accrued by the promoters/principals before going public, to pay excessive salaries and the like. Look at the intended use of the funds and the associated planning horizon to see if additional offerings or debt instruments need to be floated soon.

15 Examine not only salaries but also the compensation in the form of stock to be given to officers.

16 Scrutinize the experience of the officers, directors, and promoters; determine their track record in similar deals and in comparable markets. Invest only with well-established investment managers with proven long-term track records.

17 If not in the prospectus, any especially alluring claims about the deal should be backed up in writing by the underwriter/broker. Look not only for what is said but also for what is not said.

18 In new, diversified investment trusts, watch out for the possible unloading into the trust portfolio of one or more "dogs" previously held by the trust organizers; again, obtain and evaluate the prospectus first.

19 Remember that no matter how sophisticated the offering and associated financial jargon may sound, any nitwit or criminal with enough perseverance can float a public corporation.

20 Remember that in most states, anyone, including a charlatan, can call him- or herself a financial adviser (with or without a newsletter), since few states have licensing procedures like those for stockbrokers, real estate brokers, tax attorneys, CPAs, and the like. Whether you deal with a licensed or an unlicensed individual, be hard-nosed, and base your investment decisions on recent historical results, not simply reputation.

commitment over time (rather than as lump sums) will significantly reduce your chances of losing your entire investment.

If the investment yield is inconsistent with the general market for that investment risk, then someone is probably misrepresenting the facts.

In addition to these general protective rules, you should remember two more: First, if the investment yield is inconsistent with the general market for that investment risk, then someone is probably misrepresenting the facts. You can expect about a 3 to 4 percent real annualized return on your investment after taxes and inflation; anything more than that should alert you to undisclosed risks.

Second, when money is involved, there are no guarantees. Just because a person is a friend or a relative doesn't mean that they can be totally trusted with your money.

KNOCKING A SWINDLER OFF TRACK

FBI statistics on reported crime reveal that no one is too rich or poor, sophisticated or uneducated, old or young to escape the clever and persistent con.

It is not easy to spot swindlers. They come in all shapes and sizes and from all walks of life. They use any and all means to convince you to buy into their schemes. They use high-pressure tactics because they often work; you have to condition yourself to step back and say, "Wait a minute."

A swindler talks fast and asks questions to keep you from asking them. The National Futures Association suggests you ask these questions that will knock a swindler off track (and that anybody reputable would be willing to answer).

- Where did you get my name?
- What risks are involved?
- Can you send me a written explanation of your investment proposal?
- Would you mind explaining your proposal to a third party, such as an investment counselor or my attorney?

- Where, exactly, will my money be, and what kind of accounting statements will you provide me?
- Are the investments you offer traded on a regulated exchange? (Not all legitimate investments are traded there, but no fraudulent proposals ever are).

If the answers to these and other questions you may have (and ask a lot of them) are vague or unsatisfying, look for other avenues for investment. If you still aren't sure, check with your local police department or Better Business Bureau to see if there are any complaints on file concerning the individual or firm; keep checking, even if it means tracking the individual out of state. Your money is too important for you not to be diligent about who is going to invest it. Remember, no investment is risk-free, but you can minimize the risk.

RESOURCES FOR REDRESS

If you believe you've been a victim of fraud, you may wish to seek redress through some of the following agencies or their counterparts in your state:

- U.S. Securities and Exchange Commission, (800) SEC-0330 or www. sec.gov
- Federal Trade Commission, (202) 326-2222 or www.ftc.gov
- Commodity Futures Trading Commission, (202) 418-5000 or www. cftc.gov
- Federal Bureau of Investigation, (202) 324-3000 or www.fbi.gov
- Housing and Urban Development Department, Interstate Land Sales Registration, (202) 708-1112 or www.hud.gov
- National Futures Association, (312) 781-1300, (212) 608-8660 or www.nfa.futures.org

PART FIVE

BUSINESS AND INDUSTRY SECURITY

CHAPTER 25

VIOLENCE ON THE JOB

Crime and violence on the job not only diminishes your productivity, it can also result in loss of property, bodily injury, or possibly even death. Most of us spend at least one third of our time on the job— not counting the time it takes to get there and back—so it's worth taking steps to protect yourself during what is actually most of your waking hours.

ESTABLISHING SECURITY IN THE WORKPLACE

Every company, ranging from the one-person shop with a special hiding place for cash to the giant defense contractor with a security department numbering thousands of employees, should have some sort of security program. But you can take steps to protect yourself on the job, too.

Protecting Your Property

Don't leave wallets or keys in your coat at work. Put your purse in a desk drawer and lock it. If you are not in physical contact with your bag— actually *touching* it—then lock it away.

Hazardous Occupations

Occupational homicide is starting to be more widely recognized than ever before. Gas station attendants, convenience-store workers, and taxi drivers are among the highest group of employees who fall into this category. Check out the list below to see if your job has any of the risk factors that contribute to on-the-job homicide.

- Exchanging money with the public.
- Working by yourself or with few people.
- Working late-night or early-morning hours.
- Working in a high-crime area.
- Protecting valuable property or merchandise.
- Working outside, often in isolated locations.

A purse is not all you might lose at the office. Other favorite targets are cash, calculators, USB drives, cell phones, Blackberries, PDAs, clothing, cameras, radios, and computer equipment. If you work in a building with tenants who are strangers to each other, you are much more likely to suffer a loss than if you work in a place where everyone knows everyone else, at least by sight.

When leaving your office, put calculators and other small valuable items in your desk and lock it. Few desks have adequate locks, but you might at least prevent random pilferage this way.

A purse is not all you might lose at the office. Other favorite targets are cash, calculators, USB drives, cell phones, Blackberries, PDAs, clothing, cameras, radios, and computer equipment.

Protecting Information

The list of things that can go wrong through the inadvertent release of confidential or personal information is endless. So lock up important reports and memos when you leave the office, even if only for a few minutes. And don't be in such a hurry at quitting time that you fail to lock filing cabinets. In short, leave a clean, orderly desk when you're away from it. This way, you'll help guard against the use of confidential information against your company and thus indirectly against you.

COMMON BUSINESS CRIMES

Here are just a few of the things that you, as an employee, can do to protect yourself and your company against the most common types of crimes committed against business.

Bad Checks

Bad checks account for a significant share of crime-related business losses. If your work involves handling checks, you must guard against this type of loss. Follow all your company's procedures, and insist on adequate identification before you cash a check for anyone. If there is any doubt in your mind, or if the person offering the check cannot provide satisfactory identification, don't cash it.

Counterfeit Money

If you handle cash on the job, you may come into contact with counterfeit money. The government will not reimburse a businessperson who accepts a counterfeit bill. If he or she accepts a counterfeit bill and attempts to pass it on, knowing it to be a bogus bill, the person might well be in violation of federal laws.

The difference between most counterfeit bills and the genuine article is so striking that there is really no excuse for accepting a fake. When in doubt, make a side-by-side comparison, and refuse to accept a questionable bill.

Forgeries

Forgeries, especially forged checks, are another problem you may encounter. If you can't adequately identify an endorser, and the endorser can't adequately identify him- or herself, don't cash the check. Satisfactory identification consists of at least two items that bear the person's signature as well as a photograph, such as a driver's license and a credit card. Strictly enforced limits on the amount for which a check may be cashed are especially recommended.

Spotting a Counterfeit Bill

The easiest way to spot a counterfeit bill is to look at it and feel it. The paper on which legitimate bills are printed is of a special manufacture, available only to the government. It has a distinctive enough feel that a side by-side touch comparison will enable you to determine the difference. The authentic paper is made from fibers, and its red and blue fibers are visible even to the naked eye. The engraving reproduction quality of a bogus bill will be noticeably inferior to that of an authentic bill. The background behind the pictures on genuine bills is composed of many small dots or finely etched lines. Even if the counterfeiters use a photographic process in their reproduction, counterfeit backgrounds will tend to "close in" and be considerably darker than those on legitimate bills.

Don't assume that a check is good just because it is drawn on the federal, state, or local government. If you cash such a check and the signature of the rightful recipient has been forged by someone who stole it from a mailbox, you and your firm will suffer the loss. This is especially hazardous in the late spring or early summer, when income-tax refund checks are abundant, and also at those times when welfare, Social Security, or other assistance checks are in the mail.

Satisfactory identification consists of at least two items that bear the person's signature as well as a photograph, such as a driver's license and a credit card.

Shoplifting

The National Association for Shoplifting Prevention estimates the cost of shoplifting to be $13 billion a year, costing more than $25 million per day. Another study indicates that the estimated loss of profits resulting from shoplifting ranges from 0.5 percent to a full 5 percent, depending on the business. This may not sound like a large amount, but in most businesses a loss of 1 percent can cause heavy damage; higher losses can be crippling.

While anybody fitting any description can be a shoplifter, the great majority of shoplifting is done on impulse by amateurs, compared to planned theft by professionals. Juveniles are often involved as part of a dare, peer pressure, gang initiation, or just for kicks. Occasionally it is a cry for help; troubled children will attempt to steal, subconsciously hoping to get caught to create attention for themselves.

The National Association for Shoplifting Prevention estimates the cost of shoplifting to be $13 billion a year, costing more than $25 million per day.

There is no profile of a typical shoplifter. Contrary to common belief, men and women shoplift about equally often. About 75 percent of shoplifters are adults; the remaining 25 percent are minors.

While accounting for a small number of shoplifting incidents, "professional" shoplifters do a great deal of damage. They will go into a store, often searching for a designated item, steal it, and resell it at a much cheaper price.

The most likely target items for all shoplifters are the following: For women it's cosmetics, women's clothing, and jewelry; for men it's alcohol and cigarettes.

If you work in a place that may be victimized by a shoplifter, keep your eyes open and don't forget to ask, "May I help you?" The last thing a shoplifter wants is a lot of attention.

Apprehending a Shoplifter

It is estimated that only one in 48 shoplifting incidents ends with the apprehension of the suspect. While this data may urge you to be overzealous, be careful; stay alert and be concerned, but follow your company's policies concerning the apprehension and detention of shoplifters. No matter how well intentioned it may be, an overzealous reaction on your part could result in losses to you personally and to your company in the event of a false arrest.

How to Spot a Shoplifter

Often, especially when the thief is a nonprofessional, the suspected shoplifter will appear nervous and jumpy, with a flushed face. Usually he or she will try to distract you by requesting additional merchandise or by dropping items on the floor. Actions such as repeatedly comparing two different samples of the same item, the frequent opening and closing of a purse, or erratic movement around the store are possible indicators that something is wrong. Keep an eye out for people wearing bulky clothing (especially in warm weather) or carrying large shopping bags, partially opened umbrellas, folded newspapers, or schoolbooks.

Shoplifters often work in teams. One person may take a position to block your view of the other's theft. An accomplice may create a distraction while the partner steals. Small children, accompanied by their parents, can be un-witting accomplices or may even have been trained to steal. Pay attention to people who try on merchandise in open view of store personnel. Professional shoplifters may don sweaters, gloves, hats, and scarves and walk casually out of the store as if the merchandise were theirs.

How to Minimize Shoplifting Losses

A number of actions can aid in deterring shoplifters. Practically no one steals when store personnel are looking. It is advisable to lower displays and shelving to no more than 5 feet in height, enabling employees to see much of the store. Wider aisles and open spaces add to the visibility and make theft more difficult. This economy is achieved, however, at the expense of space that otherwise could contain merchandise. Some trade-offs will be necessary to achieve optimum use of space. Of course, adequate lighting is recommended.

You can also extend your employees' range of vision by judiciously placing mirrors (especially two-way and convex mirrors) throughout the store. A reward program for employees who turn in shoplifters can be effective (and could curtail employee theft, as well).

Security officers and/or floorwalkers are also deterrents to theft, espe-cially when they are clearly visible or placed near exits. Floorwalkers—plainclothes officers who roam the store as customers—are used to nab shoplifters after they've clearly stole merchandise.

Electronic surveillance devices, such as removable tags and disposable labels, are currently used more often than not as preventive measures. Unless removed or demagnetized, the devices will sound an alarm as the shoplifter attempts to leave the store. These are not foolproof, however; anyone determined enough will find ways to render these devices useless. Some stores actually plant subliminal antitheft messages in the music that's played over the loudspeakers.

The most expensive items in your store should be protected in locked showcases. Another protection for your better goods is to locate them as far from the exit doors as is practical. Doing so will require the thief to negotiate a longer escape route.

Just as it is practical to increase sales help during the holiday season due to the heavy volume of sales, it is wise to increase security help as well: About one-third of all shoplifting crimes are committed during the holidays.

Finally, post signs: SHOPLIFTERS WILL BE PROSECUTED. And mean it.

About one-third of all shoplifting crimes are committed during the holidays.

Employee Theft

Employee theft is a more serious threat to business than shoplifting, burglary, or bookkeeping errors combined. And unfortunately, as many as 30 percent of the nation's workers will steal from their employer at some point in their career. Despite the millions spent on security devices, employee theft costs small businesses nearly $40 billion each year in the United States.

Thefts often occur after business hours. Preparing to steal, employees put merchandise into their cars or hide it in garbage cans or empty boxes for later removal. Other common methods of employee theft include under-adding merchandise at cash registers and changing inventory counts and accounting books.

Employee Screening

Companies should thoroughly screen all applicants in order to determine character and integrity, as well as technical qualifications. Fingerprinting, background checks, and in-depth interviews are a must when selecting employees who will have access to confidential data or software.

The best way you, as an employee, can help fight theft is to abide by and respect company rules. The most dedicated scofflaw might well be stealing while attempting to make you an unwitting accomplice by undermining employee respect for antitheft rules. Such rules are necessary because some of your coworkers are undeserving of trust, and it is your obligation to do whatever you can to get rid of them.

Discovering that a coworker is stealing is a tough problem, leading to the question of how many pencils one must steal before it becomes serious. Knowledge of an obviously serious theft might place you in actual physical danger. Yet failure to do anything about it would make you a morally, if not legally, culpable accessory. Your obligation to your employer should outweigh any loyalty that you might have to a thief who also happens to be a friend.

Experts estimate that stealing by employees accounts for almost half of business losses. In addition to as much as the $15 billion annual take of employee thieves, there are other losses impossible to quantify, such as the company time wasted, for example, trying to figure out these sudden and unexplainable losses.

Experts estimate that stealing by employees accounts for almost half of business losses.

WHO CONTRIBUTES TO WORKPLACE VIOLENCE

According to the National Institute for Occupational Safety and Health (NIOSH), homicide is the third-leading cause of death in the workplace for all workers, after deaths from motor vehicles accidents and falls.

Homicide is the leading cause of death among women in the workplace. Nearly 1,000 workplace homicides occur annually, most involving attacks on police and security officers, taxi drivers, and retail clerks.

Assaults on workers occur much more frequently than occupational homicides. These are no longer isolated events. Assault and harassment can occur at anytime. Estimates suggest that workplace violence costs American businesses at least $4 billion in employer medical/legal expenses and lost work time.

Estimates suggest that workplace violence costs American businesses at least $4 billion in employer medical/legal expenses and lost work time.

Disgruntled Employees and Ex-Employees

Disgruntled employees and ex-employees can pose a serious threat to everyone around them if they become violent. While this is relatively uncommon, the results can be devastating when it does happen. And in most cases, the rage that leads to workplace violence is usually detectable prior to the incident, with various red flags indicating the killer's rage and frustration. So by recognizing these warning signs, you could possibly prevent this type of violence from occurring.

Recognizing Red Flags

There are usually three stages that employees go through before becoming violent at work. First, they become argumentative and hostile, oftentimes swearing loudly and spreading rumors. Next, they begin making threats and remarks about hurting other people at work and may begin destroying work property. In the final stage, the employee starts getting in fights at work, makes threats about getting even, and finally becomes violent.

Below are the typical warning signs that may indicate that a disgruntled employee could become violent.

- presence of a concealed weapon
- history of violent behavior

- obsession with weapons and firearms
- intimidating or threatening coworkers
- holding grudges for a long time
- extreme disorganization
- paranoia
- making unwanted romantic advances toward coworkers
- inability to accept criticism
- family/financial/custody problems
- making comments about murder or suicide
- high level of stress on the job.

Of course, this is not to say that people who fit this descriptions will definitely become violent at work, but it is important that management catch these red flags and intervene with counseling. In addition, it is important that businesses have strict drug abuse policies and zero tolerance policies for violence in the workplace. Background checks should be performed on all applicants in order to weed out anyone with a history of drug abuse or criminal behavior. Ex-employees should not be allowed on the premises unless they receive proper authorization from a manager.

Angry Customers, Clients, and Patients

In many occupations, you have to worry far more about dealing with angry customers, clients, and patients than about angry coworkers. If you work in retail, chances are you will frequently have to deal with angry customers who are intimidating and verbally abusive. When customers have to wait in long lines before being helped, this only serves to increase their anger and frustration. You must protect yourself in the event that these angry customers become violent. When working with the general public, you may also come into contact with people who are mentally ill or abusing drugs/alcohol, which can create dangerous situations for the employee.

Everyone who works with customers, clients, and patients should be trained in how to deal with angry encounters, and employers should have procedures in place for dealing with violence. The best thing we can do to avoid violence is to treat people politely and with respect. Learn to keep an eye out for signs of anger and potential violence, such as avoiding eye contact, adopting an aggressive stance, and nervousness. Avoid triggering violence by steering clear of people's personal space, never turning your back on them, or shouting or swearing at them.

> The best thing we can do to avoid violence is to treat people politely and with respect.

Hospital workers must be very cautious when working with angry patients. This anger may result from long waits in the emergency room. Patients who are brought in for emergency care may be armed, intoxicated, or mentally ill. Nurses and physicians must respect a person's right to refuse medication or hospitalization. Patients or their family members may also be angry about poor outcomes if, for example, an operation or procedure was not fully successful. Or they may simply be tense and on edge because they do not feel well and do not understand what is wrong with them, or because they just received an upsetting diagnosis. Doctors must be patient and understanding and be sure to listen carefully to what their patients have to say.

WHAT TO DO IF YOU ARE CONFRONTED

If you are confronted with a volatile situation on the job that appears to be heading toward physical violence, don't take a confrontational stance; walk or run away. Say you have to go to the bathroom, retrieve a file, or get a cup of coffee. If it's impossible to leave, try to position yourself near an exit or avoid being blocked in an area you can't easily get out of. If an employee becomes hostile toward you, try to divert him or her by redirecting the conversation, using calming words and a reasonable tone of voice. If this doesn't work, agree with the individual's point of view or complaint and explain that you share similar feelings. Lower your voice, and talk slowly and politely. Never, ever argue or humiliate the aggravated person.

DEALING WITH DOWNSIZING

One of the major triggers of workplace violence by a disgruntled employee is when an individual gets laid off. When a business decides to downsize and reduce its number of employees, the employer must be aware that those people who are fired will be extremely upset, and if they are not handled with care, they may come back to seek revenge for what they feel was unjustly taken away from them.

Communication throughout the downsizing process is key. Rather than pretending that negative feelings don't exist, employers should speak openly to their employees about the reasons for the downsizing and about employees' responses. Morale at work is likely to go down as a result of downsizing. Employers must be aware of this and should make sure that they stay attuned to the feelings of their workers.

Downsizing should be done as fairly as possible. One way to do this is to publish the criteria used for deciding who will be laid off. This way, long-term performance can be stressed as an asset rather than criticizing an individual's recent performance at work.

If whole groups of people are getting laid off at once, then a social environment may develop in which people support each other's feelings of anger and frustration. In this scenario an individual may receive encouragement for violent behavior from the group. Therefore, employers should try to downsize across different office units to prevent feelings of solidarity among those getting laid off.

On a more personal level, it is a good idea to have human resources personnel meet one on one with individuals who are getting laid off in order to explain that the downsizing is being carried out reluctantly and that the decision was not a personal one. By humanizing the process and taking the time to explain to these employees the reasons behind the downsizing, they are less likely to feel that they are being unfairly persecuted. Subject to any state-law privacy restrictions, the human resources personnel should also discuss other domains of the employee's life, and if it appears that there are also problems at home or in other areas, the laid-off employee should be referred to counseling.

INSTILLING A HUMANE ENVIRONMENT IN TODAY'S WORKPLACE

While security measures such as metal detectors and surveillance cameras might serve to make everyone feel safer, the best way to truly prevent workplace violence is through awareness and education.

- Enforce strict policies regarding violence and drug/alcohol abuse at work.

- Encourage employees to report all incidents of harassment, threats, or violence or mention of suicide by seemingly troubled employees.

- Have the human resources department handle all minor policy infractions reasonably and fairly.

- Immediately report repeated and more serious violations to the security department and/or to the authorities.

- Train all employers and employees to recognize the signs of a potentially violent worker.

- Provide unhappy and disgruntled employees with a healthy outlet for their frustrations and a way to communicate their grievances in a non-violent way.

Businesses that treat their employees like valuable resources are less likely to experience workplace violence. Providing a comfortable and stress-free work environment is probably the best security a business can have.

Providing a comfortable and stress-free work environment is probably the best security a business can have.

DANGER OFF THE PREMISES

A company obviously has less control of its security once employees leave its facilities to perform work off premises. Even a company with state-of-the-art security systems, highly trained security officers, and best intentions can't always provide proper protection from dangers lurking

Who's in Danger off the Premises?

Many workers today are employed in service industries and perform the majority of their tasks off company property. Who are these people? Many include delivery people, tourist guides, repair personnel, consultants, computer specialists, gardeners, home-care workers, traveling salespeople, caseworkers, law-enforcement personnel, exterminators, and meter readers.

outside. A company's employees may become the victims of crime or violence in a split second. And you can expect the problem to balloon, because most workers today are employed in service industries and perform the majority of their tasks off company property.

Follow these few simple rules to increase your personal safety:

- Arrange with your employer to call in every hour or after each service call.

- Try to work in pairs or in threes in high-risk areas, and avoid these neighborhoods after dark.

- Wear a company uniform or jacket and cap, along with an employer-issued ID badge, so you won't be mistaken for an intruder.

- Make sure the name of your company is visible on your vehicle or uniform.

- Don't carry excess cash on the job.

- Always lock your vehicle, and never leave in it anything of value, especially if it is visible.

- Ask your employer to paint a large, clearly discernible number on top of your company vehicle so that it can be easily identified and followed in the event of an emergency.

- Most important, when outside the company perimeter, remain attentive and very alert.

CHAPTER 26

ROBBERY IN SMALL BUSINESSES

Planning how to respond to a robbery attempt is always a wise measure. Every employee—especially those who handle money—should know what to do to protect themselves.

DECREASING YOUR CHANCES

Unlike other crimes, robbery represents a threat to both your person and your property. Surprisingly, injuries occur most frequently when no weapon is used, because in this instance a victim is most likely to fight back. But do not be a hero and resist the robbers physically or verbally. While it is true that robbers may use force even if you don't resist, they will become frustrated if you attempt to thwart their goals and will be more likely to become violent.

If you own a small business or store, follow these simple guidelines to decrease your chances of becoming victimized.

- Keep the premises orderly and clean. A cluttered store gives the impression of carelessness.
- Make sure the back room is out of public view so that the robber is not drawn to property that may be stored in it. Also, the robber will not be certain if someone else is on the premises.

- Keep a television or radio on in the back room to give the appearance of the presence of others.
- Keep the inside of your store well lighted.
- Be active; move around the store.
- Maximize the amount of space inside that is visible from the outside by using adequate lighting.
- Display security decals in the window.
- Constantly be on the lookout for suspicious-looking people standing inside or outside the store.
- Avoid obstructions near the window that might block the ability of pass-ersby and the police to observe what is happening inside the store.
- Instruct employees not to disclose information about alarm systems, security, the number of employees, or any other information that would assist anyone interested in robbing your store or business.

Be Selective When Hiring Employees

Many robberies are accomplished with the assistance of an insider, as was the $1 million heist of Tiffany's on Fifth Avenue in Manhattan in 1994. Once the robbers were apprehended, the police learned that a Tiffany's operational security officer was involved in the robbery. He had provided his accomplices with confidential information on the security precautions used by Tiffany's to deter robbery.

Handling and Safeguarding Money

Be serious about protecting your money. Keep a minimum amount of working cash in your store, especially at night, when most robberies occur. Put larger bills in a drop safe as soon as you receive them. Never allow cash to accumulate in your register. Make bank deposits during the day, and vary your route and timing. If possible, take someone else with you.

Display burglar alarm decals in a prominent place. Post signs on the door stating that a second key, not kept on the premises, is required to open safes. If you belong to a special citizens' robbery prevention program, post signs to this effect inside and outside the store. Since many robberies occur when you open or close the store, try to have someone else present at these times. Robbers case their potential targets and know when only one person will be on hand.

Employees should be reminded regularly that they devote about 30 percent of their lives to their jobs, and with that sort of commitment, they need to do everything they can to protect the environment in which they spend so much of their time.

Do not balance registers or count receipts in full view. This actually tempts robbers, customers, and even other store employees. Have cash drawers taken to a secure location to count the money. Record the serial number of a few bills that you permanently keep in the cash register. This can aid the police in tracking down the robbers and help in the identification of your property if it is recovered.

It is best not to rely on firearms. Alarm systems, electronic surveillance equipment, safes with time locks, and other robbery-resistant items may provide better protection and should be considered for your store.

Securing the Workplace on the Outside

A determined thief will exploit every weakness that you fail to remedy adequately. Your place of business should be as secure as your home, if not more so. Small businesses are not immune to crime. In fact, small businesses are particularly vulnerable because they have more difficulty absorbing a loss compared to a large company.

Obviously, your protection must begin outside the workplace, for that's where you want to contain an intruder. You should avoid leaving ladders or stacks of pallets outside the building. Either of these could provide above-ground-level entry into your business. Parking up against the building should be discouraged, because an auto not only can be used as a stepladder to the second story but also because it is a convenient method of removing the loot.

The very best protection, however, is to be found in alert and caring employee groups. Employees should be reminded regularly that they

Vigilance Is the Best Strategy

Always greet customers in a friendly, personable manner. This will not only benefit your business but also make potential robbers feel that they may be identified later. Robbers seek to remain anonymous and to avoid friendly contact with potential victims. Be alert for anyone appearing to loiter inside or outside the store, seemingly waiting for you to be alone. Err on the safe side and call the police if you notice suspicious people. You should prepare signals with fellow employees so that if a robbery takes place, you can alert a coworker who may be in a position to notify the police.

devote about 30 percent of their lives to their jobs, and with that sort of commitment, they need to do everything they can to protect the environment in which they spend so much of their time. Much of what is stolen is their property. And what is stolen from the employer affects them as well, since their job security and prosperity depend on the employer's continued survival.

Securing the Workplace on the Inside

Today's office is much more sophisticated than in days past, and the equipment used is much more expensive. A generation ago a steno pad and a typewriter were the tools of the trade for secretaries and typists. Today's equipment can command much higher prices. The wonder computers of the 1960s, which revolutionized our banking industry, had less computing power than the PC sitting on the secretarial desk of today.

Among many truisms about crime is this: If you have something both valuable and small, someone will try to steal it. Even if your office has no other easily portable and valuable equipment, a thief may steal your telephone in a second or two.

An intruder in your building may be looking for a physician's office and drugs; on the way out, the thief may take your purse. At lunchtime, most office personnel take a break, leaving one person to take care of the office. If safeguards are ignored, much mischief may follow.

Robbery Realities

Robbery accounts for more than 30 percent of all violent crime. In 40 percent of the cases, no weapon is used. Studies also reveal that robberies seldom involve people who are known to each other. More than three-quarters of all robberies are committed by strangers.

A building security officer, a strong deterrent to the would-be thief, is good protection against stealing. Designated areas where valuable items, including the personal property of those working in the building, can be kept under lock and key are additional protection. Installing your cash register as near to the front of the store as possible will allow passersby to note an in-progress robbery or an after-hours burglary. This is also a good deterrent to shoplifters, since they will have to pass the cashiers on the way out.

Cooperate with neighborhood merchants for your mutual self-protection. In one of the toughest areas of the South Bronx, a group of merchants banded together. They installed buzzers that sounded in the buildings next to their own. It was thus relatively easy for an in-progress crime to be reported to the police, without a confrontation with the thieves. These "buddy buzzers" proved to be excellent security weapons, at the cost of only a few dollars.

VIOLENCE PREVENTION PROCEDURES

Though robbery is a crime in which the threat of violence is always present, there are things you can do to decrease that threat.

During a Robbery

Obey the instructions of robbers immediately. Never argue with them. Robbers are less likely to injure you if you cooperate. The shorter the time it takes the robbers to do their work, the less chance there is for injury or even death. In fact, the average robbery is completed in under 2 minutes. Remain calm and reassure your employees and customers. Do not fight with the robbers or attempt to use weapons. By the time you are confronted by a robber, it is too late for such actions.

Assume that any firearm is real and loaded. If you need to reach for something, or put your hand in your pocket, or do anything else that the robber may perceive as threatening, tell him before you do it. For your own safety, alert the robbers to any possible surprises, such as an employee working in the back room or a delivery person who may return to the store at any moment.

Some stores and businesses have marks on door frames or a wall that aid an employee or witness in estimating the robber's height. This may be easily done by placing two pieces of colored tape at about 5 feet 6 inches, and at 6 feet on the door frame.

Take mental notes about the crime and the criminals. Pay attention to the number of robbers, their ages, sexes, ethnic backgrounds, appearance, clothing, shoes, weapons, voices, nicknames, special characteristics, and unusual behavior or identifying marks. Some stores and businesses have marks on door frames or a wall that aid an employee or witness in estimating the robber's height. This may be easily done by placing two pieces of colored tape at about 5 feet 6 inches, and at 6 feet on the door frame.

One anti-robbery technique sometimes recommended is the installation of a doorbell in your place of business. The bell should ring in an adjacent store, enabling your neighboring merchant to notify the police when you are unable to do so. For your neighbor's protection, you can reciprocate.

Caution: If the robbers observe you signaling, they will typically do you harm. Therefore, signal only if you feel certain it will not be detected by the robber. Surviving the robbery without injury is your number one goal.

After a Robbery
Note the make, color, and year of the vehicle used in the robbery, and the license plate number and state of registration. Check the direction

Corporate Offices a Rising Target for Burglaries

Cash-heavy businesses such as service stations and convenient stores aren't the only locations prone to burglaries. These days thieves are targeting corporate offices as well. The reason for the increase? Traditional targets have beefed up their security, and the recession has driven some people to desperate measures.

The most likely to be hit are small companies with ground-level offices that offer easy access, and sometimes the perpetrators are armed. Last year Crisis Care Network Inc. provided crisis counselors to employees at 206 workplaces nationwide, including offices and retail stores, after armed robberies took place.

Federal law requires employers to provide a safe work environment. As such, if an incident occurs in your workplace, worker's compensation laws prohibit employees from suing employers unless in circumstances involving gross negligence.

in which the offenders were heading, but do not chase or follow them under any circumstance. The robbers may try to kill you, and the police may even mistake you for the criminals.

Notify the police immediately. Stay on the phone until they get all the necessary information, then remain close to the telephone. Lock the doors until the police arrive. Take inventory of exactly what was stolen, but do not give this information to the responding officers. Reveal this information only to the detectives assigned to your case; the police may talk to reporters, and publicity about a substantial loss may convince other robbers to attack your store, too.

Record the names and addresses of witnesses. Do not disturb any objects the robbers may have touched or held, and avoid discussing the robbery until the police say it is okay for you to do so.

PART SIX

PROTECTION FROM VIOLENT CRIMES

CHAPTER 27

RAPE, SEXUAL HARASSMENT, AND STALKING

*Crimes of rape, sexual harassment, and stalking affect everyone.
No man, woman, or child is exempt from being a potential victim.
But understanding the crimes—and the criminals—will give you
insight into ways to protect yourself from this violence.*

RAPE

Rape is a not a sex crime, but a crime of violence that includes dominating and imposing power or will over the victim. Victims of this crime are primarily women. More than any other type of crime, the physical and psychological effects of rape tend to be long-lasting. Rape carries with it the immediate physical dangers of being beaten, injured, or killed, as well as the possibility of pregnancy or sexually transmitted diseases, including AIDS. The victim is also subjected to psychological stress and trauma that may last a lifetime. The rape victim often feels humiliated and ostracized.

Forcible rape involves attempted or completed sexual penetration of a person against her will. Statutory rape consists of an adult having sexual relations with a person under a legal age of consent (16 in most jurisdictions), even with her consent.

Protecting School-Age Girls from Rape

One of the more common forms of rape involves an assault upon a school-age girl by an older man. The assailant is alone, has no weapon, and is probably known to the victim, at least by sight. Too often, these young victims are too trusting and too inexperienced to take proper safeguards. How can you protect your school-age daughters? Always know where your children are, what they're doing, and with whom. You should also follow these guidelines:

- Make sure she never entertains her male friends at home without supervision and never admits strangers.
- Teach her that there is safety in numbers, but with the caveat that she is safest in the company of other girls.
- Make sure she is home by the time that most people in the community are asleep.
- Tell her to exercise caution and awareness through astute observation when she is home alone during the daylight hours, such as after school.
- Teach her to avoid one-to-one relationships in after-school activities or situations in which she might be the only female in a group.
- Help her exercise extreme caution in accepting dates. Always insist on meeting her dates and engaging them in dialogue. Make sure that her friends or other parents know the date.

If You Are Attacked

Since self-protective measures help in the majority of attacks, you should be prepared to defend yourself by kicking, clawing and screaming. If you are not serious about, or simply not capable of, inflicting pain or physical harm on your assailant, you shouldn't attempt it. If you are determined to defend yourself, your best defense is escape.

The best time to make a break for it is as early during the assault as possible. Authorities suggest that the optimum moment to react is during the first 20 seconds. The attacker won't expect an escape then. Also, the less time you are under the control of the rapist, the less likely you are to be hurt or intimidated. Moreover, your chances of escape are better before the rapist gains total control and before he has the chance to throw you to the ground or force you to a secluded spot. The longer you submit passively to his demands, the less likely you are to react later on. Fear of antagonizing your assailant will worsen, and overcoming inertia will become more difficult in time.

Scream as you run to distract the rapist and alert others to the danger. Some suggest that screaming "Fire!" rather than "Help!" will get assistance more quickly. A loud scream tells the assailant that he picked the wrong target. Hysterics are not recommended; they may panic the assailant and alert to him your fear and vulnerability. If an attacker points a gun at you and orders you into a car and you run, the odds are high that he will not shoot. But if you get into the car, your chances of surviving are very slim.

If you are trapped and have little chance of escape, should you fight or not? There is no simple answer to this question. If you do fight, statistics indicate that you *will* be attacked physically—maybe even suffer a brutal beating. The best policy is never to fight an assailant armed with a knife or gun, but if his only weapon is superior strength, resisting may be worth the risk of getting hurt. Only you can decide whether and how to resist a rape attack, and since every situation is different, no one can second-guess you.

Some suggest that screaming "Fire!" rather than "Help!" will get assistance more quickly.

You may be able to change the rapist's intentions. He may be reluctant to have sexual contact with you if he believes you have a sexually transmitted disease—even AIDS. You may be able to persuade the rapist that you want to have a sexual relationship with him, but in a more comfortable setting. Pretend to invite him to your place, with the intention of escaping or summoning assistance. Try to make yourself unattractive by telling him you are at the peak of your menstrual period or you have stomach cramps. This may distract the assailant or perhaps cause him to loosen his grip. Some women have vomited or relieved themselves to ward off a persistent assailant, and others have been successful by feigning mental retardation.

Defensive Weapons and Tactics

Using a weapon in the attack may help you defend yourself and even get away. Although you should avoid weapons such as handguns, knives, tear gas, and Mace since they could be a violation of the law—and might be taken from you and used against you—other items that aren't classified as concealed weapons might be even more effective because they can be hand-carried or hidden in a coat pocket. These include hatpins, keys, a pen or pencil, a corkscrew, pepper, lemon juice in a squeeze bottle, or hairspray—all of which can be used against the attacker's eyes. An umbrella can be a good weapon if used like a spear or sword rather than a club. A pocket-size, heavy-duty flashlight can be used as a thrusting weapon or to temporarily blind your assailant. (See chapter 11 for more on defense weapons.)

Some items of self-defense you should keep in your pocket include hatpins, keys, a pen or pencil, a corkscrew, pepper, lemon juice in a squeeze bottle, or hairspray—all of which can be used against the attacker's eyes.

However, you should be warned: Many men have had boxing or other self-defense training, and your assailant may be able to parry your thrust and block your swings. Even so, his switch from offensive to defensive tactics may give you a chance to flee, and if you're lucky, you'll at least discourage him from his initial objective. But remember, if you do attack, be prepared to keep it up.

Some authorities tell you to attack the assailant in the groin area. While this is his most vulnerable spot, he is also likely to protect this area, both through instinct and from a lifetime of street fighting. Instead, go for the pit of the stomach, the throat, the eyes, the temples, or even the kneecap.

Other vulnerable and easily accessible parts of the body include the kidneys, solar plexus, pinkie finger, nose, and ears. However, if the rapist makes an embracing type of attack from the front, smash a knee into his groin. Or grab his scrotum in the groin area with both hands, squeeze, twist, and drop to the ground so the full weight of your body is on the scrotum. This technique should disable the attacker.

Some experts recommend you punch his trachea or Adam's apple with your fist. At the same time, use your other hand to yank his head forward. Or cup your hands and, with all your force, in one continuous sweeping motion, strike your assailant's ears and then forcefully press both thumbs into his eyes. This tactic is particularly useful when the rapist is facing you and pressing you toward him.

If you are grabbed from the rear, jab an elbow into your attacker's stomach. Stomp on his foot—about halfway between the ankle and the toes—to break it. The pain of this might well discourage any further attack. Even if it doesn't, it might make it easier for you to break free and run.

Other aggressive actions include eye gouging, biting, scratching, and kicking. Additional natural weapons include your head, heel, palm of your hand, thumbs, hips, and forearms. The rapist will usually try to throw you to the ground. Once you are on the ground, your chances of defense are lessened but not hopeless. For the best chance of defending yourself, take a self-defense course geared toward helping women defend themselves from such threatening situations.

If you are trapped and so threatened that you cannot escape, you may still be able to avoid attack by crying. Sobbing may save you from an attack. You might also try to establish some sort of conversation to de-escalate the situation.

You may encounter circumstances that make it impossible for you to resist. If, for example, he threatens not you but your child, you may feel that there is no alternative but to accede to his demands. The decisions you make when face to face with an attacker must be based on circumstances as you see them at the time. In addition, your body will release chemicals in your bloodstream that will help you fight, run, or outsmart. Once the incident is over and you reflect on what you did and how you might have done otherwise, remember that your actions were dictated by your body as well as your mind.

Self-Protection

What can you do to protect yourself from rape?

- Never walk alone after dark.
- Avoid public parks, areas with a lot of trees, bushes, and shrubbery, parking lots, alleys, and deserted areas.
- Cross the street if you see a group of males approaching you.
- Be alert when waiting for a bus, a traffic light, or a friend. Your stationary position makes you more vulnerable to attack.
- If you are on foot and a car pulls up next to you or drives by several times, change direction or run away.
- Pay attention to your instincts. If you feel uncomfortable getting into an elevator with a strange man, do not get in. Better to offend a stranger than to risk your safety.
- Be aware that a date could degenerate into a rape; maintain defenses at all times.
- Always be aware of your exact location in case you need to contact the police.
- Follow all instructions and answer all questions posed by a 911 operator. Do not hang up until the 911 operator tells you to.

ACQUAINTANCE RAPE

Acquaintance rape is a rape in which the perpetrator is someone the victim knows. Date rape occurs when what appears to be a friendly, innocent sexual overture suddenly becomes a sexual attack.

Acquaintance rape can involve relatives, casual friends, coworkers, and other people familiar to each other. Men of all descriptions and backgrounds have been accused of acquaintance rape, including attorneys, businessmen, physicians, and dentists.

The best defense against acquaintance rape is the ability to identify and avoid men who are likely to engage in sexual assault. Potential rapists:

- Tend to think violence is an acceptable means of attaining goals and resolving disputes.
- Have an unhealthy obsession with violence on TV and in movies, and may have an obsession with guns or hard-core pornography.
- Often have problems with alcohol and/or drugs.

- Tend to display minimal respect for other human beings generally, and they may be cruel to children and animals.
- Intrude on the personal space of others, psychologically and physically.
- Act "macho," exhibiting sexist conduct and attitudes.
- Will be satisfied with nothing less than complete control of their acquaintance's mind and body.

Acquaintance rape can involve relatives, casual friends, coworkers, and other people familiar to each other.

How to Protect Yourself on a Date

Experts say early warning signals for date rape include intimidating stares, standing too close, enjoying your discomfort, acting as if he knows you better than he does, calling you names that make you uncomfortable, constantly blocking your way and following you, touching you in sensitive places "by accident," ignoring what you say, and becoming angry when you disagree with him.

Here are some concrete suggestions for protecting yourself on a date:

- Be certain you know the full, real name of every man you date, where he lives, and something about his occupation. Take his phone number, but do not give out your own.
- Consult your friends or any other people who know the person before you accept a date with him to obtain information about personality, life activities and habits before you accept a date with him.
- Never invite a man you have met in the street, a bar, or any other public place to be alone with you in your home or any private place until you know him well.
- For your first date, arrange to meet him at the date location, which should be a public place like a movie theater, museum, library, mall, cafe, coffee shop, or restaurant. Insist on taking a cab or public transportation; avoid driving with him, especially in his car.
- Make certain you take along your cell phone and at least enough money for a taxi.

- Offer to pay for part of the date or arrange to go "dutch" so that you set a tone of equality.
- Always maintain a measure of reserve and distance on the first date. This does not mean you should be cold, uncooperative, or impersonal. You can be reserved and, at the same time, warm and compassionate.

Insist on taking a cab or public transportation; avoid driving with your date, especially in his car.

- Remain sober or drink moderately on dates with men you don't know well, to maintain control of your faculties at all times. If you are at a party or on one of the first few dates with a new person and he is drinking and ordering or pouring drinks for you, have just one glass of wine or cocktail and then insist on switching to a non-alcoholic beverage, such as club soda. Alcohol and drugs lower inhibitions and set the stage for unwanted sexual behavior, which can easily turn into sexual assault.
- Never leave your drink unattended. Drugs such as "roofies," or Rohypnol, known as the "date-rape" drug, can be added to your drink without your knowledge. Stay alert to symptoms—if you are suddenly feeling excessively tired, dizzy, or nauseous or are having trouble walking or speaking, immediately tell a friend or person working at the restaurant or club that you are not feeling well and need to leave so that they can make sure you get home safely. Call a family member or friend if you need someone to pick you up and possibly stay with you.
- Be sure to tell someone before you go anywhere other than a public place with him, and be certain your date knows you have done so.

Preemptive Action

Learn date-rape danger signals, and be alert for any strange behavior. Is he trying too hard to convince you to accompany him to an isolated location? Has he suddenly steered the conversation toward sex? Is he making lewd statements or describing sexual acts in detail? Is he using foul language? Does he suddenly try to hug, kiss, hold, or touch you without permission? Does he start to push and hit you lightly?

If you detect any of these signals, you must take the next steps to keep the situation from getting out of control:

- Be assertive and firm in your tone of voice and body language. Lethargy and passivity send the wrong signals, especially to a "macho" type. Ambiguous signals tend to confuse your date, making it more difficult to stop sexual improprieties later on.
- Do not allow the would-be rapist a small liberty in the hope it will appease him or prevent further aggression. Remember, the assailant seeks to dominate the victim with rape. A token concession is unlikely to stop him.
- If you have made a strenuous objection and your date does not stop the unwanted behavior, threaten to call the police.
- Do not allow yourself to become isolated.

Confrontation

If you still can't stop your date from forcing himself on you sexually, you can try these additional strategies that may work as well with an acquaintance rapist as with a stranger. (See page 318.)

- **Use a verbal defense.** Try to talk the rapist out of the attack. Use conversation as a stalling tactic. Convince the rapist that you do not want sex under any circumstances with him or anyone else. Explain to him that what he intends is rape. This approach is more likely to be effective with an acquaintance or date than with a stranger.
- **Invent a surprise.** Tell the attacker that you're having your period or that you feel sick. Tell him you are going to throw up. If you can make yourself vomit, do so. Try to make the attacker disgusted. Tell him you have AIDS. Strange or bizarre behavior may also throw a date-rapist off guard. Rant and rave; flail your hands; make sudden body movements; act out hallucinations.
- **Escape.** Think of the above strategies as ways to buy time until you can figure out an escape. As soon as he lets his guard down, run out of the house or apartment or get out of the car. Attract the attention of other people if possible; scream if you have to. Or tell him you have to go to the bathroom, then use a cell phone to call for assistance or leave through the bathroom window if you can.

- **The best time to attempt an escape is at the very beginning of the confrontation.** During the first few seconds or moments, the date-rapist will try to get you under his control. The further the situation escalates, the more important that control will become for the rapist, and the more difficult it will be to pry yourself loose.

SEXUAL ASSAULT ON CAMPUS

Acquaintance rape flourishes within the social and dating structures of teenagers, but teenagers are particularly likely not to report sexual assaults because many are convinced no one will believe them—not their parents, best friends, acquaintances, employers, or coworkers. Often, teens who are unfamiliar with sexual encounters aren't sure that what they experienced constitutes rape.

On college campuses, young people—most right out of high school, many away from home for the first time—often live together in co-ed dorms and regularly attend unsupervised parties. They are thrown into situations in which acquaintance can escalate into intimacy within minutes. Add alcohol and drugs, and you have an explosive mixture. The student least likely to be a victim of sexual assault is the student who is best informed about it.

A recent survey reported that many men involved in date rape had consumed alcohol or drugs immediately prior to the assault. Moreover, 55 percent of the victims had consumed alcohol or drugs before the incident.

Self-Protection on Campus

The two most significant factors associated with campus rape are how often a woman dates and her lack of sobriety. The more men she dates, the more likely it is she will at some time find herself with a man with the characteristics of an assailant. In addition, a recent survey reported that many men involved in date rape had consumed alcohol or drugs immediately prior to the assault. Moreover, 55 percent of the victims had consumed alcohol or drugs before the incident. If you do drink, you should do so in moderation and stop before you feel dizzy or drunk. Determine your tolerance level before exposing yourself to potentially dangerous social situations.

The following rules will provide some protection from campus date rape:

- Be extremely selective in the men you date. Note any signs that may signal a tendency toward assaultive behavior.
- Be alert to "rape hazards" like isolated places, first dates, and weekend parties.
- Avoid parties where alcohol and drugs are consumed. If you must drink, know and observe your limit.
- Refrain from dating "macho" men who demean women.
- Tell your partner as soon as possible (only you can sense the right moment) your sexual limits, describing the behavior you consider acceptable and unacceptable. Tell him that kissing, hugging, and touching are not a license for total intimacy.
- Terminate your date if the man attempts any form of force or intimidation, even if the man is a classmate or friend.
- Memorize the campus security or emergency telephone number. Write it down and keep it in an easily accessible place and program it into your cell phone as well; if a disturbing situation develops, you may have trouble remembering it.
- Ask a female friend or campus security officer to accompany you home after a late-night party.
- Never leave a party with a man who makes sexual comments that are unwelcome or that make you uncomfortable.
- If your date engages in behavior that makes you uncomfortable, be assertive. Tell him if he does not stop, you will end the date.
- Leave immediately with a girlfriend if you find yourself one of few women remaining at a party.
- Always trust your intuition and instincts about a person or situation.

Keep in mind that your college has probably established a safety escort service that is available at night and on weekends or a bus or van shuttle to dormitories that operates after dark. Your college may also have security phones at convenient locations throughout the campus that automatically dial the security office in case of an emergency.

In the event of sexual assault, the victim should not shower, bathe, or change clothes. Immediately seek medical attention at the college infirmary or the nearest hospital emergency room. Medical personnel will notify law enforcement if the victim has not already done so and will offer medical treatment and counseling regarding sexually transmitted diseases.

What Parents Can Do

Here's what you can do to help protect your daughter from rape on campus.

- Discuss with your prospective freshman the issues of acquaintance and date rape and the potential dangers of fraternities, athletes, alcohol, drugs, and parties—especially during the first few weeks of class, the most vulnerable "window" for assaults, when your daughter is unfamiliar with campus lifestyle and policies.
- Teach her the warning signs of potentially dangerous behavior and the fact that she should never to go to an isolated place with someone she does not know well.
- Remind her that the dating process is a very serious matter and should not be treated casually.
- Make sure her school has a meaningful rape prevention program, takes a strong stand against sexual assault, and mandates meaningful and just penalties for men found guilty of rape.

SEXUAL HARASSMENT

Sexual harassment and stalking are each violations of the law. Both involve subtle ways of destroying the confidence, well-being, and security of women, who are the primary targets.

Sexual Harassment on the Job

Sexual harassment is defined as unwelcome sexual advances, requests for sexual favors, and other verbal or physical conduct of a sexual nature where:

- Submission to such conduct is made explicitly or implicitly a term or condition of an individual's employment.
- Submission to or rejection of such conduct by an individual is used as the basis for decisions affecting on-the-job status of the individual.
- Such conduct has the purpose or effect of unreasonably interfering with an individual's work performance, or creating an intimidating, hostile, or offensive working environment.

One major form of sexual harassment involves *quid pro quo*, or giving something in exchange for something else. This abuse of power occurs when one person holds institutional control over another—for example, a physician over a nurse, a manager over an employee, a professor over a student, or an officer over a lower-ranking officer or enlisted person. It is illegal for you to be terminated or denied an employment benefit because you refused to grant sexual favors or because you complained about harassment.

Similarly, you've been subject to sexual harassment if you've had to resign from your job rather than accept aggressive sexual behavior or an offensive work environment. Unwelcome sexual advances, familiarities, remarks, off-color jokes and comments about people's anatomy, slurs about gender, unwanted touching, spatial encroachments, requests for sexual favors, work discussions that suddenly turn to conversations about

Sexually Transmitted Diseases

In addition to the emotional and physical trauma of rape is the reality that you could also be at risk for herpes, gonorrhea, syphilis, or AIDS. All of these diseases can endanger the victim's health and may even be life-threatening.

However, the list of consequences does not end with the victim. Their sexual partners are also at risk, as are gynecologists, emergency-room personnel, and others who may have offered assistance. If the beleaguered woman is pregnant (or becomes so as the result of being attacked), the fetus she carries is at risk from a variety of venereal disorders.

Claiming you suffer from an STD may help deter an attacker. Although they may not believe you, you'll have nothing to lose.

sex, and obscene and suggestive letters or notes all may constitute sexual harassment. Sexual harassment may also involve visual conduct, such as leering and sexual gestures. This is especially the case when the behavior is unwelcome, coercive and persistent.

Another aspect of sexual harassment is known as a hostile work environment, which is created when superiors or coworkers engage in physical or verbal sexual improprieties that a reasonable person would find unwelcome and abusive. A constant stream of offensive sexual comments, repeated sexual propositions, constant display of pornographic materials, or repeated unwanted touching creates a hostile work environment.

If You Are Harassed

Take these steps if you are harassed in the workplace.

- **Inform the harasser.** The first step is to inform the harasser immediately and clearly that you consider his attention, remarks, or behavior offensive and unwelcome and that he is engaging in sexual harassment. Be specific, providing concrete examples of exactly what offended you. Use body language to indicate that you do not want the behavior to continue, like taking a rapid step backwards when the harasser comes too close or suddenly stopping and staring angrily into his eyes. Your primary aim is to have him stop the offending behavior before it escalates. Notification also supports your contention that you were harassed.

- **Write a memo.** If a verbal warning fails to stop the harasser, write him a memo about what he did or said, what you don't like about it, how it made you feel, and the action you will take if he does it again. Deliver the copy in the presence of a witness, or send it certified mail, return receipt requested. Keep a copy of the memo in your personal files away from the office. These actions will counter the harasser's argument that he didn't realize the behavior was unwelcome or that he thought it was good, clean, harmless fun.

- **Document the situation.** Thoroughly document your situation. Write down everything that takes place; leave nothing to memory or chance.

Maintain a precise written record of what happened or what was said: when it was said, the location, your response, and all witnesses, including those who can confirm that you spent time with the harasser. Include a description of how the offensive behavior hurt you and the names of those you told about it. Also, make certain you gather all evidence, including cards, letters, notes, and memos sent to you by the harasser, and keep a careful record of all his telephone calls to you.

Make certain you gather all evidence, including cards, letters, notes, and memos sent to you by the harasser, and keep a careful record of all his telephone calls to you.

- **Document your work performance.** Document your performance, showing the work you have done and that you have performed it well. Maintain a record of written materials and verbal statements that indicate positive performance, and keep copies of evaluations by your superior. This is to prevent the harasser from being able to justify a claim that you are raising charges of sexual harassment as an excuse or a smokescreen for poor work.
- **Report the harasser.** If unwanted comments or familiarities continue, and your verbal and written warnings prove futile, report the behavior to your superior, your union, and your personnel office. Follow your complaint up the company hierarchy until strong action is taken to stop the behavior. If your complaint is ignored and no action is taken, file a formal complaint with the Equal Employment Opportunity Commission (EEOC). (You can find the EEOC in your telephone directory under U.S. Government listings or online at www.eeoc.gov/offices.) You have 180 days from the time the behavior occurred to file the complaint with EEOC; otherwise, the complaint may be considered untimely.
- **Go public.** Write a letter to your local newspaper or contact your local radio or TV news station about your situation. Join a women's support group or a lobbying organization. Publicizing your situation may help other women who are experiencing sexual harassment, as well as you.

Sexual Harassment in Schools

A group of guys corner you in a school hallway, press you against the wall, and tell you what they'd like to do with you. A classmate passes around a note with your name and telephone number that says you're the one to call for "hot sex." Your adviser insists it's acceptable for a young woman to fall in love with an older man, like himself. These are typical examples of sexual harassment that take place in high schools every day.

Sexual harassment in schools involves more than obvious and unwelcome flirtatious advances by teachers or students. Sexual harassment includes touching and grabbing; sexual remarks; conversations that are too personal; dirty jokes; obscene gestures; and persistent staring so as to make you feel uncomfortable. Graphic descriptions of women's bodies, pornographic pictures, graffiti, and denigrating language also constitute sexual harassment when they promote a hostile and unequal environment in which girls are precluded from attaining their full potential. Statistics show that girls in schools are four times as likely as boys to experience sexual harassment.

What a Student Should Do

If you're harassed at your school, here's what you can do:

- Find out exactly what conduct is considered sexual harassment.
- Familiarize yourself with your school's policy on sexual harassment.
- If any harasser, especially an adult, tries to convince you not to tell anyone, always bothers you when you are alone, or threatens to hurt you, then *immediately* tell a trusted adult.
- Tell the harasser that the behavior makes you uncomfortable and that you want it to stop.
- Speak to a family member, especially your parents, and ask for their help in lodging a complaint.
- Keep a record of the harassment.
- Avoid being alone with the harasser.
- Write a letter to the harasser detailing exactly what behavior occurred, what it is about the behavior that you object to, that you want him to stop, and what will happen if his behavior persists.

- Report incidents of sexual harassment to your principal, counselor, or appropriate administrator charged with responsibility for this issue.
- Be prepared to press your complaint through the school hierarchy. If your school does not have a written policy and mechanism for handling complaints, speak to your student council, teachers, guidance counselors and principal, and urge them to formulate guidelines.

What a Parent Should Do

If you think your child may have been sexually harassed, here's what you can do to help:

- Discuss with your child her feelings about various kinds of sexual attention. Explain sexual harassment, and provide concrete examples.

It's best for your teenager to learn appropriate tolerance levels from you instead of from her peers.

- Raise the issue with your child to determine if she has been sexually harassed. Explain that certain forms of flirting constitute sexual harassment, even though she may find it exciting and flattering. Teenage girls may not be fully aware of what kinds of behavior demean women. Boys can also be victims of sexual harassment, so parents should raise these issues with boys as well as girls.
- Be certain your child will come to you with an issue of sexual harassment. Keep the lines of communication open. It's best for your teenager to learn appropriate tolerance levels from you instead of her peers.
- Acknowledge the injury that your child feels as a result of sexual harassment.
- Ensure that there will be no retaliation if your child comes forward with a claim of sexual harassment.
- Be loving and supportive.
- Take seriously all charges of sexual harassment. Report any incidents to the appropriate authorities.
- Guide your child through all the necessary steps to stop the behavior.

STALKERS AND STALKING

Stalking involves the unwanted harassment of, following of, and obsession with another person. Most stalking involves harassment, such as repeated and annoying phone calls and letters, and may include threats or violence against the victim. The worst possible outcome is murder.

While some stalkers may be psychologically disturbed, studies suggest that the majority of stalkers are not mentally ill. Stalkers may be male or female, heterosexual or homosexual, but most are men who have been rejected by women. Most murders by stalkers occur because the stalker is unable to accept the end of a relationship with the victim.

Stalking and Evidence

Many victims of stalkers are typical, everyday people; their stalkers are ex-spouses or lovers, acquaintances, or even strangers. The remaining victims are entertainers, sports figures, executives or supervisors with unhappy employees, or psychotherapists stalked by patients.

If you are being stalked, notify the police immediately. Request that a file on your case be started. Give the police a photo of and all the information you have about your stalker.

Save and date all evidence—including letters, notes, cards, and voicemail messages—and take pictures of any damaged property. Wear cotton gloves when opening letters. Hold them at the corners and store them in clear plastic bags so they may be read without directly touching them. When you have contact with the stalker, note the date, time, what was said, and any witnesses. This account may be admissible as evidence in court. You may also get an order of protection from the courts, which may increase the offender's punishment if he is convicted of stalking you. Finally, ask the police to drive by your home, and ask them to also conduct a home-security assessment.

Protect Yourself from Stalking

Stalking is against the law. However, each state has different requirements. Check with local law enforcement. If you believe that someone is stalking you, trust your instincts and seek help. Most people can't afford personal protection, such as a bodyguard or a security officer for their home. Instead, here are more practical guidelines that will help you protect yourself:

- Put a deadbolt on your door and secure your windows. If the stalker has a copy of your keys, change the locks.
- Vary your routes when walking or driving.
- Get an unlisted telephone number or caller ID, or screen your calls with an answering machine.
- Get an order of protection that imposes a penalty (of money or imprisonment) on your stalker if he keeps contacting you.
- Do not try to meet, talk, or reason with the stalker.
- Do not return the stalker's letters or gifts. Doing so may incite him further. Besides, you want to keep them to use as evidence later.
- Do not respond to his cries for help, such as threatening suicide. The purpose of these attempts is to make you feel guilty or to trap you.
- If your assailant is a former spouse or lover, do not reconcile in the hopes of warding off an attack. This only reaffirms his motivation for making you the object of his obsession.
- Do not develop a cyber relationship with a stranger, and never meet a "cyber friend" in an isolated circumstance or location.

CHAPTER 28

HATE CRIMES, KIDNAPPING, AND MURDER

When you think of violent crime, you probably think of murder. But other crimes that threaten bodily harm—such as hate crimes and kidnapping—fall into the category of violent crime as well.

DEALING WITH HATE-MOTIVATED VIOLENCE

A hate crime is any threat or act of violence that targets an individual, a group, or property, and is motivated by the race, color, religion, national origin, age, disability or sexual orientation of the victim. The impact of hate crimes goes beyond any specific act, because they incite fear, distrust, hostility, anxiety, insecurity and confusion. Even if only one individual or group is targeted, this particularly violent form of crime affects us all, personally and collectively.

The acting out of racial, religious, and homophobic hatred has been evident in widespread reports of disrupted religious services, church, synagogue, and cemetery desecrations, cross burnings, fire bombings and hate-motivated assaults, beatings and gunshots. At the same time, distribution of hate literature has continued to be a problem; radio talk shows, which often provide an open mike for hate talk, have been winning big audiences and high ratings; and studies suggest that over 10 percent of bias-motivated hate crimes occur on school property.

What steps can you take to stop hate crimes?

- Teach your children the importance of tolerance and lead by example. A child who grows up in a tolerant family is more likely to resist hateful propaganda and the hateful influences of others.
- Help schools promote anti-hate programs, and encourage them to swiftly punish any negative remarks or behaviors directed at minorities.
- Demonstrate that you will not tolerate hate crimes in your own community by reporting all such incidents to a government or private agency combating this kind of bigotry.
- If you are a college student, report a hate crime or any information you may have about its perpetrators to the campus police, the dean, or other designated representatives of your college.

If you are a victim of hate-motivated threats, harassments or acts of violence, you or a government attorney may be able to apply for a restraining order against the perpetrator. The laws vary from jurisdiction to jurisdiction. Once the perpetrator is convicted, you may be entitled to compensation for medical bills, property damage, lost wages and psychological counseling. Also, you can bring a civil action to recover legal fees and monetary damages. Above all, have the courage to persevere until justice is done and the problem has subsided.

KIDNAPPING

The chance that your child will be kidnapped is relatively small, as only a handful of the millions of children in the United States are kidnapped each year. However, this should not cause you to have less concern for the safety your children, particularly if there is a serious domestic situation, you have observed a suspicious person within the vicinity of where you live or your child's school, or there are other indications that an unknown or suspicious person is taking a special interest in your child.

At Home

Make sure that outside doors, windows, and screens are securely locked before you retire at night. Confirm that your child's room is not readily accessible from outdoors. If your home has an intercom system, leave the transmitter in your child's room open at night, or keep the door to the room open so that you can hear any unusual noises. Since leaving the door open removes some fire protection, an intercom is preferable. (See chapters 16 and 17 for more information on child protection.)

If you leave your children at home without adult supervision for a short time, keep the house well lit and the garage door closed. Tell your kids not to open the door for anyone, even if you are expecting a package. Discourage your children from publicly discussing family finances and routines, and do not permit advance publicity for business trips or other occasions when you will be away from your home and family.

Consider organizing a "relay" system in which a parent walks with a group of children for a block or so, followed by another parent, then another, and so on.

At School

Escort your children to the school bus or to school, if possible. If you feel especially susceptible to kidnapping, do not let them take taxis or public transportation. Consider organizing a "relay" system in which a parent walks with a group of children for a block or so, followed by another parent, then another, and so on.

Make sure your school follows these security procedures:

- Before releasing a child to anyone except the parents during the school day, a teacher or administrator should telephone one of the child's parents or guardians for approval.
- When a parent requests by phone that a child be released early from school, the caller's identity should be confirmed before the child is permitted to leave.
- If the parent is calling from home, the school should check the request by a return telephone call, with the child identifying the parent's voice.

- If the call is not being made from the child's residence, the school should ask questions about the child's date of birth, the courses he or she is studying, or names of teachers and classmates.
- If there is any doubt about the child's safety, he or she should not be released. (See chapter 20 for more information on school security.)

Dealing with the Media

After a kidnapping occurs, news reporters will no doubt seek information as soon as they get wind of it. While being as cooperative as possible, be sure not to release information that could jeopardize hostages or witnesses, or hamper the police investigation. Only a specifically designated spokesperson should speak to reporters, who should be asked to protect the identities of all witnesses. The press should not be permitted to enter your home or office or examine the scene of the abduction.

IF YOU ARE A KIDNAP VICTIM

If you are kidnapped, there are things you can do that may save your life. Take a moment to compose yourself; consider your plan; then act on it.

Strategies for Survival

Above all, stay calm. Don't threaten anybody. Kidnappers may well be mentally unbalanced, perhaps dangerous psychotics, so don't push them into anything rash. Never fight physically with your abductors; they have probably planned your abduction carefully and will have sufficient manpower to handle you. If your abductors direct you to talk to someone—your spouse or employer, for example—don't attempt heroics.

Cooperate with your abductors as best as you can, but do not tell them what actions your family or employer might take. Assume that you will get out of this situation alive and that everyone connected with your abduction—family, police, FBI—is, first and foremost, working with that objective in mind. Recovering ransoms and apprehending offenders can wait until you are returned safe and sound.

Try to determine where you are and to remember everything you can about your abductors and their methods in order to help police when you're released. Having thoroughly researched you and having spent a great deal of time planning the abduction, your abductors will not give you much opportunity to escape. They will transport you to a previously prepared location, designed for the purpose of holding you as long as they see fit. You will almost certainly be prevented from knowing where you are being taken, and you may be forced to make part of the journey in an automobile trunk. Trunks in most late model cars come equipped with a truck release lever or button, some of which glow in the dark. Of course, safely escaping can still be tricky, especially if the vehicle is moving.

Gather as much information about your confinement as possible. Utilize as many of your five senses as you can. You will be able to hear sounds and detect odors; these details might be important in finding those responsible.

Keep your mind active. Try to keep track of time. Even if you are unable to see outside, you may be able to differentiate night from day by temperature patterns or the mealtimes of your captors.

Personalize your area of captivity. Keep your space clean, and as much as you are permitted, keep yourself clean as well. Designate part of your space as a bedroom and sleep there; eat only in your "dining room." If your captors permit you to have the personal items from your wallet, display snapshots of your family. The odds are great that you will be released. Nine out of 10 kidnapping victims are.

MURDER

You've seen murderers on TV: raving, ranting, vicious-looking, glassy-eyed maniacs who randomly select victims and strike without warning or mercy. Protecting yourself from this type of random psychotic killer seems nearly impossible.

It is important to realize, however, that we are more likely to be murdered by someone we know—a spouse, relative, friend, coworker, or other acquaintance—than by a stranger. And you can, indeed, develop a defense against what at first appears to be a totally unpredictable phenomenon by removing yourself from an environment of threat, rage, depression, mental and physical abuse, alcohol or substance abuse, or a history of prior violence.

Oftentimes the victim is intimately related to her murderer, such as a spouse, ex-spouse, boyfriend, girlfriend, or former boyfriend or girlfriend. Intimate homicides account for about 11 percent of all murders. Women are more likely to be killed by an intimate, with intimate murders accounting for a third of all female-victim murders, but only 3 percent of all male-victim murders.

Murder is also common among other family members. Children are most commonly killed by their own parents, and this is the only type of homicide for which women kill at nearly the same rate as men.

About a third of all murders are committed by non-strangers who are also non-intimates, such as friends and acquaintances. Men are more likely than women to be killed by acquaintances or strangers.

Serial Murder

Serial murder involves the killing of many individuals over a period of at least several weeks or a few months.

Obviously, protection against these individuals is very difficult because you are unlikely to recognize their evil designs until it is too late. You can nevertheless increase your security by following the standard practice of being cautious with strangers.

- If someone you don't know approaches you for no apparent reason or initiates conversation, be suspicious of their actions. Walk away as rapidly as you can.
- If you cannot avoid a conversation, your response should be terse and to the point. Under no circumstances allow a stranger to manipulate you.
- Never give out your address or telephone number to people whom you do not trust.
- Do not allow anyone into your home that you fail to recognize or who does not have a specific, legitimate reason for being there.
- Avoid situations that put you at the mercy of strangers, like hitchhiking or walking alone in isolated areas at night.
- Above all, don't be complacent. Convincing yourself that victimization by a serial killer happens to other people but not to you tends to make you vulnerable.

- Be sure the company you work for has your security as a priority, with good systems and controls that protect you from intruders.

Mass Murder and Random Attacks

It is even more difficult to protect yourself from mass murderers whose multiple homicides are generally fueled by rage and frustration. These tragedies may occur on the job.

Be on guard for the warning signs that surface just before these explosive, violent events. For example, a highly verbal worker may suddenly withdraw or become depressed; a cheerful, reliable employee may turn irritable or begin arriving late for work. Also, be particularly alert for coworkers or employees who suffer from chemical dependency, marital stress, or other exceptional pressures. They should be urged to utilize your company's employee assistance program.

> If you encounter a person's blinding rage, there is little more to do than try to run away.

Above all, remember to be courteous and fair to such people. Do not antagonize or insult them. This strategy will turn the odds away from you as the object of the murderer's wrath.

If you encounter a person's blinding rage, there is little more to do than try to run away. Do not try to fight or reason with the killer. These tactics will only further enrage the individual. If you are unable to escape a building, lock yourself in a closet or other secure area as soon as you hear gunshots or understand what is happening and wait for help.

CHAPTER 29

TERRORISM

Since 9/11, fear of terrorist attacks has remained heightened in the United States. These threats can come either from other countries (international terrorism) or from someone within one's own country (domestic terrorism). Although you should not let this fear run your life, you should be aware of the steps you can take if an attack were to take place.

TYPES OF ATTACKS

Terrorism takes place in many forms, from viruses and bombs to weapons of mass destruction. Although some cause more widespread devastation than others, all are intended to instill fear with total disregard for the safety of civilians.

Bombings

Bombings are by far the most common incidents perpetrated by terrorists. They can easily be concealed because they can be made to look like anything. Bombs are typically concealed in garbage cans, file cabinets, under or in desks, and in mailed packages or letters. Plastic explosives are even easier to conceal, because there is no detectable odor and can be hidden in everyday items, such as clothing, luggage, toys, and cameras.

Suicide bombs. There have been more than 2,000 suicide-bomb attacks since 1983, half of which have occurred since the 2003 U.S. invasion of Iraq. Most suicide bombers carry explosive devices in backpacks and target mass transit or public marketplaces.

Dirty bombs. Also known as a radiological dispersal device (RDD), these bombs combine conventional explosives with some sort of radioactive material. Thus, they can cause injury or death not only through the initial explosion but also via airborne radiation and contamination. A dirty bomb is not a nuclear weapon; nuclear weapons involve complex fission reactions and are far more devastating. The amount of radioactive material is not likely to cause serious injury or sickness, but its presence causes people to panic and is also costly to clean up. Thus, dirty bombs are commonly referred to as "weapons of mass disruption."

Mail bombs. Also called a letter bomb, this is a favorite implement of fear utilized by terrorist groups. While other bombs are undiscriminating, the mail bomb is specific in whom it is addressing. See page 343 for mail-screening procedures.

Bioterrorism

This type of attack entails the use of bacteria, viruses, and other disease-causing microorganisms as a weapon to harm or kill people, animals, or plants. These biological agents can spread through air, water, or food. Bioterrorism can be very hard to detect, because weeks may go by before any symptoms begin to develop. To protect yourself, wash your hands regularly and get vaccinated against measles, rubella, mumps, and influenza. But be aware that any vaccine can cause side effects. You should discuss these with your doctor.

Weapons of Mass Destruction

WMDs are nuclear, radiological, chemical, and biological weapons that have the potential to cause massive death on a catastrophic scale. Today security, military, and intelligence communities are more concerned about WMD than they are about explosives and other small arms.

Mail-Screening Procedures

Another way a criminal can reach you is via the mail. Any unusual mail merits careful inspection. Look for the following characteristics; they may indicate that something is amiss.

- Excessive postage
- Poor handwriting, sloppy typing, or unusual handwriting style
- Incorrect titles or titles used alone without names
- Misspelled names or words
- Oily stains on the envelope or package (which may be caused by an explosive)
- No return address, or a postmark that doesn't match the return address city
- Envelopes that are uneven or lopsided
- Unevenly distributed weight
- Extremely large amounts of masking tape or string on the envelope
- Wire, metal, or aluminum foil protruding out of the envelope or package
- Mail with an unusual odor, especially if similar to almonds or marzipan
- Damaged pieces of mail

If you spot a suspicious-looking piece of mail, don't touch or move it; leave it alone. Open all windows and doors in order to reduce the effects of a potential blast. Leave the premises, notify the police, and don't return to your home until it is absolutely safe.

Cyberterrorism

As new technology develops, so too can we expect the tactics used by terrorists to evolve over time. One of the most recent developments is cyberterrorism, in which terrorists use computer technology to intimidate or coerce a group of people or their government in order to further their own political or social objectives. To be considered cyberterrorism, a computer-related act must result in violence against people or properties, or at least instill feelings of fear and terror.

Government and business activities are now largely based on computer networks, making them vulnerable to terrorist tampering via "cyber weapons." Thus, cyberterrorism has the potential for causing serious devastation. In the mid-1990s, when the Internet became commercialized, the term "Digital Pearl Harbor" came about, referring to the various scenarios by which terrorists could use computers to wreak havoc—for example, causing citywide blackouts, interfering with traffic signals, and causing planes to crash into each other.

Fortunately, no cyber attack of this size has yet occurred. Terrorists tend to be more interested in explosives and other types of non-cyber weapons than computer networks. Nonetheless, cyber security should not be overlooked. Not only can cyberterrorism potentially lead to physical damage, but terrorists can also use computers to access vital information. And as the war on terror becomes increasingly successful in preventing more conventional attacks, terrorists may begin to turn toward cyberterrorism as an attractive alternative: It's cheap, anonymous, can be conducted remotely, and can reach a vast number and wide variety of targets.

RESPONDING TO A TERRORIST ATTACK

In the case of a biological or chemical attack, listen to your radio for instructions as to whether you should remain in your home or evacuate the area. If you are told to stay inside, turn off your ventilation system. Stay in a room that has no windows, if possible, and seal the doors with duct tape or plastic sheeting.

If you are exposed to a biological or chemical agent, seek clean air and obtain medical help as soon as possible. In the case of a nuclear or radiological attack, get to shelter that is either underground or in the middle of a large building. If there is a nuclear attack, do not look at the flash or fireball, and take cover (preferably underground) as quickly as possible. Remain there until instructed by officials to leave. It may take days or weeks before it is safe to come out.

PREPARING AN EVACUATION PLAN

In the event of a terrorist attack or natural disaster, it is critical to have an evacuation plan already in place. Of course, the safest course of action depends on where the threat is located. If, for example, the threat is within your place of business or home, then evacuation may be the safest route. However, if the threat is in the near environment, it may be safer to remain indoors. Find out what the authorities are telling people to do by listening to the television or radio. Make sure you know where all the emergency exits from a building are located.

Prepare a disaster kit ahead of time so that you'll have the supplies you need. It should include:

- a first-aid kit
- an area map and a map of your state
- clothing
- battery-powered radio and extra batteries
- necessary medications (watch expiration dates of medicines)
- flashlight
- small pry bar
- canned food and bottled water for all in your household for a minimum three days.

If the authorities have asked you to evacuate your home, take clothing as required by the existing weather conditions. Take your pets with you, and lock your dwelling's doors and windows prior to leaving.

Have a predetermined plan to contact other family members or friends in case you become separated. Make sure you all have the contact person's telephone number memorized. Although cell phone circuits may be jammed, text messages often can be transmitted and received.

If the authorities have established an evacuation route, be sure to follow it—don't attempt shortcuts, as such routes may be dangerous or blocked. Be sure to stay away from downed power lines.

PRECAUTIONS WHEN TRAVELING ABROAD

Most countries are safe for Americans to visit with little fear of terrorism. Others, notably those on the U.S. State Department's list of troubled countries, are less friendly and merit extra precautions. When traveling in these countries, you'll need to take steps to avoid being a target, in addition to other precautions for safe travel (see chapter 13).

Before You Get to the Airport

- Don't have an "It can't happen to me" attitude; anyone can be involved or targeted.
- Don't be an obvious tourist. Carefully choose your clothing; if it's too expensive or screams "American," it can make you a potential target.
- Remove stickers and personal ID tags from luggage whenever possible.
- If you have a title or military rank, you might want to consider not using it, and if possible don't dress in a uniform. In short, avoid anything in your appearance that would attract attention. Just blend into the background.
- Write down your passport number, the issuing office, and its expiration date. Place a copy in your wallet and your baggage.
- Make two copies of the page in your passport that contains your photograph and personal information. Place one in a safe location at home and bring the other copy with you, but keep it separate from your passport.
- Leave a detailed itinerary with someone you trust.
- Use your office address and telephone number on baggage and for hotel registration.
- When flying to a troubled land, choose your airline based on its safety and security record and policy, not on economics or comfort. Avoid flying first class; first-class passengers are the most likely to be targeted.
- Keep in mind that wide-bodied jets are the least likely to be hijacked, and direct flights are less risky than flights with stopovers.
- If possible, avoid airlines flying the flags of nations involved in hostilities or non-combatant nations supporting those that are at war.
- Carry only your passport, credit cards, and driver's license in your purse or wallet. A little money, of course, is also necessary, but remember to change your U.S. currency to local money as quickly as you can.

At the Airport and on the Plane

- Try not to arrive too early at the terminal—many terrorists strike when they know the most people will be present, such as groups of people waiting for a plane.

Staying Safe in Your Car

Over 85 percent of all kidnappings and assassination attempts occur while the victim is in transit. So how can you protect yourself when traveling by car?

- Always have your car keys in hand, and don't dawdle outside the car.
- Make sure your car is unobtrusive.
- Always lock the car when leaving it, and inspect it when you return, particularly the undercarriage, wheel wells, and exhaust pipe. Drive defensively and keep a safe distance between your car and other vehicles.
- Vary your route to and from work and social points.
- Keep your gas tank at least half full.
- Try not to park your car in an unattended area.
- Look for unusual objects or wires before unlocking or opening the door of your car.
- Be alert for anything unusual or out of the ordinary, such as the hood slightly ajar or a window left open when you know you closed it.
- Keep your vehicle orderly so you can tell if it has been tampered with.
- Check hubcaps; they are a common hiding place for bombs.
- Marking your hubcaps and the wheel rim with paint or a small scratch will help you determine if they have been switched.
- Check the underside of your car for unusual attachments.
- Fill up keyholes with soft wax and place clear tape across doors to determine if someone has gained entry.
- If you are at high risk, do a complete visual check of your vehicle every time you return to it.

- Proceed through the passenger-screening checkpoint soon after arriving at the airport.
- Visit airline club lounges if possible. In addition to the convenience of a peaceful place to wait, they usually provide another level of passenger screening.
- Keep an eye out for people who act suspiciously, and do not hesitate to inform a security officer if you have reason to believe that someone might be a terrorist, or if you see any unattended packages or luggage.
- Always note where the emergency exits are located.

- In the air, avoid intense, serious discussions with other passengers, particularly regarding religion or politics.
- Don't mention your firm's name or your position to others.

Spend as little time as possible in airline ticket areas, cocktail lounges, pre-boarding screening areas, departure gates, and anywhere in the terminal that is adjacent to large plate-glass windows. These areas are favorites for terrorist attack and are likely to be high-injury locations in the event of an explosion or gunfire.

At Your Destination

- Before arriving, have a local business associate arrange transportation from the airport.
- Do not agree to carry or watch a briefcase or package for a stranger.
- Allow only baggage handlers at both the airport and the hotel to handle your luggage.
- Request a hotel room at the back of the building, away from the main entrance. Ask for a room no higher than the seventh floor; this is about the highest an aerial rescue ladder can reach.
- Be sure that your room is neat and orderly when you leave it. If your possessions are disturbed, you should be able to notice the difference, and this will put you on guard.
- Leave a TV or radio on when you leave; unwelcome visitors will likely assume you are in the room.
- Avoid Americanized bars, restaurants, and nightclubs; you will certainly be safer, probably will spend less, and will be able to enjoy the authentic local atmosphere.
- Read local newspapers, and learn and use at least some of the local language and customs.
- Know how to contact the police, your embassy, and consulates.
- Know where the hospitals are.
- If you smoke, make certain you smoke a local brand of cigarette. Your preference could identify you as a tourist and American citizen.

CHAPTER 30

THE CRIMINAL JUSTICE SYSTEM

If you have been involved in a police dispute, arrested, or are a victim of a crime, there are important facts you need to know about the criminal justice system and your rights. Most people have no idea.

LAW ENFORCEMENT AND YOUR RIGHTS

The most visible line of defense in our criminal justice system is the police, who are responsible for confronting crime in the community. Police agencies exist at each level of government. At the federal level there are 50 law-enforcement agencies, while at the state and local levels there are more than 17,500 agencies in operation. Each one of these police agencies has five major duties:

1. keep the peace
2. apprehend violators
3. combat crime
4. prevent crime
5. provide social services.

However, it is important to understand that police are sometimes forced to make quick decisions or at times use poor judgment. If you are ever stopped, questioned, searched, or arrested by law enforcement, it is essential to know your rights. A good place to start is the question-and-answer booklet produced by The American Civil Liberties Union entitled Know Your Rights When Encountering Law Enforcement, available on the Internet. Remember, though, that while the booklet is an extremely helpful guide to helping citizens and non-citizens understand their basic rights, it is not a substitute for legal advice.

Excessive Force

In 1991 the beating of Rodney King by Los Angeles police officers drew worldwide attention. Throughout the past quarter century, such incidents have made the public aware of the issue of excessive force by police.

A police officer's job sometimes requires him or her to use force, such as when making arrests, controlling disturbances, or dealing with drunk or mentally ill people. By law the police do have the authority to use force if necessary. This typically occurs in cases when a suspect resists arrest. However, most officers do not usually have to resort to such tactics, and when they do, it's usually only minimal: grabbing, pushing, or shoving.

There are, however, incidents in which police officers unnecessarily use force, or use more force than a situation requires. In the worst-case scenario, their use of excessive force can result in the death of a suspect or bystander, and in these cases the public often responds with outrage, especially if racial issues come into play.

For example, in 1996 a white police officer in St. Petersburg, Florida, killed a black motorist during a routine traffic stop because the motorist refused to roll down his window and appeared to be trying to drive away. The resulting riots caused $5 million in property damages. In November 2006, police officers in Queens, New York, shot and killed an unarmed man as he was leaving his bachelor party with his friends, only hours before his wedding—at least 50 rounds were shot at the men's vehicle.

Although it is impossible to completely prevent the use of poor judgment when police officers are forced to make quick decisions, many police departments today have taken steps to reduce these incidences, especially because victims of excessive force or their families are likely to file lawsuits. One way of doing this is to teach officers ways of applying force without causing injuries, such as through specific holds and pressure points. Police officers are also trained to use weapons that use less-than-lethal force, such as electric shock devices; soft, nonlethal projectiles; and chemical sprays. These allow the police to maintain order without resorting to gun power. However, even these devices can be extremely dangerous, as was unfortunately demonstrated in the case of Victoria Snelgrove, a 21-year-old college student who was killed after being shot in the eye by a projectile as police tried to disperse the crowds of celebrants following a Boston Red Sox championship game in 2004.

Illegal Searches

People's rights under the Fourth Amendment protect them from illegal searches and seizures. An illegal search is one in which the police fail to obtain a search warrant when one is legally required. In addition, a search may be considered illegal when the search goes beyond the scope specified by a search warrant.

In the 1961 case of Mapp v. Ohio, the Supreme Court ruled that evidence produced during an illegal search cannot be admitted in court. In that particular case the police had forcibly entered Mapp's home without a warrant to search for a bombing suspect. Even though the suspect was not found, the police proceeded to search Mapp's home and discovered illegal pornography, for which they arrested her. Mapp was convicted, but the Supreme Court later overturned the verdict.

The Supreme Court has since established what is known as the "exclusionary rule," which states that any evidence obtained by the police in a way that violates a person's constitutional rights cannot be used against them in court. There are, however, several exceptions to this rule, such as the "good faith" exception (when the police officers honestly believe that they were following the proper rules when they conducted the search) and the "inevitable discovery" rule (when it is believed that the illegally obtained evidence would have eventually been found anyway). However, if you consent to a search, the search automatically becomes legal and renders the resulting evidence admissible in court.

Filing a Complaint against Law Enforcement

If you believe you have been mistreated by a police officer or that police misconduct has occurred, you should file a complaint. First, try to remember every detail of the incident and write them all down—particularly the police officer's name and badge number, as well as the officer's car number. You should also take note of any witnesses. If you have been arrested, you can find out the police officer's name by requesting a copy of your arrest report.

When you file a complaint, be sure to get a notary's signature on any forms you fill out and to get your own copies.

Every police department should have some sort of internal affairs or professional standards department where you can file a complaint. When you file a complaint, be sure to get a notary's signature on any forms you fill out and to get your own copies. This way, you have an official backup in case the forms get mixed up or lost by the police.

COMPLEXITIES OF THE LEGAL SYSTEM

Over the centuries, a complex system of legal justice has evolved, requiring constant response to changing conditions. To combat the cost of crime, society has two weapons: laws and those who enforce them. While this is clear, however, it is not always apparent why some cases are deemed suitable for prosecution and why others are not.

Why Cases are Declined for Prosecution

There are a number of reasons why the prosecutor's office may decline to prosecute. The arresting officers may lack sufficient cause to arrest or have violated the suspect's rights. There may be insufficient evidence to move forward with prosecution. Or there may be other cases more deserving of the attention and the available resources in the prosecutor's office.

Possibly your attacker might not be brought to trial because he or she has an excellent reputation with no previous criminal record. First offenders frequently are not tried. The burden of proof upon the prosecution

Courthouse Security

If you must go to court to seek a restraining order because your ex-partner is stalking and/or threatening you, insist that he undergo a thorough search every time he enters the courthouse. Also insist that the court have an adequate staff of court officers trained to deal with emergency situations. Be sure you are guarded every second you are in the courthouse. Whoever you are facing in court should never be permitted to confront you. If your courthouse does not have metal detectors, insist that they install them. If they don't do so, contact your local newspaper, radio station, and TV news stations.

Don't get too caught up in the symbolism of "the court" as a place where justice prevails and the bad are punished; the courthouse itself is a building, nothing more and nothing less. Criminals and defendants don't leave their violent and destructive tendencies outside; as with any situation, be prepared.

in a criminal case is that it proves the defendant's guilt beyond a reasonable doubt.

A final reason that might prevent your case from heading to court is the possibility that the attacker might be a prominent individual who is owed favors or is a close relative or associate of such an individual.

If this happens, the matter is usually dropped immediately by law enforcement, and it is difficult to receive any further response from them on the subject. You can't sue the police and force them to arrest someone. And if you respond by making a citizen's arrest, you might open yourself up to charges of false arrest.

If the Case Is Headed for Prosecution

If the case is prosecuted, there are still several ways a defendant can go free: through an acquittal, a not guilty verdict, or a plea-bargaining. Still, there are many trials that end in sentencing by the court. Victims may be given the right to enter into the court record a statement of the impact that the crimes have had on their lives. This is a relatively new concept, however. Traditionally, victims testify at the trials and bail hearings.

HOW TO REPORT A CRIME

If you are a victim of crime, remain calm. Remember that the only way to ensure the arrest of the offender is to call the police. The probability the offender will be arrested will increase if you call the police within 2 minutes of the crime. If you have been injured, go to the nearest emergency room for treatment. Then report the crime. If more time has elapsed, notify the police anyway. Note the name and shield number of the investigating police officer, and also record the special police report number assigned to your case for future reference.

What can you do to help the police?

- Remember as many details as you can about the crime scene and the criminal, including all unusual occurrences and characteristics.
- Try to record the names and addresses of all witnesses.
- Record what property was lost, stolen, or damaged.
- When a suspect is apprehended, be sure to press charges.
- If you have been physically assaulted, do not change your clothing, wash, or shower until the police have had an opportunity to process any physical evidence.

The probability the offender will be arrested will increase if you call the police within 2 minutes of the crime.

Failure to report a crime can have several repercussions.

- There is no way the criminal can be arrested unless the police know that a crime has been committed.
- The police must allocate their resources wisely. Your failure to report a crime can mean you're not getting your fair share of protection.
- Unless a crime is reported, you may not be able to obtain reimbursement from insurance for losses.
- You may be eligible for an income-tax deduction if the crime is reported.
- Many jurisdictions have victim compensation programs, but this requires a police report.

- It is your duty. Your assailant may strike again unless you do something. You have an obligation to do what you can to protect not only yourself, but all of us from crime.

COMPENSATING CRIME VICTIMS

All states have a crime victim compensation program. In 1984 Congress passed the Victims of Crime Act (VOCA), which allocated funding for support of victim compensation and assistance programs, and established the Office for Victims of Crime. Reimbursement, which can be made directly to victims of crime or be made on their behalf, can be used to cover medical costs, funeral and burial costs, mental health counseling, and lost wages or loss of support, in addition to various other expenses.

Each year, states and territories receive VOCA funds to support community-based organizations; these include domestic violence shelters, rape crisis centers, and child abuse programs. (Domestic-violence victims comprise 20 percent of all adult victims who receive compensation.)

If you suffered physical or emotional injury or monetary loss because you were a crime victim, a family member or dependent of a crime victim, or an individual who happened to be present during the crime, you may be eligible for compensation. If you paid for medical or burial expenses for a crime victim, you may be entitled to receive reimbursement.

If you suffered physical or emotional injury or monetary loss because you were a crime victim, a family member or dependent of a crime victim, or an individual who happened to be present during the crime, you may be eligible for compensation.

Most programs also pay for loss of earning power, property damage, support, counseling, and rehabilitation services. Some states allow compensation for victims who suffer undue financial hardships; other states pay moving or relocating expenses and the cost of a course on self-defense if you are in imminent danger. In most states, you are eligible for an award if you are innocent and did not contribute to your victimization. But you must report the crime to the police, usually within three days, and cooperate fully with the investigation. The deadline for filing a compensation claim in most states is one year, but verify this matter, because deadlines vary from 180 days to three years. Ask the police or prosecutor's office for an application for your state's compensation program. Generally, the offender does not have to be convicted for you to receive payment.

SEEKING CIVIL RESTITUTION

Increasingly, crime victims are using civil litigation against their assailants as a means of restitution. They seek compensation for financial losses, such as lost wages, counseling and hospital expenses, and property loss. A civil judgment may be awarded even if the defendant was found not guilty of the crime. Time limits for filing suits vary from about three months to three years.

Third parties may also be liable for their failure to provide "reasonable and adequate" protection from crime. Institutions such as businesses, hospitals, hotels, and government agencies may have contributed to a crime by their negligence in security. Check with your attorney or a local prosecutor to determine liability.

While it isn't possible for a civil suit to undo the crime or its effect, civil suits do help compensate for expenses and give victims a greater sense of control over their lives. These suits also help heighten public awareness of the need for increased crime prevention.

The criminal may be sued for income and property. Portions of wages, benefits, tax refunds, and government payments can be awarded to the victim. Real estate, personal property, financial holdings, and bank accounts are also possible resources for satisfying civil judgments.

Civil remedies on behalf of child abuse victims may be sought against negligent third parties who failed to prevent the abuse from occurring. These third parties often include schools, daycare facilities, camps, churches, and youth groups. The statute of limitations may be extended for victims of sexual abuse because of the delayed discovery rule—the fact that the effects of the abuse may not be fully determined until much later, as the victim may repress memories of the abuse.

PREPARING FOR YOUR DAY IN COURT

Now you are ready for your day in court. This will not be an easy task. You may have experienced apathy, aloofness, and bureaucratic behavior on the part of the police, and you very well may be in for more of the same once judicial proceedings begin. You will arrive at a large, strange building, where you may even encounter the criminal who victimized you.

Whatever you do, avoid contact with the defendant. Criminal defendants or their friends and relatives have been known to intimidate, threaten, and harass victims. If this occurs, report the incident to the prosecutor immediately. Threats away from the courthouse should also be reported to the prosecutor, the police, or both.

One of the most depressing and infuriating aspects of your court experience is the ease with which your trial may be postponed. You may take time off from work, arrive at the courthouse, wait around for hours, and then learn that the proceedings have been delayed. These delays may occur over and over again throughout the trial, and they may last for months.

Lesser problems include difficulty with parking, finding your way around inside the courthouse, and uncomfortable waiting conditions. You might even find it difficult to determine the status or progress of your case. Try to find someone in the prosecutor's office who is willing to update you on your case. This may be the best way to mitigate frustrating experiences. In addition, you can contact your victim/witness assistance program for help and support.

The Witness Stand

Now you are ready to testify. Your evidence can make or break the case. If you follow these simple instructions, your testimony will be greatly improved.

- Review your testimony before your court appearance. Picture in your mind what occurred, so that you recall details. Make notes, but do not memorize your testimony, because it will appear staged.
- Dress appropriately for court. Initial impressions are important.
- Remain alert and calm, and never lose your temper.
- Be attentive and listen carefully to each question.

- Answer all questions precisely, but never volunteer information.
- Keep your testimony objective.
- Above all, be yourself. Judges, jurors, and attorneys, like most people, appreciate sincerity and integrity.

Victim Assistance

Victim/witness assistance programs are intended to lessen the impact of crime and judicial procedures on the innocent, while maintaining the constitutional guarantees for those accused.

Each community provides different types of crime victim services, but most include sexual assault centers, child abuse treatment centers, domestic-violence shelters, and victim/witness centers. These programs usually provide emergency and long-term support to victims and their families. Services may include counseling, temporary shelter, clothing, food, transportation, and medical care. These programs may also provide assistance throughout all criminal justice proceedings and for filing your crime victim compensation program. Additionally, many programs notify your friends and relatives and intervene with your employer to minimize loss of pay and benefits due to your absence from work.

If you or someone you care about has been the victim of crime, call the National Organization of Victim Assistance (NOVA) for immediate support, referrals, and help at (800) TRY-NOVA. NOVA, online at www.trynova.org, will provide information for serious forms of criminal victimization, including homicide, rape, assault, robbery, burglary, child abuse, spouse battering, stalking and sexual harassment.

Neighborhood Watch groups and block clubs may also provide assistance to victims (see pages 239–240). These groups can assist victims in numerous ways, such as helping the victim until the police arrive at the scene; offering emergency assistance to victims right after the crime occurs; repairing broken windows or locks and fixing damaged property; providing referrals to neighborhood-based victim assistance programs; offering transportation to the hospital or to the police station; babysitting; and helping the victim recall a description of the offender. A similar program to aid victims can be established by any community.

INDEX

E

elder abuse, 188–93, 259–62
elevators, 98
E-mail viruses, 230
emergency phone list, 57, 171
emergency rooms, 256–67
employees
  computer theft and, 223
  disgruntled, 299–300, 302
  hiring, 305–11
  safety, 258, 303–4
  screening, 298
  service, 64–70
  sexual harassment of, 326–29
empty home, 84–90
environmental design of
  neighborhoods, 245–46
escape plan
  carbon monoxide, 41
  fire, 39
  spousal abuse, 179–83
  terrorist attack or natural disaster,
    344–45
evidence of stalking, 332
excessive force, police and, 350–51
ex-employees, 299–300, 302
exterior
  of home, 76–83, 89
  lighting, 71–73
  of workplace, 307–8

F

family security. See also children;
  seniors
  carbon monoxide and, 41
  fire and, 39
  intruders and, 33
family violence, 175–93
FAST LANE transponders, 107
fencing, 76–77
financial forecasting fraud, 280–81

fire
  arson, 79–80
  detection, alarms and, 38–41
  escape plan, 39
  hotel, 158–59
firearms, 25–30
food safety, 90
forcible rape. See rape
forgeries, 293–94
fraternity hazing, 254
fraud. See also scams
  consumer, 91, 266–77, 280
  financial, 278–87, 293
  help for victims of, 275, 287
  holidays and, 91
  Internet, 232–34
  mail, 269–71
  real estate, 273–74, 283
  against seniors, 265–66
  street swindles, 272–73
  telephone, 269–71
  ticket, 136
French doors, 13
funerals, 91, 272

G

gambling, 92–93
gangs, youth, 215–16
garage doors, 13
GPS (Global Positioning System)
  unit, protecting from theft, 106–8

H

hacking, 227–35. See also
  cybercrime
Halloween, 91, 210
hallway watch programs in nursing
  homes, 262
handguns, 25–30
hatchback cars, 109
hazardous occupations, 292

television violence, 211–12
tenants' associations, 101
terrorism, 341–48
theft prevention. *See also* home, security in
cars, 105–6
by employees, 297–98
in hospitals, 255–57
in nursing homes, 261–62
for seniors, 263–65
in workplace, 291–92
Third World travel, 166
timers for lighting, 74
towing for cars, 114–15
tracking devices for children, 205–6
trash, protecting from identity theft, 78–79
travel, 111–14, 152–66. *See also* car(s)
by mass transportation, 132–35

U
university campuses, 251–54
unwanted calls, 59–62

V
vacations
home security and, 84–90
spousal abuse and, 176
valuables, 20–25
in hotel rooms, 157–58
marking of, 21, 244–45, 261
at work, 291–92
vandalism, 80–81
vans, 121–22
vigilantism, 242–43
violence, 247–51
crimes of, 315–48
family, 175–93
in the media, 211–13
prevention, 309–11

in schools, 248–51
workplace, 298–304
viruses (computer), 227–31

W
walking
at night, 130
to school, 247–49
warranties, 269
water safety, 90
weapons
firearms, 25–30
of mass destruction (WMD), 342
against rape, 318
for self-defense, 126–29
webcams, 53, 205
weddings, 91–92
weekends, spousal abuse and, 176
whistles, 129
Wi-Fi security, 233
wilderness vacations, 160–61
wills, storage of, 21–25
windows
alarm systems for, 42–43
apartments and, 96
home, 14–17
witness to a crime, 137
women. *See also* rape
battered, 175–83
self-protection and, 320
workplace
hostile, 328
humane, 303
security, 291–311
sexual harassment at, 326–29

Y
yards, 76–79, 89

367